## Here's What Seasoned Sailors are Saying About "The Essential Galley Companion"

"Amanda Swan-Neal has cooked under every condition imaginable and her book is full of tips on how to turn onboard cuisine from a simple fare to a pleasurable experience. Her favorite ingredients are a good dose of common sense with a pinch of subtle humor.

Jimmy Cornell, author of World Cruising Routes

"Chock full of sea-tested recipes based on ingredients available worldwide, this book also includes invaluable advice for the ocean epicure from filleting a tuna to managing waste. Amanda has brought to bear all of her 125,000 miles of offshore experience to create a useful and useable reference for anyone whose kitchen moves from place to place, and then added her wit and wisdom in the form of anecdotes from her days of Whitbread racing and world cruising. This book will be aboard wherever I cruise from now on.

Beth Leonard, author of The Voyager's Handbook

"The Essential Galley Companion is a breath of fresh air. Compiled and written by someone who knows how to provide good food in often impossible circumstances, it is packed full of essential practical advice."

Tracy Edwards, MBE, skipper of *Maiden*,
1989-90 Whitbread Race

"Amanda's spirit and wide of experience shows through on these pages."

Dawn Riley, CEO *America True*, watch leader on *Maiden*

"This is a seagoing Joy of Cooking, but with a difference; laced throughout the quite simple and savory recipes are vignettes that serve as windows into worlds that most of us may never see – a farmer's market in the Chilean channels; an anchorage near Cape Horn; a rough watch on a Whitbread boat; or the embrace of a devoted New Zealand family. The Essential Galley Companion is the first truly unusual offshore-sailing cookbook to come along in our memory."

Nim Marsh, editor, Blue Water Sailing

"I love to cook but I'm not creative in the galley. So, I really need a book like Amanda's to provide the impetus for me to try new things. The Essential Galley Companion provides a well thought out guide to menu planning and that is the heart of galley success and the most difficult aspect to manage."

Robert Perry, yacht designer

# THE ESSENTIAL GALLEY COMPANION

## Recipes and Provisioning Advice for Your Boating Adventures

AMANDA SWAN-NEAL

MAHINA EXPEDITIONS
PUBLISHING
FRIDAY HARBOR

Printed by Publishers Press, Salt Lake City, Utah

Library of Congress Catalog Card Number: 99-80127
Swan-Neal, Amanda 1964-
The Essential Galley Companion : recipes and provisioning advice for your boating adventures / Amanda Swan-Neal.

ISBN 0-9676904-0-4

Cover design by Suzy Wilson
Cover and book illustrations by Ron Wilson
Cover photograph by Larry Hartford
Copy editors: Nim Marsh, Molly O'Neil and John Neal

Mahina Expeditions Publishing
P.O. Box 1596
Friday Harbor, WA 98250 USA
360-378-6131, fax 360-378-6331
www.mahina.com
sailing@mahina.com

# Contents

## Dedication

To
mum and dad,
who gave me the passion to experience life,
my nanna and poppa,
who gave the strength and tenacity to believe in my endeavors,
and to John,
who gives me love, the joy of life, and the encourgement to share what I've achieved.


## Acknowledgements

I thank Ron Wilson for his amazing artwork and support, and Suzy Wilson for her incredible creativity.

I thank Carol Noel for her energy, love of life and enthusiasic input into this book, Lisie Knowles my adventurous buddy, for always being there on the end of the phone, miles away but close in spirit, Christine Webb for being my guiding light, and my fellow Maidens for proving that dreams do come true.

I thank Tami Oldham Ashcraft for her powerful example of determination in publishing, Robert Hale, Oscar Lind, Steve and Linda Dashew, Don Douglass, Réanne Hemmingway-Douglass and Bruce Conway for their advice and encouragement. Thanks also to Kim Schmidt and Nim Marsh at Blue Water Sailing Magazine for their terrific help in editing and layout.

I thank all the Mahina Expeditions members who were taste testers, vegie choppers and recipe contributers. Thanks too to fellow boaters and the resturants who eagerly shared their favourite recipes.

I thank the cover crew, Larry Hartord, Kathy Mohrweiss, Sharon Stuckey, Donna Donnahoo and John for a sucessful day.

And I especially thank the warrior goddess of computing, Molly O'Neil and her assistant Hille, for their awesome computer guidence, hard work and dedication.

# Introduction

*The Essential Galley Companion* has been designed to introduce you to onboard cooking, both at anchor and underway. I wrote this book to answer the frequent requests seminar students and expedition members have, wanting to know how to make their lives at sea simpler and safer.

When I joined John Neal in 1994 aboard *Mahina Tiare* and started conducting sailing expeditions between foreign ports, I began gathering information ranging from how to prepare local seasonal produce, to easy solutions for feeding a large crew on an extended passage. I learned that a well-provisioned and efficient galley is essential in providing easy, quick and nutritious meals for a hungry crew.

Material for the book came from discovering terrific recipes while sharing memorable meals with cruising friends, from new friends ashore, from local restaurants, and from fellow expedition members, some of whom are great cooks, and others who definitely needed a helping hand.

*The Essential Galley Companion* was written while underway on an 11,000 mile, six month series of passages from New Zealand to Alaska, ending in our beautiful homeport in the San Juan Islands of Washington.

I hope that you will gain as much enjoyment reading and cooking from this book as I have realized in writing it.

AMANDA

## Guide On Using the Recipes

I have made the assumption that you are already familiar with a basic knowledge of cooking, the terminology, and ingredients used.

All recipes are designed to serve four people.

Each recipe is streamlined to enable you to quickly determine if the recipe is suitable for your available ingredients, time frame, and weather conditions. I want to avoid overloading you with excessive instructions, especially if you are following a recipe while under way and the pages are dancing before your eyes.

The ingredients are listed in order of most-required to least-required, allowing quick scanning down the list to determine the quantity of ingredients required – and if they are not available, what could possibly be substituted.

Wherever possible, I have tried to adapt the recipes applicable to worldwide use; for example, in the fish chapter I have not specified a particular variety of fish unless the recipe works only with that type, such as salmon.

You are welcome to vary the vegetables used in most dishes; when cruising you are often forced to do with what you have or need to consume before it perishes. I did not consider it necessary to continue mentioning this throughout the book.

I specify fresh herbs in most of the recipes, and generally prefer to use them in my cooking. When substituting dried herbs for fresh, remember that 1 t of dried herbs is the equivalent of 1 T of fresh chopped herbs.

## Symbols in the Text

Symbols are included to work as a quick guide.

T Tablespoon

t Teaspoon

 Pressure-cooker option

 One-pot dish

* Optional addition to a recipe

# Weights and Measures

## Conversion Chart for Weights and Measures

| **Kilograms** | **Ounces** | **Cups** |
|---|---|---|
| 1kg. | 32 oz. (2 lbs.) | 4 cups |
| 750g | 24 oz. (1 1/2 lbs.) | 3 cups |
| 600g | 20 oz. (1 lb., 4 oz.) | 2 1/2 cups |
| 500g | 16 oz. (1 lb.) | 2 cups |
| 300g | 10 oz. | 1 1/4 cups |
| 240g | 8 oz. | 1 cup |
| 180g | 6 oz. | 3/4 cup |
| 60g | 2 oz. | 1/4 cup |

## Oven Temperatures

| | | |
|---|---|---|
| Very slow | 250°F | 120°C |
| Slow | 300°F | 150°C |
| Moderately slow | 325°F | 160°C |
| Moderate | 375°F | 190°C |
| Hot | 400°F | 200°C |
| Very Hot | 450°F | 230°C |

Chapter 1

# Outfitting the Galley

# Galley Design

The size of your boat will detmine the minimum space allocation for the galley area. I've sailed and cooked on many boats; a 28-foot stripped-out raceboat on a one-burner camping stove, a 50-foot motor yacht with an electric range, a Whitbread 60 with its ergonomically-designed cook-pod, cruiser/racer yachts that try to emulate the kitchen at home, a 1909 76-foot restored Fife yacht with the galley forward of the mast on a sloping cabin sole, and a 175-foot sail-training vessel for 50 crew. The lesson I take away from this experience is that more important than size is a layout that takes many critical factors into consideration.

## Layout

Personally I like a U-shaped galley that you are able to wedge your bottom in and perform simple galley tasks without worrying about what the boat is doing and which way you are heeling. The other option is a long fore-and-aft galley running along the hull, though this takes up a lot of space in what is traditionally the main saloon area. On larger yachts the galley is often located beside the cockpit in the walkway through to the aft cabin as on Oyster Yachts. With a long galley, you need some means of keeping yourself in place, and a strap that sits across your bottom is the common solution, though this allows you no quick means of escape to dodge a flying pot. On our 46-foot Hallberg-Rassy, with its U-shaped galley, I'm right in front of the stove but can easily escape missiles.

On a motor yacht, space is less at a premium because of the increased volume. Most often the galley is equipped as it would be at home, with electrical appliances including stove and refrigerator, large counter space, pressure water, and adequate stowage facilities. As there often is far less motion on a motor yacht than on a sailboat, it is not as critical to design the galley area as if it were a continual moving platform.

## Sinks

- A **deep sink** is my paramount choice for the galley. It doesn't have to be extremely large, just big enough to be able to comfortably hold large dinner plates.
- If space allows, a **double-sink** arrangement works best. The

sinks on *Mahina Tiare III* are 12" x 12" and 12" x 9", and both are 8" deep.

- Installing the sink relatively **close to centerline** will allow it to drain on all angles of heel.
- If your sinks are positioned **close to the waterline** or against the hull, you will need either a manual or electric pump to drain away the water – or at least an easily accessible ball valve to shut off the salt water which gurgles up the drain when heeled over.

## Soap Dispenser

We have installed two soap dispensers in our galley. One is for antibacterial hand soap and the other is for dish soap. I've since found a product available in gallon jugs from Costco and Wal-Mart that does both these jobs, so I could have installed just one pump.

## Water Pumps

- Having a **manual freshwater foot pump** instead of a hand pump allows you to use both hands while working in the galley.
- Most boats on which I've cruised also have a **saltwater galley pump** to help reduce water consumption.
- When we purchased our current boat, I was surprised to discover that there was no saltwater pump in the galley. John assured me that as we have large water tanks and a high output watermaker we have adequate water to be able to wash the dishes without using salt water. For the first few months of cruising, I felt extremely guilty every time I used the freshwater for a job that I would have previously used salt water. After a while I realized that and the dish towels stayed fresher and that none of my galley utensils were rusting as they normally did each year.
- A **pressurized water system** with the added convenience of hot water makes the galley area feel more like home.

## Counter Space

- Counter space is **often limited**, and when the boat is underway items can't be put down unattended.

- At sea I place **Scoot-gard** or a similar nonskid material on the countertop to prevent objects from moving when I set them down.
- You need to train yourself to **be a tidy cook**, cleaning up as you progress though a meal, not only in stowing away equipment used, but also staying on top of the dishes.
- A **fiddle** should surround the countertop to stop articles sliding off, and on our yacht these have slots cut into them for handholds.
- Having a **chopping board** custom made for your sink or stovetop will increase counter space.
- Our chopping board is **a pullout block** like a drawer that can also serve as additional counter space.
- I have been on a few cruising yachts that have an **extra countertop** that swings up and is propped open with a leg.

## Storage Lockers

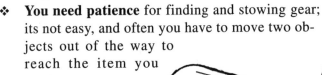

- You want to **utilize the space** you have available for the items you use frequently while cooking. Give careful consideration to each item you place in a prime, easy-to-reach location, and check that nothing sits dormant in a location that could be otherwise occupied by a more frequently used item.
- **Transfer large containers** of food such as oil, jelly, mayonnaise, honey, mustard, salt, cereal and rice into small containers that fit your galley space. Before each ocean passage, top up the containers so you don't have to do it the first week at sea.
- **Always return items** to their stowage space; its very frustrating to have to dig around in lockers looking for a rearranged or misplaced item.
- **You need patience** for finding and stowing gear; its not easy, and often you have to move two objects out of the way to reach the item you want.
- Rubbermaid manufactures an extensive range of **plastic drawer-dividers** that allow you to separate and organize items.

- Use **Scoot-gard** to prevent items for sliding around in lockers and drawers.
- Ensure that your drawers have a **sturdy locking catch** and a stop that prevents the drawer from totally sliding out.
- To organize and divide lockers, use baskets, wooden/plexiglass dividers, or install adjustable pegs into the base of the cupboard.

## Ventilation

- Generally, the galley is situated **near the companionway**, ensuring plenty of fresh air and easy access to the cockpit, though alternatives are needed when the main hatch is closed.
- A **dorade vent** placed above the galley helps supply ventilation.
- The addition of a **small electric fan** – such as a Hella Turbo – greatly aids in cooling down the cook in the tropics or in heavy weather when hatches and ports are closed.
- An **opening port** above my stove is a quick solution for fresh air, but it requires constant monitoring for spray or waves.

## Stove Installation

To save galley space when building our second cruising boat, my dad decided not to gimbal our kerosene stove. His reasoning was that we had big deep pots to keep the food inside and strong adjustable arms on the stovetop to prevent the pots from jumping off as the boat lurched. When the sea conditions were calm enough, my dad would let my brother and I bake a cake. Once in the oven, the initial baking process required constant monitoring, turning the cake this way and that to be sure that the cake didn't develop an uneven tilt. All of our cakes inevitably did, and we would name it a port or starboard tack cake depending on it's resulting angle.

- A **stainless steel grab-bar** should be mounted across the front of the stovetop to prevent people falling on the elements and grabbing the stove for support when the boat rocks.
- Stoves are generally mounted **fore and aft** against the hull.
- Check that your stove **gimbals with ease** and has no erratic movement. You may need to add some more weight down low to dampen its movement.

- A gimbaled stove requires a **locking catch** to secure the gimbals when not needed. I always lock the gimbals before opening the oven door on my Force 10 stove as the change of weight when a meal is baking causes the oven to tilt drastically.
- A stove that is mounted **athwartship**, against a bulkhead, won't be able to utilize gimbals, but is considered safer by some people as it does not rock and lurch with the boat's movement.
- A stove top needs a high fiddle, an even grill surface on which different-sized pots can sit flat and adjustable **pan-locking arms** or **pot-holders** to keep pots positioned over the burners.

## Fire Safety

- In the event of a galley fire, a **fire extinguisher** should be readily accessible.
- A **Fire Towel** mounted near the galley can be used to quickly snuff out grease and alcohol fires.

## Treating Minor Burns

In my first restaurant kitchen job, I received a nasty burn when I picked up a hot frying pan that the cook had tossed into the sink. I instantly placed butter on it, which I quickly learned was a myth, as butter fat stays hot adding heat to the burn. Thank goodness another chef noticed my lack of knowledge and administered the correct treatment saving me more pain.

- **Immerse burns** immediately in cold water.
- **Clean seawater** or salt solution is preferable, with ice or chemical cold packs added. Soak until the heat dissipates, at least half an hour.
- Apply**Silvadene ointment** (Silver-sulfadiazine) thickly to the burned area and cover with clean gauze (somewhat loosely so as not to constrict blood flow). If two burned surfaces are touching each other, between the fingers for example, place sterile gauze between them.
- Several times a day, **soak burns** in a sterile container of salt water and reapply Silvadene ointment and gauze. Silvadene is an antibacterial agent that prevents infection of burns far more effectively than any other antibiotic cream.

# Equipping the Galley

## Small~Handled Utensils

Bottle opener with cork screw
Can opener x 2
Garlic crusher
Knife sharpener
Measuring spoons
Measuring cups
Stove lighter
Scissors
Vegetable knife
Vegetable peeler (2)

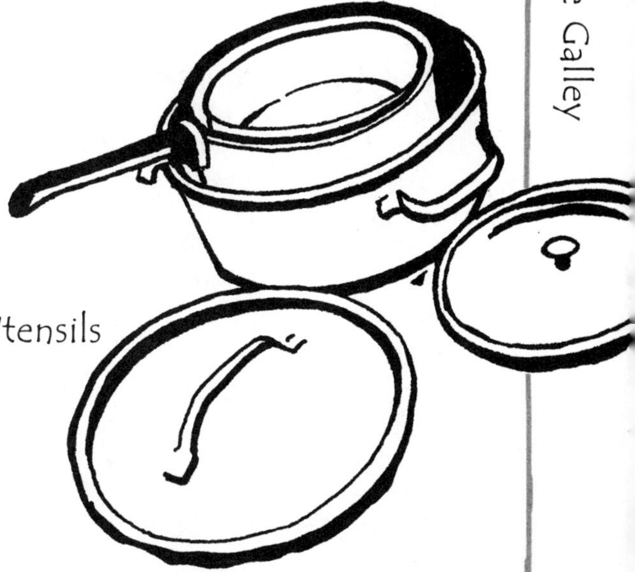

## Large~Handled Utensils

Barbecue tongs
Bread knife
Fish slice
Fish filleting knife
Gas stove lighter (2)
Grater
Knife – large
Rubber spatula
Salad tongs
Serving spoon
Slotted spoon – large
Skewers – for barbecues
Whisk
Wooden spoon

## Galley Helpers

Funnel x 3 – assorted sizes
Measuring cup – mine is like a saucepan, and I use it to melt butter or toast small amounts
Mortar and pestle – not necessary, but handy for mixing spices
Rolling pin – I tend to use a wine bottle instead
Sieve/strainer
Sprouting jar with stainless steel mesh lid

Wooden chopping board x 2 – 1 large and 1 small
Yogurt maker or large-mouth thermos

## Pots and Pans

Revere stainless steel teakettle with whistle
6-quart Cuisinart pressure-cooker
3 nesting Cuisinart stainless pots with 2 removable handles and one shared lid
5-quart Cuisinart soup pot with lid and steamer basket
8" Teflon sautéing pan
11" high-sided Teflon frying pan with lid or cast-iron skillet
Wok (if you enjoy Asian cooking)
8 x 12 Pyrex baking dish
11 x 14 Pyrex casserole dish
2 x stainless steel bread pans
Cookie tray
Muffin tray
2.3-quart stainless Nissan thermos. Top-plunging, I have it installed on my galley counter top for hot water. Model number TAA 2200, priced at around $125.

## Electrical Appliances

Blender/food processor
Bread machine
Cake mixer
Coffeemaker
Coffee grinder – also used for spices
Crock pot
Hand blender and chopper – Braun MR380; I really enjoy having this aboard, its my only piece of electrical galley equipment

## Galley Supplies

Aluminum foil
Apron
Containers for leftovers – I use empty plastic salsa tubs
Dish towels
Garbage bags – large and small – I recycle plastic supermarket bags
Hand towel

Hot pads – for placing hot dishes on the table
Paper bags – 5" x 10" brown paper for organic waste disposal at sea
Paper napkins – work out cheaper than paper towels when purchased in bulk
Paper plates – for barbecues ashore and potlucks
Paper towels – I cut the roll in half to make it last longer
Plastic wrap – I very rarely use it, and in fact don't even have a roll onboard
Plastic cups, forks and knives – for barbecues and potluck dinners ashore
Ziploc bags – freezer bags are the sturdiest; carry various sizes
Nonskid matting to stop objects sliding
Oven mitts

## Tips on Cookware

- **Pyrex baking dishes** are great onboard, are extremely sturdy, cook evenly, and clean easily.
- **Teflon-coated baking pans** may rust out in a couple of years.
- We have a **Teflon-coated frying pan** that we replace every two years as the Teflon coating gets scratched off.
- My mum has a **cast-iron frying pan**. It needs to be seasoned by hot heat and wiped with oil so it won't rust.

## Wok Cooking

- A steel wok will need to be **seasoned** by wiping it with oil and baking it in a hot oven three or four times before using it. Once seasoned correctly, it will be sealed and won't tend to rust as quickly. My mum's wok is so seasoned from her Chinese cooking that when she heats it up it smells divine. The only trouble is that when she uses her wok to make any other ethnic dish – such as Italian tomato – it ends up with a hint of Chinese.
- The **secret to wok cooking** is to keep the heat hot and the food sliced evenly so that it cooks at the same rate. Another option is to add the food at different times, ending with an item such as cabbage that requires the least amount of cooking.
- To **clean and care** for your wok after cooking, wipe it out with soapy water and place it back on a hot flame to dry it out. If your wok starts to rust, just season it again.

## Bread Machine

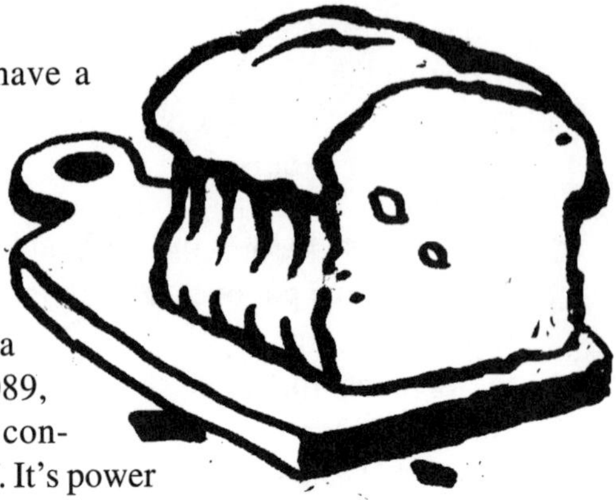

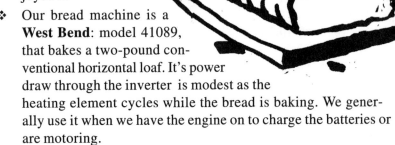

- It is **not necessary** to have a bread machine onboard, but in the three years I've been cruising with ours, I've really enjoyed it.
- Our bread machine is a **West Bend**: model 41089, that bakes a two-pound conventional horizontal loaf. It's power draw through the inverter is modest as the heating element cycles while the bread is baking. We generally use it when we have the engine on to charge the batteries or are motoring.

## Pressure Cookers

My first offshore passage as a child was extremely rough. I have memories of my mother making banana custard using milk powder and the whole dish having an awful burnt flavor to it. I was rather excited by the prospect of having pudding at all. Visions of that same passage feature mum struggling, strapped in at galley, and throwing all sorts of wholesome food into the pressure cooker.

Patiently, she lights the kerosene stove, and sits down wearily to observe its progress. Five minutes later, as the cooker is in full pressure and hissing steadily, an extra large wave throws the entire pot off the stove and onto the floor. It continued to move, bouncing around the cabin and venting even more steam like some demented giant beach ball with a hole in it. I thought my whole world would soon explode, sending me out into the dark blue ocean. Mum started laughing, and she calmly stood up, scooped up the pot, still hissing away, and placed it gently on the stove.

- Pressure-cooking is **quick, efficient, and a one-pot method** to preparing meals, casseroles, soups, stews, and baking.
- **In the tropics**, the shorter cooking time of pressure-cooking results in reduced cabin heat.
- Pressure-cooking reduces conventional **cooking time** by up to 70%.

- With the top locked down, it **prevents food from sloshing** over the top of the pot in rough weather.
- Carefully **read the instruction booklet** that comes with cooker.
- **Brown meats** to seal their flavor, and simmer the meal for a few minutes to even out the heat before locking on the lid.
- Never fill the pot over **2/3 full** incase the food or liquid blocks the vent.
- Always **use plenty of liquid** to avoid the contents drying out and burning.
- When the **cooker reaches pressure** its time to monitor the cooking period.
- Don't use **high heat**, just enough to sustain the pressure.
- Never remove the lid until **all the pressure** has been released from the cooker.
- Once your timing has finished, **cool the pot** by placing it under a cold water tap.
- It is best to **season** your cooking after pressurizing, as flavors tend to become concentrated while under pressure.

### To Use Pressure Cooker as a Mini~Oven

1. Remove the rubber-sealing gasket in the lid so it won't dry out.
2. Place a metal trivet on the bottom of the pot (an empty tuna can with the bottom and top removed works well). This trivet acts as a spacer, and should be at over 1/2" high.
3. Inside the pressure cooker, place a metal pan that provides a 1/2" space between its sides and the cooker allowing even distribution of heat.
4. Be sure to use a low heat or the bottom of your baking will burn. A flame-tamer on top of the burner helps to evenly distribute heat.
5. When baking bread, grease and coat the inside baking dish with flour.
6. Don't remove the lid until you are sure the baking is cooked, as the heat escapes.

- Foods cooked under pressure, then left sealed inside with the pressure cap still on, **remain sterile** for a couple of days without refrigeration. Repressurizing before eating kills most organisms. This process works well for meats or if you catch a large fish and don't have refrigeration.

- **Food that does not pressure-cook well**: milk products, eggs, and pasta, as it tends to froth.
- ***Cooking Under Pressure*** by Lorna Sass is great book for pressure-cooking advice and recipes.

## Romantic and Guest Entertaining

*Remember that the boat is now your home – so there is no need to feel as though you are forever camping out.*

On our first offshore cruise in 1977, my mum outfitted our galley with plastic bowls and plates. This was a move she regretted, because the plastic soon scratched and she missed her china dinnerware. When we built our second boat in 1980, mum purchased two identical dinner sets (one as a spare) and had dad build them into their own storage locker in the galley. She never regretted the extra expense, and rarely did we break a dish – even with my brother and I handling them.

My first date with John transpired when he asked me out for dinner while I was working on his rigging. I was rather shellshocked that he asked. I hadn't even noticed that he was even remotely keen on me, especially since we had only met while I was wearing my work attire. He gave me a choice of a restaurant meal or dinner on his boat. I had not seen his boat, and it occurred to me that I might have to sit through a restaurant meal knowing that I would still be given the standard chat-up line, "Do you want to come see my boat?" So I decided to have dinner onboard, where I could be assured of an easy getaway if I felt uncomfortable with the situation.

Arriving down at the boat after dark, nervously clutching a bottle of wine, I gingerly knocked on the hull. A smiling face appeared out of the hatch and called, "Come on down!" As I step down the companionway, I was impressed. *Mahina Tiare*'s interior had a tropical flare, small lamps draped with flower leis lighted the corners, and soft Hawaiian music quietly played. In the center of the

table set for two sat a bottle of my favorite wine, perfectly chilled. John was in the galley adding the finishing touches to chicken fettuccine and a tossed salad brightly contrasted with a tidy bench top. I sat down with a sigh and thought to myself that I'd sail anywhere in the world with this guy.

If you don't picture yourself as the perfect dinner host, just invite friends over for sunset drinks rather than for dinner. Sharing a cool drink and munching snacks while watching the sun go down is nice way to end the day, and it certainly takes the pressure off the cook.

The cruising lifestyle lends itself well to entertaining, and a few treasured items onboard help create a special event. Here is my entertaining list, and although these items are not a necessity to have onboard, both John and I receive a lot of pleasure when using:

Attractive salt and pepper grinders
Candles and candle holder
Cheese board and knife
Crystal wine glasses
Flower vase filled with fresh flowers
Interesting dishes for serving appetizers (carved bowl, woven bread basket, colored glass dish)
Napkins (cloth and paper)
Place mats
Table cloth
Wooden carved dish (for nuts)

# Cooking Appliances

## Propane Stoves

Propane is the cooking fuel most commonly used on cruising boats. Propane provides instant and easy heat simply by lighting the gas burner.

## Propane Installation

- ❖ The **hazard with propane** is that it is heavier than air. If a leak occurs, the gas will collect in lowest point, where even the smallest spark can cause an explosion.
- ❖ Most boats have a **built-in propane locker** with a drain hole in

the bottom that leads directly overboard.

- **Aluminum propane cylinders** are double the price of steel propane cylinders, but are maintenance-free and lightweight. We carry two 20-lb. tanks and with 8 people onboard a tank lasts 6 weeks. A full tank weighs 30 lbs. so I use our Ruxxac folding dock cart to transport it.
- You need to keep **steel cylinders** painted to prevent rust. White is the best color to prevent the tank heating up, causing a dangerous pressure level if placed in the sun.
- An electric **solenoid valve** should be installed immediately after the tank with a remote control switch near the stove. A Xintex propane Monitor & Control not only controls turns the gas on and off, but also monitors the system for leaks, in which event it automatically shuts off the flow and sounds an alarm.
- Propane or butane is **available worldwide**, though quality differs in some countries. Many countries use **different pipe threads** for their propane tanks that might not be compatible with your tank. We have found that, when filling our propane tanks in different countries, the local propane refilling station will have an adapter to fit U.S. pipe fittings, often given to them by a previous visiting yachtie.
- Some countries may **only exchange propane tanks**, so you might have to shop around for a facility to refill your tanks with correct attachments. In Chile and the Marquesas, we resorted to **filling our tanks by gravity**:

  **Connect the two tanks.**
- Place the larger full tank over your small tank.
- Turn the large tank upside-down or on its side and open the bleed valve on your tank.
- The liquid gas slowly flows into your tank. It is impossible to fill a tank completely this way, but sometimes it is the only option.

## Kerosene Stoves

Kerosene used to be the fuel of choice for cruising in isolated places, but now with propane more readily available, kerosene stoves are less common on cruising boats.

*Advantages:* Kerosene is cheap and nonexplosive, and produces the most heat per volume of any fuel.

*Disadvantages:* It requires priming with alcohol and periodic decarbonizing of the burners, which is a nasty job!

## Microwave Ovens

When outfitting our new boat, a microwave was on the option list, but I didn't give it a second thought. I would rather have the storage space, and I realize that I'm not a microwave cook at home, only using it for reheating leftovers, drinks and making popcorn. Microwaves are common on liveaboard, dockside boats, but I see few long-distance cruisers using them and I'm not sure why.

Many large, modern yachts are fitted with microwaves. Steve and Linda Dashew aboard their 78-foot *Beowulf* enjoy theirs, especially in the tropics as it produces less heat below than a conventional oven and in rough weather it quickly heats precooked meals.

## Electric Stoves

Requiring a generator to operate, electric stoves are fitted on power yachts and very large sailboats, but are uncommon on cruising sailboats.

*Advantages:* No chance of explosion from propane or additional fuel system. Simple and safe for dockside living.

*Disadvantage:* Generator needs to be running when stove is in operation.

## Diesel Stoves

More common in high-latitude cruisers because, when operating, the entire range serves as a heater.

*Advantages:* Diesel fuel is cheap; stove is used as a heater and to supplement the waterheater. Stove removes moisture from the cabin.

*Disadvantages:* In warmer climates the radiant heat is hard to bear. Consideration should be taken when stove is on to avoid unnecessary contact, especially while under way, as the entire unit is very hot. Attention needs to be given to the exhaust to ensure that nothing is in the way. Can't be gimbaled. Combustion process often results in sooty decks and sail covers. Strong winds may create backdrafts, resulting in smoke in the cabin, particularly if the chimney isn't long enough. Can only be used when the boat is not heeling much.

## Alcohol Stoves

I have not recently met a cruising yacht using alcohol, and personally I don't recommend it for long-distance cruising.

*Advantages:* Alcohol fuel burns clean, and is safe as it evaporates when spilled. Fire can be extinguished with water.

*Disadvantages:* Alcohol fuel is expensive and hard to find worldwide. Burns at a low temperature, so you need to allow 15% more time to cooking.

## Camping Stove

Carry a multi-purpose camping stove as a backup for your main stove. I use mine when we go on extended hiking trips.

## Barbecues

The first time I became aware of marine barbecues was when my parents were outfitting to go cruising from New Zealand in 1993 and my dad asked me to purchase a charcoal barbecue from the marine store on my way home. Looking at its size in the shop, I was surprised that my father was willing to carry such a large item, plus the charcoal, aboard their 36-foot yacht, but they have had many years of dining pleasure with it.

They had considered gas, but having experienced a few windy potluck evenings when the flame keep blowing out, they thought they would try their luck with charcoal. I was undecided as to whether or not I wanted to have a barbecue on our new boat. Visions of half-cooked meals instantly came to mind, but John assured me that we would purchase the large Force 10 gas barbecue to make barbecuing quick and easy.

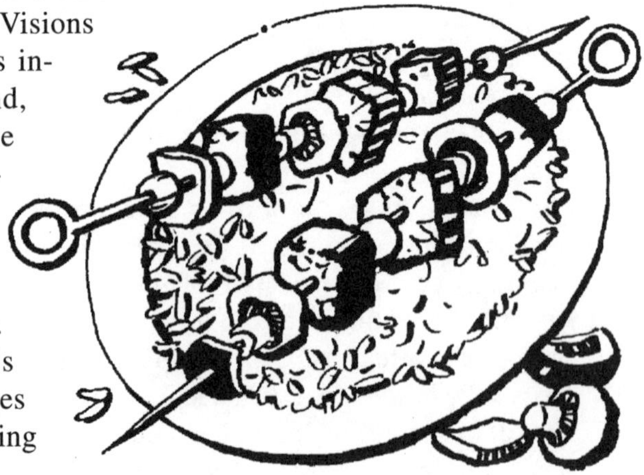

It certainly is large, and on passages we don't want it hanging off the aft rail getting in the way. We stow it inside its cardboard box in the cockpit locker when we go to sea and its 10-lb. propane tank in the side deck gas locker. We've enjoyed many barbecue meals, and it's certainly fun and easy for entertaining. Barbecuing on deck helps decrease the smell and heat from the galley area, especially in the tropics.

I've discovered that barbecuing is a "guy kind of thing," so I'll often be quick to suggest a barbecue meal as I know it's one less thing for me to do in the galley. I've noticed that few Europeans have barbecues, as it's not often a cooking style they enjoy at home, but for many Kiwis, Aussies and North Americans, a barbie and cold beer are the essence of cruising.

### Barbecue Do's

- Choose a **marine barbecue** constructed of stainless steel so to avoid corrosion.
- **Stow your barbecue** when making passages to avoid complications in heavy weather, while sailing and when docking.
- Consider a **canvas cover** for your barbecue when in port, as even marine brands don't hold their lovely shine for long.
- Take care to **avoid sparks** when it is lit.
- Plan on using your barbecue as an **alternative cooking source** if your main stove fails.
- **Take your barbecue ashore**, as its fun to use for interesting picnics and potlucks. Both Force 10 and Magma have optional dock stand brackets.
- For shoreside barbecues, I generally use **paper plates** to save washing up when back on board.
- **Be careful when flipping your cooking**. Many chefs have lost precious morsels to the sharks. Perhaps it's a substitute for feeding Rover at the table.

### Barbecue Don'ts

- Never mount your barbecue near your outboard **fuel tank** or anything flammable.

## Gas Barbecue

- Quick **easy lighting** system.
- Choice of **two gas options:**

- ❖ Disposable high-pressure 1-lb. LPG cylinder. Approximately 2.5 hours cooking.
- ❖ Can adapt the barbecue for use with your onboard low pressure system.
- ❖ **Be aware of the hazards** of using propane.
- ❖ Option of purchasing a model that has a **radiant burner plate** for use as a stovetop, oven, or barbecue.

### Charcoal Barbecue

- ❖ Prevent **spontaneous combustion** by keeping the charcoal dry in a safe place.
- ❖ Don't use **stale charcoal** as it takes forever to light and maintain its heat.
- ❖ **Cheaper to purchase than gas**, with no complicated systems.
- ❖ A trick of mum's and dad's to obtain **three meals from one set of coals**. When a meal has finished cooking place the lid on the barbecue to starve the air and stop the coals from burning.

### Cleaning the Barbecue

Gas and charcoal barbecues are not the easiest item to clean. You need to take your barbecue ashore, spray it well with oven cleaner, scrub it with a metal brush, and wash and wipe it down well.

### Beach Barbecue Grill

Several friends we've met cruising carry stainless oven grates or metal grills that they prop over a fire on the beach for cooking. If you're on a budget, this is a no-fuss and very easy to stow option to purchasing a proper charcoal or gas barbecue – and the food is just as tasty!

## Refrigeration

It is not necessary to cruise with refrigeration, but in the tropics I rarely meet a yacht that doesn't have a small fridge installed. Refrigeration gives you a healthier diet, more meal options, and reduces waste since produce does not spoil as quickly.

## Refrigeration Systems

*Evaporator:* Similar to a household refrigerator, the compressor is controlled by a thermostat and runs on a continual power supply cycling on and off 24 hours a day. Cold gas runs through the plates, cooling the surrounding air, which is called cold-air evaporation.

*Holding plate:* Used if you don't have a continual power supply. The compressor cools a solution in the plates, which retain the cold, which in turn cools the air, hence the name *holding*. You need to visually monitor the temperature controlling it by turning on the compressor. The compressor is either driven by an electric motor or a belt-drive off the engine and is run for a period of time, usually a minimum of 1 to 2 hours a day when the engine is on. Maintaining constant fridge temperature can be difficult as you tend to freeze the lettuce when the engine is running and melt the ice cream if left to long between operating times.

## Icebox

An option to running your refrigeration on its power supply is to utilize the fridge compartment as an ice box. If a boat is hauled out or has inefficient or broken refrigeration, just place large blocks of ice in the insulated fridge box. Some cruisers frequently do this in port to avoid running their engine.

# Galley Rules

- **Wash hands** after using the toilet, before preparing food, and after touching raw meat, for a minimum of 30 seconds with plenty of friction between the hands.
- **Clean cutting boards** and knives thoroughly after preparing raw meat. Do not place cooked meat back on a cutting board until after it has been thoroughly washed.
- Cook meat to a temperature of about **170° F** (77° C) internally.
- Use a **meat thermometer** for roasts, or cut up meat in small

pieces to assure thorough cooking.

- **Refrigerate leftovers** promptly, and heat thoroughly to kill bacteria that grow after an hour or more of room temperature incubation.
- **Crew with infected hand sores**, strep infections, or diarrhea should not prepare food for others.
- Use **clean towels** for drying, and change them frequently as they harbor bacteria. Another option is to air-dry dishes.

Chapter 2

# Provisioning

# Galley Provisions

## Dry Stores

Baking powder
Baking soda
Cake mixes
Cereals - breakfast
Chocolate – drinking, eating, cooking
Cocoa
Coconut desiccated
Coffee
Cookies
Cornmeal
Cornstarch
Couscous
Flour – self rising and whole wheat
Legumes – black beans, chickpeas, sprouts, lentils, and navy beans,
Nuts – almonds, hazelnuts, peanuts, pine nuts, and walnuts
Oats – rolled
Pasta – various
Popcorn
Powdered milk
Rice
Salt
Sugar – brown, white, and confectioners
Taboule – bulgar cracked wheat
Yeast
2- minute noodles

## Condiments

- **Chutney** includes many varieties from smooth to spicy. Generally made with fruit and virtually any fruit, fresh or dried can be used. Specific for Indian dishes and great added to dressings, sauces, marinades, chicken salad, sandwiches, fruit salad and to accompany chicken and fish.
- **Dill Pickles** are tangy additions to salads and sandwiches.
- **Fermented Black Beans** are used with garlic, ginger, sugar, and rice wine to create Chinese sauces and stir-fries. Black beans have a distinctive bold pungency and need to be used sparingly.

Stored in an airtight container and kept cool they will keep indefinitely.

- **Fish Sauce** the salt of Asian cooking is a robust liquid resulting from the fermentation of anchovies and salt. Use in curries, stir fries, dips and sauces.
- **Ketchup** lasts well in the tropics. American brand names are expensive outside U.S. and locally produced ketchup may have a different flavor and is often sweeter.
- **Honey,** I prefer a runny honey which I keep in a squeeze bottle so it's easier use and saves dirtying a spoon.
- **Jelly** is purchased in small containers as it spoils quickly in the tropics once opened unless refrigerated.
- **Maple Syrup,** even though it is expensive, it is nice treat on pancakes and French toast.
- **Mayonnaise** is purchased in one-quart containers. I transfer mayonnaise into a small squeeze bottle and thin it out with cider vinegar to make it more squeezeable. The squeeze bottle takes up less space in the fridge.
- **Miso** is a Japanese fermented soybean paste that goes terrifically in soups, salad dressing, and marinades. Available in Asian and health food stores it is long lasting and protein-laden.
- **Olives** are nice additions to salads, pastas and Mediterranean cooking.
- **Peanut Butter** is every galley's heavy weather standby. Use for quick peanut sauce and to quell your appetite.
- **Sambal-Oelek** is a hot chili paste from Indonesia made from red chilies, salt vinegar and garlic. Both the paste and the oil are useful together or separately for marinades, sauces and dressings. Found in Asian Markets. Can substitute chili sauce and add extra garlic.
- **Soy Sauce** is excellent for sushi and sashimi. Good substitute for salt in oriental dishes even when not called for. Use in marinades (it is a natural meat tenderizer), dressings and sauces.

- **Sweet Chili Sauce** is a treat with chicken, spring rolls. Add to salad dressings, sauces and stir-fries.
- **Tabasco** is a hot chili sauce.
- **Tahini** is a toasted sesame seed butter of Middle Eastern origin. It has a mild delicate flavor and is used in sauces, spreads, and dressings. Two popular spreads using tahini are hummus, made with chick peas, and baba ghanoush, with smoked eggplant.
- **Wasabi**, a hot Japanese horse radish sauce is essential for sushi and sashimi. It is also good in dressings and sauces. Available in plastic tubes that last a long time or in powered form that you mix with water.
- **Worcestershire Sauce** is a rich spicy sauce of vinegar, molasses, anchovies, garlic and spices. Used in red meat dishes and marinades.

# Alcoholic Beverages

## Wines

- **Red Wine** is a nice addition to hearty meals such as stews and wild game, it gives an added zing to tomato sauces, and a rich dimension to red meat marinades.
- **White Wine** goes well with fish, seafood, and poultry.
- **Sherry, Port, Rum, Brandy, and Whiskey** give a sweet flavor to sauces and deserts.

## Liqueurs

I'm not suggesting that you carry all of these liqueurs onboard but we often have a bottle of something interesting that I find is a treat to use in cooking. I've included this list as guide to help you add an extra zing.

- **Bailey's Irish Cream** is made in Ireland from Irish whiskey flavored with cocoa, vanilla, and cream. Use with chocolate, coffee and vanilla flavors. Avoid mixing with citrus.
- **Crème De Cacao** is made from cocoa beans and vanilla. Use with chocolate, coffee, mint and orange flavors.
- **Drambuie** is made from Scottish malt whiskey base with herbs and heather honey. Use with honey, spices, chocolate and dried

fruit.

- **Grand Marnier** is made in France from cognac and oranges. Used as a flambé in sweet dishes and savory sauces. Great with chocolate and fruit especially citrus and berries.
- **Kahlua** is made in Mexico from a brandy base, flavored with coffee. Use with coffee, vanilla, and dried fruit.
- **Midori** is also made in Mexico from honeydew melons. Use with fruit, ice cream, sorbets and sweet sauces.
- **Tia Maria** is made in Jamaica from a rum base with coffee flavor. Use with coffee, chocolate, vanilla flavors and dried fruit.

## Oils

- **Olive** oil has a distinct flavor, useful for salad dressings.
- **Vegetable** is the most versatile of the oils and can be used interchangeably (corn, soy etc.)
- **Sesame** has a strong flavor, a small bottle goes a long way. Used for oriental dishes.
- **Nut** includes walnut, almond etc. Excellent novelty for salad dressings with a fruit vinegar.

## Vinegars

- **Red Wine and White Wine** are more versatile as you may add a sprig of herb for flavor.
- **Balsamic** is good to add to others for a richer, sweeter flavor and for roasting vegetables - just brush it on undiluted or with a bit of oil.
- **Rice Wine** is essential for sushi rice, oriental sauces, marinades, and dressings and as a light vinegar for other dishes. If unavailable substitute dry sherry or scotch.
- **Cider and Malt** is used less often but important in marinades, dressings, sauces, chutney, and pickles.
- **Fruit** is terrific with nut oils for salads and with some vegetables.

## Herbs

I find that in most countries I voyage to the locals grow a favorite herb that is readily available at local markets. In some places, herbs such as dill, basil, cilantro and mint grow wild and are unused by the locals, I often enjoy picking these for use in my cooking.

It is only in the last 5 years that I have come to enjoy cooking and experimenting with fresh herb, and in many of the recipes I have omitted the amount of fresh herbs used as I consider this to be a matter of personal taste.

The French are masters at drying herbs, and I urge you to provision with French herbs whenever you can. One of my most precious galley gifts was a small paisley fabric bag of mixed dried herbs form Provençe, given to me whilst we were cruising Patagonia. Réanne had sent it to us just after completing a cycling trip through the south of France and every meal that I cooked using the smallest pinch out of the bag instantly transported me to the other side of the world.

*Remember that **1 t of dried herbs is the equivalent of 1 T of fresh chopped herbs***

- **Anise** is the seed of the plant, called aniseed. It has a subtle licorice flavor and is used as a condiment, and in the preparation of the liqueur anisette. Aniseed has an aromatic, agreeable smell, and a warm, sweetish taste due to its oil, called oil of anise.
- **Chinese Anise** is also known as star anise from the starlike form of its fruit. The qualities of the fruit closely resemble those of the common anise. Used in baking, Indian cooking, and pickles. Not commonly used.
- **Basil** is a versatile sweet herb that improves the flavor of most savory dishes with a wonderful affinity for tomatoes, meat, and eggs. Keeps well in the refrigerator, minced and covered in olive oil. Add dried basil towards the end of cooking, but well in advance in a salad dressing so the flavor has a chance to develop. Use fresh basil to create pesto and lively basil-garlic vinegar. Historically, basil has been used to induce romantic passions, while in Italy it represents love.

- **Bay Leaves** are from the evergreen laurel tree a native to the Mediterranean. Used in soups and stews, the dish is most often cooked using the whole leaf, which is then removed before serving. Add to par boiled potatoes for added flavor.
- **Capers** are the green flower buds of the Mediterranean caper bush that taste similar to tiny sharp gerkins. Used for seasoning in tartar sauce, salads, pasta and sandwich mixes. Capers placed in a white wine sauce add a subtle zest to fish.
- **Caraway Seeds** are spicy, resembling cumin in flavor. They are a wonderful addition to dark breads, cheeses, confectionery and stews. Crush the seeds to release their flavor when adding them to salads and vegetables, especially cabbage (sauerkraut).
- **Celery Seeds** have a strong flavor and need to be used sparingly. Ground and mixed with salt it is called celery salt. Can be used whole or powdered in stews, salads, pickles, vegetables, and seafood. They are a good substitute for the flavor of celery.
- **Cilantro,** also known as Chinese parsley, is the leaf of the coriander plant. It is often a basic ingredient for Asian, Italian, French and Latin American cooking. Cilantro offers a lemony-fresh flavor for salads, soups, seafood, meats, salsa and guacamole. When fresh it keeps well in a cool place with it's feet in water that should be changed daily. Another option is to keep it packed in an airtight container with a moist paper towel on the bottom.
- **Coriander Seeds** from the cilantro plant are strong smelling. Use in gingerbread, salads, apple pies and as an ingredient for curry. Often used in Middle Eastern and Indian recipes.
- **Cumin** has a strong and earthy flavor, resembling that of caraway seeds in taste. It is popular in Middle Eastern and Latin American foods. Use a 1/8 t in 1 cup of mayonnaise or salad dressing. Use in pea, bean, lentil or chicken soups. Add to bread, cabbage, cheese, tomato sauce, curry dishes, lentils, stews, meat loafs, Mexican-style baked eggs and marinades for shish kebab and wild game. It is the main ingredient in curry.
- **Dill** has aromatic and mildly bitter leaves and seeds. Used in cabbage dishes, potato salad, sour cream, fish, and beans. The seed is good in pickles and vinegar.
- **Garlic** is a strongly-scented herb of the lily family, the bulb of which is related to the onion. Used freely by garlic lovers, it is

the basic ingredient for many hot meals, always going hand in hand with onions and salad dressings. Keeps up to 8 weeks in a dry, dark place.

- **Italian Herbs**. See *pg.164*
- **Marjoram** more commonly called oregano, is a perennial while sweet marjoram is an annual, or warm climate perennial. Use in stews, tomato dishes, meats, vegetables, cabbage, eggs, pizza, and salads.
- **Mint,** although the most common mints are peppermint and spearmint you may be lucky enough to come across other varieties including orange, pineapple, lemon and apple. Always an attractive garnish, the main use for mint is as a refreshing flavor. Use in fruit punches, coleslaw, peas, new potatoes, lamb, jellies, assorted chocolates, mint sauces and teas.
- **Oregano** ~ see marjoram
- **Mustard** is prepared from powdered seeds of either of the two mustard plant species, black mustard and white mustard. The seeds vary from white to yellow to brown. Yellow is the most common for making mustard, though the rare white English seed is superior. Use in cheese, chicken, hot and cold sauces, cold meats, salad dressings,and pickles. Mixed with garlic and sage, it is a tasty rub for pork roasts or try it combined with rosemary for lamb roasts.
- **Parsley** is renowned for it's high vitamin capacity and versatile flavor that mixes well with other herbs. Use in salads, meats, egg dishes and soups. Keep as you would cilantro.
- **Rosemary Leaves** leaves have a strong flavor. Use in marinades, on vegetables especially new potatoes, stuffing, meats, seafood and fruits.
- **Saffron** produces a bright-yellow flavoring and coloring. Used in cakes, breads, paellas and risotto.
- **Sage** is member of the mint family. The leaves are used in stuffing, stews, meat loaf,

goulashes and wild game.

- **Sesame Seeds** are pearly, nut-flavored seeds favored in Middle Eastern cooking. They are at their best when toasted in a dry pan for a few minutes. Black as well as white sesame seeds are excellent additions for breads, vegetables, salads and pastas and as a substitute for nuts. The oil extracted from sesame seeds is used in marinades, Chinese cooking and salad dressings. Grind toasted seeds to make Tahini.
- **Tarragon** is an aromatic, bitter, herb. The green parts of the plant are used in mustard, sour cream, tartar sauces, meats, salads, pickles, vegetables and often placed in a bottle of vinegar to season it. Adds savory flavor to chicken salad and green beans.
- **Thyme** has a flavor that is milder than sage, with a smoky hint. Leaves are used with meats, stews, stuffing, soups and Southern creoles and gumbos.

## Spices

- **Allspice** has a flavor that suggests a blend of cinnamon, cloves, nutmeg and juniper berries. It is both warm and sweet. Use in relishes, soups, vegetables, eggs, French toast, spice cookies and fruit pies. Add to tomatoes, barbecue sauces and meat loafs. In Peru it is used as condiment like black pepper.
- **Cardamom** is available in black and green. The fruit is a small capsule with 8 to 16 seeds that are ground to form the spice. Use as the likes of cinnamon and cloves. Goes well with lentils, Indonesian rice, Indian curries, plain cakes, barbecues and pickles.
- **Cinnamon** is yellowish brown bark with a distinctive fragrant aroma and a sweetish, pungent taste. Grown in many countries the flavor varies slightly. Use the quills in hot chocolate, mulled wine and pickles, and powered cinnamon in curries, baking and desserts. Don't forget a sprinkle on your morning cappuccino.
- **Cloves** were once used by Chinese courtiers to keep their breath pleasant when conversing with the emperor. Their sharp bitterness adds a warm, rich aroma and flavor to sweet foods such as oranges and ham. Use in stewed fruit, chutneys, pickles and stews.
- **Curry** is a composite of various spices and the ingredients vary

according to the type of curry. Curry leaves are used in some Indonesian dishes and curry powder can be used as a substitute.

- **Ginger** was the first Oriental spice to be consumed worldwide. Available fresh, dried, preserved, ground, pickled, minced and crystallized, it's hot, biting flavor is essential to curry powder, yet also contributes to sweet baked goods such as gingerbread. Excellent results when added to fruit dishes and juices. Ginger helps to allay motion sickness and a small piece of root in hot water is soothing. It was also used in the Far East as a digestive aid.
- **Nutmeg and Mace,** apple seed is dried to form nutmeg, while the skin is peeled off and dried to form mace. Used on eggs and baked goods, it can be kept in a powered form or whole and gated with a nutmeg grater as required. Excellent with cabbage.
- **Pepper** is available in black, green and white and is a basic addition to most recipes and the dinning table.
- **Poppy Seeds** of the best flavor have a black/blue color. Add to salads, fruit salads, dressings, French toast, buttered noodles or rice, bread or cookies. For poppy-seed cake, add 1/3 cup to a pound cake mix and bake as directed.
- **Turmeric** is a yellow color and often used as a food colorant, replacing saffron. With a slightly bitter and acrid flavor it is used in pickles and Indian curries.
- **Vanilla** is a climbing orchid native to tropical America and Asia. It is derived from the bean mixed with alcohol. For best flavor it is added to food when cooking has finished. Use in baking, deserts, and ice cream, and as an accompaniment with almonds. Vanilla enhances most if not all sweet bakery and egg dishes.

## Freeze Dried Food

- **Shelf-stable** with locked in freshness, color, flavor, texture, aroma and nutrients.
- Excellent in **heavy weather** since they don't require cooking, thus reducing galley spills and burns. Also great in and **emergency** situation.
- Useful on smaller boats with **storage** and weight limitations.

- Less packing and expense if purchased in **#10 1 gallon tins**.
- Complete meals are available, but tend to be **more expensive** than other food.

## Dried Food

- Beef and turkey **jerky** keep for en extended period of time if kept dry.
- **Chicken stock** purchased in powdered form keeps well and saves space.
- **Dried coconut milk** works great for most, recipes including poisson cru - Tahitian marinated raw fish.
- **Eggs** are available dried as a powder and can be used in baking and omelets.
- **Dried fruit** makes a good substitute for fresh and is great for treats and snacks.
- **Prunes, raisins, and dates** help prevent constipation on ocean passages.
- **Instant dried milk powder** tastes better chilled. Available in whole cream or nonfat outside the U.S.
- **Dried mushrooms** taste great in stir-frys, soups and stews.
- **Dried refried beans** reconstitute quickly and taste just like the canned.
- **Dried shrimp** go well in rice curries and soups.
- **Sun dried tomatoes** are a tasty addition to salads, quiche, pastas and mixed with olive oil and basil make a great pesto spread for melba toast.

# Lucky Dip

Carol Noel~Yacht Elyxir

While visiting one of the more remote San Blas Islands, a dugout canoe came alongside with two Kuna Indian women and their molas. Each 18" x 16" mola tells a story created from bright layers of cloth with a top fabric cut in a pattern to reveal the colors beneath. The cut edges are carefully folded under and finished with tiny stitches and top embroidery. Mola designs are religion, mythology, animal and plant life, and geometric mazes. Sewn by hand they can easily take two months to complete a design, while also performing daily chores.

We had already visited a few islands where I had purchased a number of molas, and decided that I was not going to acquire any more. I had been told that it is best to pay cash for molas so that the women can afford a plane ticket to Panama where they are able to sell more of their molas.

I gestured to the old women alongside that I was not interested in purchasing any more molas. She looked rather forlorn and held up and exquisite piece of work. She had caught my interest, but I just couldn't afford any more molas and told her so.

She then placed her hand down inside her blouse, brought out a package, and began peeling off papers holding them up to me. After the third article, it occurred to me that they were labels from canned goods. I was amazed at the variety of languages and items that she had obviously traded for in the past, enjoyed, and wished to try again. I didn't recognize any of the labels but decided to try my luck.

I went below and selected eight assorted cans that we'd had onboard for a while and I knew we wouldn't miss. Placing them on the deck the old lady eagerly studied each can, gave it a shake and thoughtfully placed it in one of two piles. Then with a grin she handed me over the mola, and carefully packed away the pile of cans she had selected.

## Canned Foods

- On average in **rough weather,** five cans will be consumed a day for three people.
- In **mild conditions** can consumption drops as meals are supplemented with longer-to prepare items such as beans, eggs, grains, meats and vegetables.
- Removing **labels and coating** the cans with varnish adds extra protection if you have a leaky boat and wet lockers.
- Canned **butter, cheese, milk, jellies**, **and cream** is more

# Foods Available In Cans

**Dairy**

Butter
Cheese
Cream
Milk
Sweetened condensed milk

**Fruit**

Apples - baking
Apricots
Berries
Cherries - baking
Coconut milk
Peaches
Pears
Pineapple
Fruit salad

**Meat**

Chicken
Frankfurters
Ham
Turkey
Paté
Spam

**Meals**

Baked beans
Chili con carne
Spaghetti
Ravioli
Stews

**Sauces**

Ketchup
Tomato spaghetti sauce
Stir-fry sauces

**Seafood**

Anchovies - garnish
Mixed shellfish
Tuna
Salmon
Smoked oysters - appetizers

**Soups**

Chicken
Chicken stock
Chowder
Mushroom
Pumpkin
Tomato
Vegetable

**Vegetables**

Asparagus
Beets
Chickpeas
Corn
Green beans
Kidney beans
Mushrooms
Olives
Peas
Pimientos
Tomatoes - whole, puree, paste, sauce

## Fresh Fruits That Keep Well

- **Apples,** including Granny Smiths and red New Zealand apples keep best. Wash then wrap individually in paper towel and stow snugly where they won't get bruised or roll around. Stored in a cool area they should last up to 1 to 2 months.
- **Bananas** are a favourite trade item in the tropics, though green bananas on a stalk ripen all together, so beware. Wash the stalks thoroughly by immersing in fresh or salt water for a few minutes to dislodge ants, cockroaches and spiders. Cut off the hands and place in a dark cool place to ripen. Caution the sticky stalk residue stains badly.
- **Citrus Fruits** keep longer in the tropics if refrigerated. Need to check every second day if not refrigerated.
- **Coconuts** are plentiful in many tropical areas, store well if left unhusked and make an excellent thirst quenching drink. Green husks are best for drinking and last several weeks. Brown nuts are older and contain more white meat and less liquid. They are used for making coconut milk by grating the meat and squeezing out the milk through cheesecloth. The nuts last up to a month.
- **Fruit Salads** are popular onboard and by adding a can of fruit you can supplement fresh fruit supplies.
- **Mangoes** Hard green mangoes with a slight hint of ripening yellow will keep for two weeks before becoming fully ripe.
- **Pineapples** are ripe when the center leaf of the stalk pulls away easily, but pineapples are best bought slightly green with the stalk attached and a slight pineapple smell at the base. Stored upright in the dark they will last over a week. I prefer to remove the stalk and keep the pineapples in the fridge where they are ready to use.
- **Watermelons** keep for two weeks. To test for ripeness knock and listen for a drum sound.

## Fresh Vegetables That Keep Well

- **Cabbages** are the longest-lasting of green vegetables, surviving unrefrigerated for several weeks. Start collecting a selection of tasty cabbage recipes to utilize the last of your cabbage at the end of a long passage.When needed, peel off and use the outer leaves instead of slicing through the center, as intact heads don't rot as quickly. They last up to one month in the tropics wrapped in newspaper, kept dry and ventilated.

- **Carrots** fresh from the ground and unwashed will last several weeks if stored in a cool dark place. Store–bought carrots start going limp and developing black spots after a couple of weeks. Spots can be scraped off and the carrots rehydrated by slicing them thin and soaking them in a salt solution for a few hours.
- **Cucumbers** will last a few weeks in the fridge. When they start to go bad and produce a white slime is easy to prolong their life by pickling them.
- **Eggplants** are readily available in many local markets around the world and go well with tomatoes, in pasta sauces or baked in the Greek dish *Mousaka*, that layers the eggplant with a cheese sauce.
- **Garlic** is readily available worldwide and lasts up to two months.
- **Ginger Root** bought fresh is best stored in a dark dry place. After a month it becomes a little woody but is still useable. I find it is easiest to grate when it's frozen, so I keep a bottle of ginger just inside the freezer door.
- **Green Beans** keep up to a week.
- **Onions** stowed in a dark, ventilated and dry space will last several months. Choose small to medium-size.
- **Potatoes,** truly versatile, are long lasting and are definitly the all time favourtie galley companion. Choose new or smooth-skinned washed potatoes.
- **Tomatoes**, if purchased firm, greenish pink and unbruised will last several weeks. Store them where they won't roll around and check every couple of days.
- **Sprouts** grow well on board. Best to buy fresh seeds in developed countries, as there is more variety, though you can sprout just about anything with a little trial and error. Commercially grown sprouts keep up to three weeks in the fridge.
- **Winter Squash or Pumpkins** kept cool and dry, will last several months. Choose small ones, as once opened they last only a few days.
- **Zucchini** kept in the fridge will last up to two weeks. Use in soup, stir-fry and pasta sauces.

## Preserving

Canning food in sealed jars prevents harmful organisms from entering the jars, while organisms already present in the food are destroyed in the canning procedure. The process is rather complex and care should be taken to ensure a totally safe product. I recommend that you become familiar with this process at home, before leaving, as you have access to more space and required equipment. *The Joy of Cooking* cookbook has detailed instructions on canning.

# Memories of Home

My nanna (grandmother) Phyllis is someone I always associate with the homey feeling canning creates. Bread-and-butter pickles, tomato relishes, lemon-butter spread, orange-ginger marmalade, and glistening topaz jars of summer peaches always line her shelves, labeled with her flourished cursive writing. The labels often have a flower decorating the corner, like the ones she doodles when she's on the phone. She is always at the ready with the kettle, offering a cup of tea to go with a well-stocked cake tin, and it's impossible to leave her house without a jar or two tucked under your arm, a precious memento of summer captured in glass.

When we set out to sea from home for exotic ports, our lockers contained wrapped jars, farewell presents to send us on our way. On opening a crimson jar of plums while anchored under the palm trees, I would often feel out of place as memories of home came floating out of the jar like a genie from a lamp.

I admit that I have never spent an afternoon sweating over steaming pots and canning my own goodies. Maybe this is because my modern lifestyle does not demand time spent in the kitchen – or perhaps it is due to the availability of items that are all to easy to pick off the shelf. Whatever it is, a deep sense inside me, like some forgotten gene, still pictures myself at a future date humming away in a cozy kitchen preparing the fruits of my orchard or the seasonal bounty from the local market. At present, this image does not fit into my galley and my already packed boating lifestyle, but I know that when I place my first canned jar on the shelf, it will be in memory of little nanna.

In the past five years I have only met six boats that do their own canning. In the Marquesas, I met a young French couple, cruising without refrigeration who had filled their entire bilge with canned meat, enough to go around the world. Little did they realize that they would not be able to bring this product into New Zealand, one of their planned stops. Annette on the Danish boat Scafhogg canned 110 small jars of meat for their passage across the Pacific to New Zealand from Chile. Four jars take three hours to can, and all 110 jars took two months!

My mum carries six canning jars and cans whenever they have an excess of food, such as seasonal fruit or a large fish and no freezer space. She also has the jars as security in case the freezer breaks. She can then can the meat, but only if it's not too rough, she claims.

Dee and Marshall Saunders on their 52-foot motor yacht *Penguin* are avid fishermen, and they carry a dedicated pressure pot that holds 16 pint jars on two levels. They pressure-cook their fresh caught salmon when cruising the Pacific Northwest, and tuna while in Central America and French Polynesia. It requires 30 lbs. of fish to fill 16 pint jars, about one good-sized tuna or salmon.

In conjunction with the cooker, they also carry a gas one-burner stove that they hook up to their barbecue tank. The single element allows them to maintain a constant heat more successfully than they can on their electric stove. Dee says the gas burner is also terrific for cooking up large pots of crab or lobster, as it keeps the smell and heat out of the galley.

## Two Methods of Canning

### The boiling water bath method for acidic fruits and tomatoes:

You need to sterilize the jars before packing them by placing them in boiling water for 15 minutes. The seals and rubber also require sterilizing. Sealed packed jars are placed in a pot of boiling water with a rack on the bottom to prevent the heat from cracking the jars. Ensure that the jars do not touch the sides of the pot or each other, and that water covers the jars. Process time is about 25 minutes maintaining a steady boil.

### Pressure-cooking for non-acidic fruits and vegetables, meat and fish:

Filled sealed jars are placed in a rack inside the pressure cooker that has been filled with 3" of water. Food is processed under 10 lbs. of uninterrupted pressure for from 10 to 100 minutes, depending on the food. If the pressure drops below 10 lbs., you must start timing again from zero minutes.

## Canning Foods

- **Fruit** is most often canned in sterile jars, either in water or in sugar syrup using the water bath method. Syrup gives fruit a better color and flavor. A medium syrup mix is 1 cup of sugar to 2 cups of water. Honey, brown sugar or artificial sweeteners can be used and the syrups flavored with lemon, orange rind or spices according to the fruit
- **Vegetables** are generally pre-cooked for 5 minutes, packed in jars and covered with boiling water. Process time is approximately 50 minutes at 10 lbs. of pressure.
- **Meats** are pre-cooked in the oven or stewed, packed in jars and covered with broth or boiling water. Process 75 minutes at 10 lbs. of pressure.
- **Fish** are soaked in brine (1/2 t salt per pint) for one hour. Drain well and pack tightly into containers. Process 100 minutes at 10-lbs. pressure.

### Packing the Jars

- **Fruits and vegetables** are packed firmly into jars 1/2 inch from the top and covered with boiling syrup or water.

- **Meats** should be packed to within1 inch of the top and covered to 1/2 inch from the lid.
- **Fish,** it is not necessary to remove skin and bones, just pack the jar with the skin side out
- Remove **air bubbles** by placing a knife blade down the side of the jar and slightly moving the contents.
- **Wipe** the jar rim and secure the lid.

## Processing

- **Pressure-cook** following manufactures instructions.
- **Remove** jars and allow cooling.
- The lids are **sealed after 12 hours**. The lid curves down and does not move when pressed with a finger.
- If a **lid is not sealed** check the lid and jar edge for any nicks. Change jars and lids an reprocess with in 24 hours.
- To **check a seal,** tap the lid with a spoon. A clear clinking sound denotes a good seal. If the sound is hollow either reprocess or consume the food soon.
- Once the food is processed remove the jar to a board and **cool** away from drafts.

### General Information on Processing

- Canning jars are not readily available worldwide, so **stock up** on a size that fits your pressure cooker or preserving pan.
- Canned vegetables, meat, and fish need to be **cooked** in boiling liquid for 15 minutes uncovered before serving to destroy botulinus toxin.
- If you open a jar and the food smells bad or bubbles **throw contents away**, do not taste it!

## Vacuum Packing

I don't meet many boats that vacuum-pack items but those who I do meet are very enthusiastic about it. Dee Saunders on *Penguin* uses her vacuum-packer for salmon, crab, chicken breasts, squid, tuna, and choice cuts of meat.

- **Frozen food** items that have been vacuum packed last longer, don't taint, or become icy.

- A **large vacuum packer** with a broader heat seal is preferable to a smaller one.
- Use the **sturdy plastic** for vacuum packing and stock up before departing North America.
- Vacuum packing **flour and dry goods** reduces the reproduction cycle of weevils in the food.
- Vacuum packing is also useful **for other onboard items** that require protection.

## Refrigerated Food

The following items can be refrigerated:

- **Fruit**: apples, oranges, limes, lemons and pineapple.
- **Dairy**: butter, cheese, milk, and yogurt.
- **Meat**: ham, bacon and cold cuts.
- **Vegetables**: avocados, bell peppers, cabbage, cauliflower, carrots, lettuce mushrooms, sprouts, tomatoes and zucchini.
- **Condiments**: juice, jelly, butter, and mayonnaise.

## Frozen Food

The following items can be frozen:

- **Bacon** can be packed in areas of the freezer that don't stay totally frozen.
- **Bread** will last indefinitely frozen.
- **Butter** makes good use of areas that don't freeze completely.
- **Cheese;** a mild cheddar gets a little crumbly so choose a sharp (tasty) cheddar. Works great for utilizing the areas in the freezer that don't stay completely frozen.
- **Chicken** breasts bagged in Ziploc bags are ready to go for a meal. I often cut the breast into small pieces before freezing them.
- **Cooked chicken,** pieced, and frozen in small Ziploc bags for later use in soups, stir-frys, pastas and salads.
- **Frozen chicken pieces;** 5lb. boxes of fozen chicken are imported into many countries from the U.S. The price is generally reasonable but an entire box utilizes a lot of freezer space. I generally slightly thaw the box, remove the skin and repack into meal-sized portions in Ziploc bags

- **Crab** cooked and vacuum packed keeps frozen for 6 months.
- **Ginger** should be kept in a small plastic jar in the freezer. It lasts extremely well and grates with ease for use in cooking.
- **Fish;** any firm white fish or smoked fish freezes well, dark oily fish not so well.
- **Lunch Ham and Turkey Slices** freeze well and taste much better than Spam, corned beef or similar canned luncheon meats.
- **One pot dishes,** cook and freeze **several meals** before a passage e.g. stews, lasagnas and pies, if time permits.
- **Oysters** vacuum-packed, will last for two months.
- **Sausages** can be used on the "Down Under" barbeque or smaller chorizos for paella dishes.
- **Shrimp** frozen while raw and packed in a container filled with water will keep for five months. Pre-cooked frozen shrimp are great onboard as they can be defrosted instantly in warm water for ready use in stir-frys, soups and pastas.
- **Steak;** always bag meat in Ziplocs or vacuum-packed to avoid freezer burn.
- **Vegetables** such as peas, corn, beans and mixed veggies can be used for soups and stir-frys. Packages of frozen spinach go well in quiche and green curry.

# General Food Advice

## Bread

- It's **a great treat** to have freshly baked bread at sea.
- To prolong the life of bread wipe it with **vinegar** and wrap it in foil. Store in a plastic bag in a dark cool place.
- In the tropics, I store bread (other than French bread) in the **fridge and freezer** to prolong it's life.
- **Bread machines** and **bread mixes** make easy work of a somewhat lengthy process.

- Slice left over Italian or French bread into 3/4" slices, dry in the sun in the cockpit or under the dodger, and store in a paper bag. This makes wonderful **melba** toast that keeps for weeks and is excellent for snacks with spreads, croutons, or French toast.
- **French baguettes,** available throughout the South Pacific keep best in plastic bags.
- Plain **cabin biscuits** or **pilot crackers** make a good bread alternative and aid the seasick sailor.

## Butter

- **Canned butter** is the best bet for long term storage. It may be difficult to find in the U.S. but is always available from **Downwind Marine** in San Diego.
- I usually keep butter at the bottom of the **freezer** where it is generally not cold enough for meat to stay frozen.
- I transfer butter into a 2 cup sized **plastic container** for every day use. This also makes measurement for baking easier.

## Cheese

- Fresh cheese **wrapped in a vinegar soaked cheesecloth** will last several weeks unrefrigerated.
- Large blocks of **cheddar cheese** placed in an airtight container and **surrounded with cooking oil** will last several weeks without refrigeration. We used this method when I was ten and our refrigeration broke down. I still remember a rather slimy, slippery, smelly block of cheese but once you sliced away a small piece it was fine inside. After slicing off what you want, slip the block back in the oil.
- **Feta and yogurt cheese** in small cubes or balls keeps well in olive oil seasoned with herbs.
- Cheese that is **protected by wax** will keep up to a month without refrigeration.
- **Canned cheese** will last indefinitely if stored in a cool place.
- **Processed cheese** such as Velveeta, Laughing Cow, Kraft and Chesdale will last many months unrefrigerated.

This cheese has a different behavior and I once sat aboard a French friend's boat for an impromptu lunch just after they had made landfall in the Marquesas and completed their first grocery shopping trip. Michelle kept diving into the oven and after the fourth time, 15 minutes later she had a worried look on her face. I asked what was wrong and she said, "My stove is not working properly, this cheese on toast just won't melt".

"Ah ha." I said, "You have just discovered fromage plastique! (plastic cheese). It's not the cheese of France."

- **Grated parmesan** is a tasty, long lasting, low-calorie cheese.
- **Freezing cheese** works well. Choose a hard, sharp cheddar cheese rather than a mild cheddar which tends to crumble when defrosted.

## How to Make Ricotta Cheese

2 quarts milk
vinegar or lemon juice

- Heat milk in a pot, but do not boil.
- When the milk is hot, slowly start adding the vinegar or lemon juice one spoon at a time, while continually stirring the milk.
- The acid curdles the milk and forms little lumps, keep adding the acid spoon by spoon while stirring.
- When the whey water becomes greenish-yellow turn off the heat.
- Strain the milk through a muslin cloth or fine strainer, seperating the whey from the curd.
- Herbs and spices can be added for variety.
- Fold the cloth over the curd and place a weight on it.
- Let it drain for approximately 40 minutes.
- Refrigerate and cut into cubes to serve in salad, pasta, quiche or on toast.

## Coconut Milk

- **Powdered coconut milk** in available from most Asian food stores. Once the package is opened, keep it in an airtight container to prevent it from solidifying. It is more economical powdered as you just mix the required amount with water to your desired strength before adding to your dish.
- **Canned coconut milk** is readily available but is rich and often hard to use the entire can in one dish. It will keep refrigerated

for five days once opened and placed in a container, before curdling like cream.

- To make a **less fattening** coconut milk:

  1C of non-fat milk

  1/2 C roasted or dried coconut
- simmer milk and coconut for 20 minutes, then cool
- strain out coconut

## Cured Ham

- Cured hams will last up to **8 months**.
- **Store suspended,** wrapped in paper with plenty of air around them.
- **Slice** several days supply at a time from **the bottom of the ham** and coat the newly exposed meat with salt.
- **Soak** the slices in several changes of fresh water before cooking to lessen the salty taste.

## Eggs, see Chapter 3, Stowage

## Fishing

- **Mahi-mahi, tuna, and wahoo** are easily caught off the back of the boat with a hand line and lure at speeds of 4 to 12 knots. Great for sushi, pan frying, baking, smoking, and freezing. See Pelagic Fishing chapter.

## Fresh Meat

- Fresh meat is **available** in most major cruising ports but it may be cheaper and healthier to buy imported frozen meat.
- **Vacuum-packed meats** may also be available. They will keep for over a week without refrigeration, several weeks refrigerated, and longer frozen.

## Fruit Juice

- **Concentrated frozen juice** may take up too much freezer space, and is unavailable in many countries.
- **100% concentrated juice** is available in small tetra packs and cans in Europe and South Pacific. This is an excellent alternative to frozen juices.

## Salad Dressing

- **Prepared salad dressings** can be expensive and of a lower quality outside the U.S. or Europe.
- Stock up when in **US-supplied ports** or when you find a foreign brand you like.
- Get creative and **make your own** oil and vinegar dressings.

## Salami

- Has similar **keeping qualities** to cured ham mentioned above but does not need to be soaked or cooked before eating.
- Store in a **cool dark place**.
- Peel off the protective wrapping that often molds, bofore slicing and serving.

## Smoked Food

- Smoking **chicken, shellfish and fish** is a method that can be used to extend the life of food, but these days, more often than not, it is used for flavoring.
- **Smoking is achieved** by placing prepared food in a confined area and smoking it with fragrant sawdust placed on a rack above a low flame. It may take anywhere from 1 hour (for a light smoked flavor and a moist meat) to three days (for a harder smoked meat that is dry and will keep longer).
- Fish require **salting or brining** before smoking. This provides a good surface texture and retards spoilage.
- One method of smoking is to us your **barbecue**. Place a tray of sawdust above the flame and cook the meat on the grill using a low flame.
- The **pressure cooker** can be used for tea smoking:

| | | |
|---|---|---|
| mix together | 1/4 C | back tea |
| | 1/4 C | uncooked rice |
| | 3 T | brown sugar |

- In the base of the pressure cooker place the mixture in a metal dish.
- Position food above in a metal trivet.
- Cook on a low to medium heat with no pressure until food is done, about 1 hour.

- In some places where fishing excursions are popular such as Alaska, Canada, Chile, and New Zealand, it is possible to **pay** to have your fish smoked.

## Sprouts

- The only equipment you need to grow sprouts is a **jar with some kind of mesh lid**, preferably stainless steel, so that it is easier to drain the sprouts when you rinse them.
- The most ideal **sprouting temperature is 65°-75°**.
- Beans and **seeds may become bitter** if sprouted too long where as grains become sweeter on the fourth and fifth day of sprouting.
- **Soak** measured amount of seeds in ample water following the guide below.
- **Drain** the sprouts and place the jar lid down at a 45° angle for drainage and ventilation. This is rather hard to achieve on a yacht so do the best you can.
- **Rinse** the sprouts twice a day, more often in warm climates, with fresh cool water, and position the jar to drain.
- When the sprouts have matured or taste alright place them in a bowl of water and **skim off the hulls** that float, though I generally don't bother with this step as I like the contrast of color especially on mung beans.
- Place alfalfa, cabbage, clover, mustard, and radish sprouts in **indirect light** for two days before using so that they produce chlorophyll and turn their leaves green.
- **Store** sprouts in a sealed container in the refrigerator.

## Sprouting Guide

| Variety | Soaking time (hours) | Dry measure for 1 quart jar | Days until ready |
|---|---|---|---|
| Alfalfa | 8 | 3T | 4-5 |
| Azuki | 12 | 1C | 3-5 |
| Chick Peas | 12 | 1C | 2-3 |
| Cabbage | 8 | 1/2C | 4-5 |
| Clover | 8 | 4T | 4-5 |
| Fenugreek | 8 | 1/2C | 2-3 |
| Green Peas | 12 | 1C | 2-3 |
| Lentils | 12 | 1/2C | 2-5 |
| Mung | 12 | 1/2C | 3-5 |
| Mustard | 8 | 1/4C | 4-5 |
| Radish | 8 | 1/4C | 4-5 |
| Sesame | 8 | 1/2C | 2-3 |
| Sunflower | 8 | 2C | 2-3 |
| Triticale | 8 | 1C | 2-3 |
| Wheat & Rye | 12 | 1C | 2-3 |

## Yogurt

Yogurt can be easily made by adding freeze-dried yogurt culture or plain yogurt culture to reconstituted powered milk, long-life milk or fresh milk.

❖ **Whole milk powdered** makes a thicker yogurt than non-fat.

### Yogurt making instructions

❖ Boil 1 quart of milk and let it simmer for a minute, allow it to cool to a temperature that stings your little finger when you dip it in.

❖ Whip 2 tablespoon of plain live yogurt and add the warm milk slowly while stirring the yogurt.

- Place in a wide-necked thermos. If you don't have a thermos use a container and wrap it in a towel away from drafts. If the air temperature is really cold place a hot water bottle with it.
- Leave for a maximum of 12 hours, no longer as the yogurt becomes acidic.
- Save a 2-tablespoon of yogurt to start the next batch.
- Yogurt cheese can be made by draining the whey from yogurt. Place the yogurt in a sieve lined with a damp fine cloth and set over a bowl to catch the whey. It will turn to Middle Eastern style cheese in 8 hours, when it can be rolled into balls and stored covered in olive oil.

## Tetra Packs

- Tetra Packs are **excellen**t packaging as they don't break or rust, stow safely, quietly, efficiently, don't require refrigeration, and reduce packaging.
- **Products** available in tetra packs: fruit juice and concentrate, UHT milk, cream, tomatoes, soups, tomato sauce, and tofu.

## Cleaning Supplies

Antibacterial hand soap – more difficult to find outside of North America.
Chlorine bleach – treating water tanks, disinfectant, bleaching surfaces, removing mold and mildew
Dish washing liquid – always buy a quality brand for better results rather than a cheaper local product.
Dish scrubber
Garbage bags
Metal polish
Oven cleaner spray
Pest spray
Roach bait
Sponges – large, high-quality sponges may be difficult in less developed counties.
Scrub brushes
Soft scrub – cleaning stainless steel sink and bench top
Windex – cleaning windows and wiping down bulkheads

# Substitution Table

| If you need | Substitute |
|---|---|
| Baking Powder- 1 t | 1/4 t baking soda and 1/2 C yogurt |
| Butter- 1C | 3/4 C cooking oil |
| Butermilk - 1C | 2T vinegar or lemon juice to 1C warm powdered milk, let stand 10 min, or 1C yogurt |
| Coconut milk | Simmer 1C milk and 1/2 C roasted or dried coconut for 20 min, cool, strain out coconut |
| Chocolate- unsweetened square | 3T cocoa and 1T butter |
| Egg -1 | 2T cooking oil. Baked iitem won't be light |
| Herbs- fresh 1T | 1/2t dried |
| Lemon juice -1T | 1/2 T vinegar |
| Milk, baking - 1C | 1C water and 1 1/2 t butter |
| Sour cream -1C | 1/3 C butter and 3/4 C sour milk or Nestle's reduced milk |
| Sugar, granulated - 1C | 3/4 honey, maple syrup. Reduce recipe liquid by 1/4 C |

Chapter 3

# STOWAGE

## Organizing Stowage Space

❖ Before investing in a range of **storage containers**, check that they efficiently utilize the space available.

❖ **Nets** aren't practical for stowing fruit and vegetables while underway, as bruising may occur.

❖ **Avoid using cardboard and paper** for storing food as it can harbor insect eggs and is prone to absorbing moisture and molding. If this is not possible, place the item in double Ziplocs.

❖ The **bilge** area is good for storing bulk items that are in sturdy waterproof containers: laundry soap, engine oil, or awkward items such as diving fins and spare parts.

❖ Keep **cans** dry and check frequently. Isolate cans from the hull by stowing them in large plastic bins.

❖ **Label** and date containers of bulk stores.

❖ **Keep control of inventory** by implementing one of the following methods:

❖ Write a **master list** of items and their location.

❖ Sketch **a plan of the boat** and stowage lockers and write in what goods are stowed where.

❖ Keep **lists of what is inside taped inside each locker** door or floorboard.

If you are on a small or lightweight boat you may need to be conscious of **weight distribution**. My friend Theresa did her first major provision and stowage on her boat in Mexico in preparation for their passage to Panama and was relived to have everything organized and securely stowed away before her husband Michael returned from running errands. Michael congratulated Theresa on her efforts but asked that she walk down the dock with him. Looking back at the boat Theresa noticed that it has a 10° list to starboard and quickly realized that all the heavy provisions and cans were on the same side.

## Bulk Supply Management

❖ **Bulk stores of flours, grains, cereals, and pastas** are best placed in individual Ziploc bags and kept in large plastic airtight storage bins.

❖ **Transfer dried bulk items** into square-sided containers with screwdown lids. Choose a container size big enough for two weeks supply and stow in an easy to reach location.

- **Vacuum-packing items** saves space, keeps them organized, and helps reduce bugs. It prevents goods from being exposed to moisture and thus spoiling and also helps guard against food becoming stale or tainted.

## Daily Commodities Organization

- Since **packaging** varies in size and quality, choose sturdy small containers for oil, juice, syrup, jam, vinegar, etc. that fit your galley space. Once you've left your major provisioning port, don't be too eager to throw these away. It's often easier to transfer bulk or new products into handy reliable packaging than discover you are short on space and storage containers.
- I transfer as many **liquid food products** (e.g., jelly, mayonnaise, honey, mustard, ketchup and maple syrup) into plastic squeeze or pour containers with flip lids as I can. This reduces washing up, as no spoon or knife is needed and the squeeze bottle can be used one-handed making life at sea easier.
- **Dry products** – such as drink mix, Gatorade, hot chocolate, raisins and sugar – store well in the Rubbermaid quart bottle with flip lid.

## Fruit and Vegetable Stowage

- To **sterilize fruit and vegetables**, soak them for 15 minutes in 2 tablespoons of chlorine per 2 gallons and dry them in the sun. The chlorine kills and delays mold and bacteria.
- Carol on *Elyxir* is the only person I know to do this. She first tried it for their **extended ocean passage** from Chile to Easter Island and the Marquesas, and was pleased with the results. Later, Carol cruised the **remote Lau group** in Fiji during a major drought. Knowing that fresh provisioning was unavailable, as the locals had no water to grow many vegetables, Carol used the vegetable dip to prolong the life of the

produce she purchased before sailing there.

- ❖ **Fruits and vegetables** keep best in the dark with plenty of air circulation.
- ❖ **Apples and citrus** should not be stowed together as the citrus causes the apples to ripen.
- ❖ **Onions and potatoes** should not be stowed together as the potatoes begin to sprout.
- ❖ **Plastic baskets** in a ventilated cupboard, bilge or deck box work best for fruit and vegetable stowage.

## Care and Stowage of Fresh Eggs

- ❖ **Eggs** may keep up to two months, if you use one of these methods:

  Coat each egg completely with a light coating of **Vaseline** (this is the method I use).

  **Turn eggs** over every other day.

  **Refrigerate** and turn eggs every other day.

Unwashed, unrefrigerated eggs purchased directly from the farmer will last longer, but in many provisioning stops this may not be a convenient option.

- ❖ No matter how you preserve your eggs after a couple of weeks the old eggs may become bad. At this time, break each egg into a separate container before adding it to the main dish so you don't ruin your entire meal.
- ❖ In **older eggs**, the yolk becomes weak and runny, and it is hard to separate it from the white.
- ❖ In many places, **eggs are often sold without containers**, so keep a reserve of egg cartons.
- ❖ **Styrofoam** egg cartons work well as they can reused after washing.
- ❖ **Cardboard** egg cartons may harbor insect eggs, and don't stand up too well especially if they get wet or an egg breaks.
- ❖ **Plastic** egg crates are another option for stowing your eggs but

make sure large eggs fit. The eggshells will turn moldy so you need to drill holes in the crate to allow air to circulate.

- Eggs are also available in **powdered** form in several countries. In the U.S. powdered eggs are available from REI.

## Tips on Organizing Your Fridge and Freezer

- **Motor yachts** often have a household-style front-loading refrigerator-freezer, while **sailing yachts** often have top-opening refrigerators and freezers. Generally, the space is small and often an awkward shape. On *Mahina Tiare III*, I can't even reach the bottom of my fridge without doing a head-first dive, shoulders and all, into the compartment. It does not have a drain, so washing it out at the end of a passage is a job I leave for John, who is tall.
- If your fridge has a **drain**, check that it does not drain into the bilge; otherwise, bad odors may occur. You need to install a valve or plug on the drain to prevent the cold air from escaping.
- You need to be **organized** in the refrigeration department to avoid continually opening and closing the lid or door, and having to rearrange the entire contents each time you create a meal or just generally lose stuff.
- Some foods that we might otherwise cool at home – pickles, mustard and jelly – **do not require refrigeration.**
- **Transfer bulk goods** that you might otherwise refrigerate at home into smaller containers that take up less space in your fridge.
- This also **ensures against contamination** by not continually dipping into larger jars with a dirty utensil.

## Organizing Your Fridge

- To **maximize efficient use of the odd dimensions** of our fridge, I stacked and organized it with large-lidded plastic containers that I then labeled and packed under various subjects or weeks.
- Lynn Kirwin on the yacht *Constance* had stacking clear-Plexiglas containers with fold-down handles made for her fridge. These worked extremely well for organization and space utilization.
- Here is an example of how I pack our fridge for a three-week

passage from New Zealand to Tahiti. I have three stacking rectangular tubs, in which I stow vegetables for each week of a passage:

***Week #1:*** avocados, bell peppers, carrots, cauliflower, cel ery, cucumbers, mushrooms, parsley, tomatoes, zucchini.

***Week #2:*** avocados, bell peppers, carrots, cauliflower, celery, cucumbers, mushrooms, parsley, tomatoes, zucchini.

***Week #3:*** This tub will contain hardy and long-lasting vegetables such as carrots, green tomatoes, green peppers, cucumbers and celery.

***Condiments Bin:*** On top of Week One, I have an open tub that contains the daily condiments. The tub is easily lifted out to obtain access to containers else where in the fridge. I purchase cheese in large blocks, and when I open a pack, I transfer a block into a small container for daily consumption. Once opened, a packet of ham also gets placed in a small Tupperware, as does butter. Condiment items I keep in the fridge: small squeeze bottle of mayonnaise, jelly in the tropics, juice, milk, yogurt, fresh sprouts, leftovers, and half-used vegetables, such as onion in a container.

- I refrigerate **meats and dairy** items: salami, ham, cheese, butter, and plain yogurt for making yogurt with milk powder.
- I pack **lettuce** heads into their own separate plastic containers, with a damp paper towel on the bottom.
- **Cabbages** are wrapped in newspaper and placed in a plastic bag. If space allows, I place them in the fridge, but if there is no space I store them in the bilge until room opens up in the fridge.
- **Fruit:** I pack a container of apples, oranges, lemons and limes, and these keep up to four weeks in the bottom of the fridge. I use these when we have first consumed the majority of these items, which I stored in the bilge at the beginning of the passage.
- **Bread**: Once space occurs in the fridge, I then fill it with loaves of bread.

## Organizing Your Freezer

- For the **efficiency of the freezer,** it is most critical to keep air spaces to a minimum.
- For optimum **utilization of freezer space**, and to assist in meal

planning, I package all freezer meats, seafood and vegetables into small Ziploc bags.

- **Vacuum-packing** freezer items helps avoid freezer burn, tainting, and prolongs their freezer life.
- I **alternatively layer** small foodpacks in the freezer and work through the layers. For a meal, it is then **easy to choose a pack** and defrost it.
- When space occurs in the freezer, I either **pack it with blue ice packs**, loaves of bread or bottles of water.
- **Ice cubes** for drinks can be made in "Scubs" disposable bags available from West Marine and kitchen stores. Just fill a plastic bag containing all the little pockets with water and freeze. To obtain ice simply break out a cube from the plastic.

## Dry Ice Chest

- Packing a cooler with a block of **dry ice** is more common on race yachts than on cruising boats.
- Generally, **meals are precooked**, bagged in Ziplocs and frozen before being placed in the cooler. This saves time and effort by the cook while the boat is racing.
- Big blocks of dry ice **will keep two weeks.**
- The dry-ice blocks should be wrapped in plastic. Surround the large block of dry ice with regular ice cubes or blue ice packs and place in the bottom of the cooler.
- Care should be taken to prevent food touching dry ice; otherwise freezer burn occurs.

## Transporting Supplies to the Boat

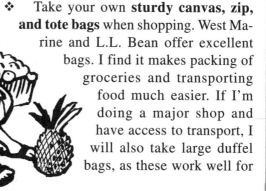

- Take your own **sturdy canvas, zip, and tote bags** when shopping. West Marine and L.L. Bean offer excellent bags. I find it makes packing of groceries and transporting food much easier. If I'm doing a major shop and have access to transport, I will also take large duffel bags, as these work well for loading light goods such as paper towels, toilet paper and bread. Purchase a **strong-wheeled cart** for moving groceries, fuel and water.

## At the Grocery Store or Market

- Plan on shopping **early** in the morning to avoid the lunchtime and evening rush. Try to **reduce all unnecessary packaging** while at the checkout counter, and pack all related items into designated bags (i.e., frozen, canned, dry and fresh goods). This makes for easier transportation (it's often a bus and dinghy ride to the boat) and stowage once aboard.

- Many supermarkets do not have people to help pack your groceries, so you need to **take someone with you** to give you a hand. Otherwise, you hold up the customers behind you, as it's nearly impossible to unload your cart, reduce the packaging and sort your groceries into their designated bag.

## Pest Control

- Try to a**void tying ashore,** as this provides easy access for pests to board your boat. When moored stern-to, lift your gangplank, and if possible, move your boat farther away (6 feet or so) from the dock at night.
- Don't leave garbage bags on deck overnight.
- Install **mesh screens** over hatches and portholes to keep bugs out.
- **Baygon** insect spray (not available in the U.S., Australia or N.Z.) is extremely effective.
- Treat all items that you bring aboard as **potential carriers** of bugs and eggs.
- **Ants** are best killed by spraying or with ant-bait traps.
- **Cockroaches** are hardy critters. They fly, have a three-week hatching cycle, and are adept at changing their resistance to pesticides. They don't like light, hiding away anywhere dark and are very wary of poisons.

- Combat or Raid **roach baits** work very well killing roaches, as they arrest their three-week hatching cycle.
- **Boric acid** is often a recommended method for killing roaches. It can be either mixed with sugar, or sprinkled around the boat, or mixed with water and sugar and painted on surfaces. I find this rather messy and prefer roach baits and spray.
- If you are still unable to kill the roaches, you will have to resort to **bombing.**
- Remove all open food, dishes and utensils.
- Block all dorades and vents.
- Open all lockers, storage areas, and bilges spraying a handheld can into each place.
- Set the bomb off and leave the boat closed for 12 hours.
- Air well and repeat bombing three weeks later, since a new batch

  of eggs will have hatched.
- To kill or repel **mosquitoes**, use smoke coils in the cockpit, which are less noxious than spraying insecticide below decks. Never scratch a bite, as staph infection can easily occur in broken flesh.
- **Weevils** are rapacious little critters that live and reproduce in cake mix, cereal, flour, pasta, grain, nuts and rice, generally preferring wholesome foods. They are able to nibble through plastic bags, and are recognized by their small, dark bodies and threads that appear throughout the packaging.

  I'm not too sure if weevils are detrimental to your health. They can be picked out of food or skimmed off the top, especially if you are cooking something in water, such as rice. Often a few herbs will disguise them. I remember my brother and I arguing about who had the most weevils in their breakfast cereal.

  **There are four ways of avoiding weevils:**

  Place a **bay leaf** or two in with the stored dry food.

  **Freeze** packets of potential weevil food for 24 hours.

  **Microwave** questionable foods for 30 seconds.

  **Vacuum-pack** drygoods.
- **Rats:** I hope that you never have the misfortune of having Mr. Ratty aboard. I meet at least one cruising boat each year that does. They are extremely difficult to exterminate and love chew-

ing through anything to wear their teeth down. I met one steel boat with a rat that was gnawing all the paint off the hull.

Suggestions to help you **eliminate Mr. Ratty:**

**Rat trap** set with cheese or peanut butter. Don't set the trap for the first few days so that the rat gets used to the idea that there is easy food available.

A **rat trap tray** with the sticky goo and tasty poison in the middle, so that when the rat steps onto the tray, it's feet get stuck.

**Insect fogger** with an escape hatch for the rat. This may not smoke it out, but it will cause it to become drowsy.

**Poison** will kill the rat, but pray that it does not go off to die in an inaccessible place.

Rats love to eat the **insulation on electrical wires**, so check all wiring closely after a rat has been aboard.

When **leaving your boat** for and extended period of time, it is a good idea to place ant and cockroach traps around the boat – even if you have no sign of them aboard.

Chapter 4

# Passage Preparation & Cooking at Sea

# Provision Planning

## Before Leaving Your Homeport

- Write down a simple menu plan for a week of the foods you generally eat. Check that these items are easy to stow onboard and prepare at sea. If not amend, your plan accordingly.
- Dee on *Penguin* writes out her favorite recipes, either on recipe cards or in a notebook. She makes the steps logical and easy to read. This way, when at sea, she doesn't have to deal with a large cookbook and fine print that provides too much information on what otherwise should be an easy-to-follow recipe.
- Use your menu plan to help with your provisioning. It allows you to calculate the amounts required and ensures that you don't forget anything.
- I generally plan a one-week rotation for my menus at sea, allowing for rough weather and the catching of a fresh fish if we are in suitable waters.
- Once your menu plan is established, you can then arrange your dry provisions, refrigerator and freezer items accordingly.
- Make a list of the items you use and the quantity you use of them several months before you set out cruising. This will give you a basic guideline when buying provisions.
- Collect and sample recipes that will take advantage of your long-term onboard provisions.
- Cabbage is cheap and keeps well. I'm always on the lookout for interesting recipes that use it so that, at the end of a four-week passage, it's not something the crew will be bored with.
- At a cruiser's potluck dinner in the Marquesas, there were 10 pasta dishes, two rice dishes and, luckily, one fish dish from a fortunate yacht that had caught a tuna just before arrival that day. I should have written down the recipes for you, as that would be 12 more for your collection!
- Make provisioning less daunting and save money on bargains by provisioning over several months.
- You may not be an avid rice, beans and pasta consumer when you set out cruising. It's rare that people change their eating habits drastically when starting their cruise, but they slowly alter them while they are cruising, usually out of necessity.

# The Cruising Diet

I was raised on a basic English diet of meat, potatoes and two vegetables. The only spaghetti I was familiar with came out of a can. Even racing in the Whitbread Race, our boat was very British with our freeze-dried meals consisting of roast beef and beans, roast lamb and peas, smoked fish and carrots, lamb stew, and macaroni and cheese. It was not until I spent 18 months cruising the remote Chilean Patagonia region – with its infrequent and minimal provisioning stops – that I became interested in using herbs and spices.

The Chileans themselves are big red meat and potato eaters, only using cumin and red chili sauce for spice. I was starting to become bored with meals onboard and, for the first time in my life, my cooking style slowly started to change. I began studying cookbooks for new ideas.

A newly arrived crewmember bought down a packet of dried Taco mix. Reading through the ingredients with gusto, I set out to recreate the mix so that I could produce future taco meals using fish instead of ground beef, and not even minding the absence of Taco shells. I was hooked!

My Dad is another example of a radical change in a diet. With English parents and 15 years as an officer in the Royal New Zealand Air Force, his eating habits were an ingrained English diet. After our first week in Tahiti, Dad slowly began to question how much of our cruising kitty Mum was spending when shopping. One day Mum threw down her wallet in disgust saying, "You go buy your pork chops, sirloin steaks and fresh asparagus." Two hours later, Dad returned and sheepishly unpacked his bags. While Mum sat in the saloon nonchalantly reading her book, Dad stowed away canned tomatoes, pasta, rice and tuna fish. He had no idea of the high cost of imported meat and vegetables and, to this day, has never complained of spaghetti for dinner.

## Tips on Provision Planning

- To Determine How Many Provisions to Stow Onboard

  First calculate your passage time.

  Next add extra days for unfavorable winds such light air or heavy weather and a few more for rigging or engine troubles.

  Double this time amount.

  This then amounts to the minimum number of days you need to provision.
- Seasickness may lay claim to your appetite for the first few days of any ocean passage. Plan for simple, bland meals when putting to sea to ensure you don't encourage your stomach to turn you green.
- Heavy weather makes cooking at sea extremely difficult. You need to have at least 20% of your passage time in easy-to-prepare meals. These may be any of the following:
- Frozen precooked meals: chilis, curries, hearty soups, lasagna, pies, pizza, and stews.
- Canned meals come in a few options ranging from baked beans, chili con carne, spaghetti, ravioli, and soups and stews.
- Freeze-dried meals ranging from complete gourmet camping meals to instant two-minute noodles.
- Research your first landfall port.
- Many cruisers crossing the Pacific from Mexico and Panama to the Marqueses are often surprised at the high cost of food and fresh produce available from the few small stores and the lack of selection. There is often another month of cruising the isolated islands of the Marquesas and Tuamotus before reaching the major port of Tahiti with its super stores and thriving local market.
- Check if any quarantine restrictions apply to food items you have onboard when arriving.
- Maintaining a well-stocked yacht gives you the freedom to stay places longer or perhaps change plans without the burden of endless trips ashore to the store.
- Find out what items are unavailable or expensive in your planned cruising ground and purchase extra provisions accordingly.
- Variety of the menu is important, so don't restrict yourself to large quantities of few items.

- Special events – birthdays, anniversaries, Equator crossings, halfway celebrations and holidays – should not be forgotten. Think of interesting ways to cater for these occasions – maybe a cake mix or special treat.
- If you are unfamiliar with the products you are choosing, it may be best to purchase one of each brand and try it out. I've often done this with different brands of canned tuna, as the size of meat flakes versus water really varies brand to brand. One label of canned stew might just taste awful, another too fatty, while too much sugar or salt is added to a different variety for our taste. Quite often, I will mix different products of ready-to-go meals, and I will stock up with extra cans when I discover a favorite brand.

## Stretching the Limit

The finish line for the Auckland, N.Z.-to-Noumea, New Caledonia, yacht race had been changed the year I did the race. Previously, it had ended at the Amandee lighthouse on the barrier reef 20 miles from the town of Noumea, but the local French sailors decided to finish the 1993 race off the yacht club headland inside the lagoon. The change was to give the race a more public spectator view and to save the committee boat from bouncing around in the surf to record the finishers.

We arrived at Amandee lighthouse after eight days of hard sailing from Auckland to discover that the wind dies at night inside the lagoon. We spent the night drifting around the coral heads in the strong tidal currents. There went all our hopes of a good result in the race as we lost 12 hours becalmed!

Our race was not the only one finishing, as Australia also had its own race arriving from Gosport. Here we were, inside the reef dodging coral heads, with an Aussie boat doing the same. Well, these Aussies weren't happy that the finish line had been changed, for they weren't notified of the switch until we told them on the radio.

To drown our sorrows we decided to have a party, for we still had a supply of rum and a few munchies, and we could get the local FM dance station on our stereo. These poor Australians were not in luck, having eaten everything onboard. Every hour or so they would contact the race committee trying to get a response. They were hoping that the race committee would let them finish at the lighthouse and just add the time spent floating around the lagoon. In this way, they could finish and all would not be lost. What they did not know was that the race committee – knowing that no one would finish in the dark due to the lack of wind – had gone home for the evening.

These Aussie's were pretty persistent, calling the race committee every hour. By 3 a.m. they were extremely agitated and were sounding quite angry, while our crew were truly merry, having demolished most of our rum. It was then that one of our crewmembers picked up the radio microphone and spoke in a very French accent: "Would you *pleeze* stop calling *zee* race committee. We are not going to talk to you, and are even prepared to deduct time off your race result if you continue to be so rude." There was a period of silence, and a very quiet voice came back saying they were sorry for being impolite.

The breeze picked up early in the morning, and at dawn we drifted across the finish line with the Australians. They were very quiet and glum, though exceedingly polite to the officials.

This just goes to show that it pays to carry a few extra provisions onboard.

## Menu Planning

Here is the menu plan I created for our 2,300 mile passage from Tahiti to Hawaii with a crew of eight. I was worried when Juha, one of our crew, informed me that he had a moderate intolerance to wheat products. I had an established supply of canned and dried goods onboard and just required fresh and frozen food provisions in Tahiti for the passage. At sea, I just generally take one day at a time, but for this trip, I decided to write up a plan for the entire passage to ensure that I could provide a balanced diet.

| Day | Lunch | Dinner with Wheat | Dinner Non-wheat |
|---|---|---|---|
| Mon. | Sandwiches | | Garlic chicken with rice and salad |
| Tue. | Sandwiches | | Quiche, baked potatoes and salad |
| | | **Depart Port Wednesday at 10 am** | |
| Wed | Sandwiches | Chicken, vegetable/ramen soup | |
| Thu. | Sandwiches | Pre-frozen lasagna and salad | |
| Fri. | Sandwiches | | Chicken lentil stew |
| Sat. | Sandwiches | | Sweet and sour shrimp stir-fry, rice |
| Sun. | Taboule salad | Spaghetti and salad | |
| Mon. | Pasa salad | | Fresh wahoo, rice, salad |
| Tue. | Poisson cru | | Chicken pumpkin curry |
| Wed. | Fish cakes | Dried cheese tortellini and salad | |
| Thu. | Macaroni and cheese | | Satay shrimp stir-fry, rice |
| Fri. | Toasted sandwiches | | Fresh tuna, potatoes and beans |
| Sat. | Poisson cru | Spaghetti carbonara and salad | |
| Sun. | Sushi | | Fish tacos and salad (frozen fish) |
| Mon. | Tuna salad | | Chili beans and coleslaw |
| Tue. | Left over chili | | Chicken tomato stew |
| Wed | Indonesian rice salad | | Fresh mahi-mahi, potatoes and corn |
| Thu. | Chickpea salad | Seafood in tomato and couscous | |
| Fri. | Toasted sandwiches | | Black bean chicken stir-fry with rice |
| Sat. | Macaroni and cheese | Shrimp pasta and coleslaw | |
| Sun. | Crackers and goodies | | Fish tacos and salad (frozen fish) |

## Breakfast

John cooks breakfast, and although most breakfasts contain wheat, Juha had the option of fruit and yogurt or eggs. French toast, yogurt, fruit (either canned or fresh), eggs, cereal, toast, fresh baked muffins, pancakes, egg muffins and porridge are all morning menu.

## Lunch

Lunches onboard are usually toasted sandwiches and the previous night's leftovers, and I always gave Juha the option of salad. French baguettes were cheap at 40 cents each, but a small loaf of local bread was expensive at $3, and imported brown bread from the U.S. or New Zealand ran as high as $6. I provisioned with 15 baguettes that lasted four days and 4 loaves of brown bread, 2 of which I froze as soon as there was space in the freezer. I counted on baking a large loaf of bread for at least two days of the trip, and I always carry a large supply of crackers for a lunch option.

## Fresh Vegetable Quantities

When provisioning the fresh food, I often count out my vegetable items per day. I allow 2 onions, 2 carrots, 1 tomato, 2 apples and 1 orange per day. Apples and oranges are best kept in the refrigerator for an Equator crossing, as they stay fresh longer. At lunch, I cut them into quarters and give each person a small slice. Such a small portion may seem stingy if you are a fruit fanatic, but a fresh, cool, crispy apple slice is a big treat especially with a tasty slice of cheese.

For this trip, I counted out four meals using potatoes, allowing two medium potatoes per person. I selected four medium cabbages, two that were red to give a dash of color in salads and stir-frys. Other fresh vegetables were imported and rather expensive, so I included four green peppers, five zucchini, five cucumbers, fresh green beans and mushrooms in small quantities. Imported frozen peas, beans and corn were inexpensive and helped supplement stir-frys and salads and stews.

Local lemons were inexpensive, and I purchased six of medium size to use in salads, poisson cru, and a garnish for fish. A bunch of imported parsley was $3 at the supermarket, but locally-grown bunches of basil, parsley and cilantro was only $1 at the market. A big bag of dried imported Herbs de Provence was $3 at the supermarket. These herbs were absolutely incredible, and I wish I'd bought several more.

## Red Meat

Red meat imported from New Zealand was good quality and inexpensive, but we generally don't eat much red meat onboard. It would be very easy to substitute red meat for the fish, chicken or shrimp dinners in the menu plan that follows.

## Chicken

Local chicken was very expensive, but 5-lb. boxes of frozen chicken thighs imported from the U.S. were only US$4. One box easily fed our crew for a meal, and before I stowed the boxes in the freezer, I slightly thawed them and removed the skin and cut the chicken into fist-sized pieces. This reduced the size of the package and cut preparation time while under way. Roasted chickens were US$7. I bought two and deboned them, freezing the meat in small Ziplocs, enough for three meals: chicken ramen, chicken lentil and chicken stir fry or pasta.

## Seafood

Shrimp were reasonably priced, and I like them as a meal plan because they don't require defrosting until you are ready to use them. Shrimp are a good standby, along with pasta dishes if you don't catch that fish you were hoping for, if weather conditions deteriorate and you aren't able to do the gourmet quiche dish you planned, or if you completely forgot to defrost the chicken.

On this trip, I only set the fishing lines on three days, because each time the lines were payed out we only had to wait a few hours before catching a fish. Each fish was a different variety, so it kept the meals interesting. I always cook the fish on the day we catch it.

## Stowage

The menu plan greatly helped in my stowage organization, as I was able to layer the refrigerator and freezer with each week's provisions.

## Surprises

We baked bread twice, and fresh bread is always a bit hit. Unfortunately, John accidentally cut the power supply to the bread machine on the second time around. He switched off the power inverter to get a clearer radio signal, and as the bread machine has no memory of its time sequence, it has to start all over again. Luckily, the loaf was on its second rise and I could punch it down, place it in two pans, wait for it to rise again, and bake it in the oven. We will now place a big piece of tape over the inverter switch whenever the bread machine is on.

For our Equator crossing ceremony, I concocted an awful mixture of oats, tabasco and coffee grounds, tinted with green food coloring to administer to the pollywogs for their initiation rite into the realm of shellbacks. A celebration batch of walnut-peanut brownies was baked, but the rest of the passage was a bit bouncy for further baking. For snacks, we have a cracker box that stays in the cockpit. Each night after dinner, we open a packet of cookies for dessert and to stock the cracker box for night watches, along with hard candy.

## Planning Overview

I was amazed at how easy my day-to-day concern of what to cook next was eased, giving me more time to concentrate on the meal of the day. Catching fish was a bonus, providing more spare meals in the bank and the chance to eliminate some repetitive meals. Most meals had an accompanying salad made with both lettuce and cabbage to stretch the lettuce further. I try to keep the evening salad interesting: Greek with olives and herbs, orange and ginger, nutty with sesame and pumpkin seeds, or mixing a tasty dressing if I feel inspired.

Many times, leftovers from previous meals were easily expanded to provide a tasty lunch. Weather conditions were good on this passage, though winds were either beam-on or just forward of the beam at around 18 knots, which made for a bumpy ride. Some nights, it was difficult to juggle the pasta pot and it was often easier to lock the stove than have it gimbal away. My next galley project is to modify the gimbal locking mechanism, enabling the oven to be locked-off at different angles for when the boat is on a steady tack.

The temperature was hot, hot, hot, and I was grateful for my galley fan; with spray over the decks, we could not open the hatches or ports. I did not use the oven, and cooked with the pressure cooker whenever possible to reduce the heat below.

At the end of the trip, my estimates had worked out extremely well. On our arrival in Hawaii, State Agriculture confiscated all my fresh food, which consisted of one tomato, two lemons, one orange and one grapefruit, so all I had left was a quarter of a cabbage, three carrots and two onions. The crew was very complimentary of the meals, saying they were better than what they eat at home and not at all what they had expected.

# Cooking While Underway

## Tips on Cooking While Underway

- Plain crackers and hard candy should be kept in a small sealed container, always at the ready for the seasick sailor.
- Have a container of snacks – cookies, dried fruit, health bars or crackers – handy for night watches or for quick in-between-meal pick-me-ups.
- Use Scoot-Gard on the counter tops to keep items from sliding.
- Prep and cooking time for a meal at sea takes twice as long as it would at anchor. Have patience, be organized, replace items as you use them, clean up as you go, and don't let it get you down.
- At sea, it's a lot easier prepare the evening meal in daylight. Remember that in the tropics it gets dark at six in the evening.
- For some reason, the wind always seems to increase at sunset, interrupting cooking. Sail reduction is often required, and conditions become more uncomfortable below in the galley.
- If my evening meals require a lot of vegetable preparation – such as with a salad, stir-fry or stew – I often do the chopping in the early afternoon so that in the evening I don't have to spend as much time in the galley.
- Quite often at sea I find it's easier to prepare and chop vegetables sitting down at the table than standing at the counter top. I place the vegetables I'm working on in large Rubbermaid containers on the table, which has a piece of Scoot-Gard on top to keep articles from sliding around.

- I really enjoy having a daily cartoon calendar on my galley wall. Being able to view a *Far Side* scenario tickles my sense of humor, especially when its rough and I'm counting down my days at sea.

## Heavy Weather Menu Planning

- The simplest menu in heavy weather is one that does not require any prep work or unnecessary time watching pots on the stove top.
- Cooking and washing dishes in rough conditions is challenging and difficult, and you can't expect just one person to do it all. You need to be able to trade off such duties.
- If you have been at sea for a few days, you and your crew will have a hearty appetite, even if heavy weather occurs. Though rich food might be a little hard to stomach, tasty one-pot meals will be welcome.

- When it is extremely rough, we generally plan only two hearty meals a day. John will cook a large brunch around 10:30, consisting of either eggs, French toast, pancakes or hot cereal, and at 4, I prepare a hot one-pot evening meal.
- When its rough, even the simple task of boiling water becomes difficult, and for this reason you need a dedicated sealed kettle and hot thermos. These will give you an convenient source of hot water for drinks and instant soups.
- When heavy conditions occur, I choose not to cook any dish that requires more than a half a potful of water – meals with rice, pasta or boiled potatoes – because the water will slosh over the edge of the pot.
- One-pot meals such as chili, curries, hearty soups and stews can be prepared before a passage and frozen. When heavy weather occurs, these meals can then be thawed and easily heated in a pot.
- Frozen meals like lasagna, pizza and pie require a hot oven or microwave to reheat them. They may be difficult to impossible

to find ready-made in less-developed countries.

- Prepared frozen meals are generally the first choice in rough conditions, but if you have already used these up, you will be resorting to canned food unless your budget has allowed you to provision with freeze-dried meals.
- Canned meals. Often I'll mix them with soup to stretch them out, and maybe add a can of meat, tuna or vegetables for variety.
- The pressure cooker provides a safe method for cooking one-pot meals in all weather conditions. My one good standby in stormy weather is a pressure cooker pot filled with potatoes, carrots and onions sprinkled with Italian or French herbs. It may sound plain, but when its cold, wet and miserable out, there's something comforting about the old spud and his pals. Toppings can vary from a knob of butter, bacon bits, Parmesan cheese, grated cheddar cheese, salt and pepper, canned tuna, or relish. Any leftovers can be diced and fried for lunch the next day see "*Bubble and Squeak.*"

## Coping In The Galley In Heavy Weather

- Know and anticipate the movement of your stove. If my stove is gimballing too erratically, I will simply lock it so I'm more in control of its movement.
- Make sure that your stove is fitted with sturdy adjustable locking arms so that all your cookware can be secured in position on the stove top.
- In heavy weather, my mum also uses a spring tie-down, a setup of a stainless spring with a hook on each end. She simply hooks one hook to the side fiddle, stretches it across the pot, lid and all, then hooks the other end onto a fiddle on the other side. It saves the worry of a flying pot, or its lid slipping off.
- Pack new sponges into gaps in galley cupboards to stop items from sliding and rattling around.
- Ensure that drawers have a sturdy catch to prevent them from jumping and sliding out of position. In heavy weather, I place a webbing strap with buckle in front if the drawers.
- Check that your drawers have a stop to prevent them from sliding out all the way. I've seen many a heavy draw go flying

across the cabin when someone has let it go after removing an item.

- If your sink is an outboard installation, make sure your shut off valve is easily accessible so you can prevent the regurgitation of water.
- Having a Hella Turbo fan installed in the galley ensures adequate ventilation for the cook. Remember that in heavy weather all ports and hatches will be closed.
- Invest in sturdy, deep, stable non-skid bowls for serving meals in storm conditions. Some people recommend paper plates, but I find that you can't set them down and that food gets cold too quickly.
- Plastic or stainless thermal mugs with tight, sealing lids are invaluable in heavy weather for serving hot drinks and meals. Their large handles makes them easy to hold, and the insulation keeps food and liquids hot in cold weather.

Chapter 5

# Appetizers & Light Meals

# Drinks

## Sangria

Sangria always reminds me of summertime afternoon yacht club lawn functions in South England. Great for a large crowd where you don't want to go to the trouble of attending "the bar," sangria can be served in jugs, though I prefer a punch bowl with ladle as you can scoop up which fruit you wish to nibble on.

| | |
|---|---|
| 1 bottle | wine – white or red |
| 1 bottle | soda – cold ginger ale, 7-Up or equivalent |
| | sliced fruit such as lemons, oranges, apples and strawberries |
| | mint leaves to garnish |

- ❖ Combine wine and fruit in a punch bowl and let soak for at least 2 hours.
- ❖ Add soda, mint leaves and ice cubes.

## Hot Buttered Rum

While wintering over in White Rock, Canada, my dad and I would row out from the pier in the afternoons to check our three crab pots. Often the weather was miserable and upon arriving back to the boat we would share a hot buttered rum before cooking up the crabs.

| | |
|---|---|
| 1/2 C | brown sugar |
| 1/4 lb. | butter – salted |
| | *cinnamon, nutmeg and allspice |

- ❖ Combine ingredients.
- ❖ Spoon 2 T of mixture into a mug, add desired measure of rum and fill with boiling water.

# Nibbles

## Spicy Fruit and Nuts

| | |
|---|---|
| 2 C | cashew – toasted |
| 1 C | almonds – toasted |
| 2/3 C | dried apricots |

| | |
|---|---|
| 2/3 C | raisins |
| 2/3 C | dates – chopped |
| 1 | egg white |
| 2 T | olive oil |
| 2 T | lemon juice |
| 1 1/2 T | lemon zest |
| 1 T | ground cumin |
| 1 T | ground coriander |
| 1 t | hot paprika |
| 1/2 t | turmeric |

- Heat oil, add spices, cook and stir until fragrant.
- Whisk egg white until it peaks, stir in spice mixture and remaining ingredients.
- Spread mixture onto a greased oven tray.
- Bake 25 minutes or until crisp and dry, stirring occasionally.

*Makes 5 cups of mixture that keeps well in an airtight container.*

## Sugared Nuts

| | |
|---|---|
| 1 C | almonds – whole |
| 1 C | pecans |
| 1 | egg white |
| 1/3 C | sugar |
| 1/4 C | butter – melted |
| 1/2 t | cinnamon |

- Bake nuts until slightly roasted.
- Beat egg white until it forms soft peaks, gradually beat in sugar and cinnamon.
- Mix in melted butter, add nuts, stir and spread onto a greased oven tray.
- Bake 25 minutes, stirring occasionally.

## Devilled Nuts and Seeds

| | |
|---|---|
| 1 C | walnuts |
| 1 C | pecans |
| 1 C | peanuts |
| 1 C | pinenuts or pumpkin seeds |
| 1/2 C | Brazil nuts |

| | |
|---|---|
| 1/4 C | butter |
| 4 T | Worcestershire sauce or chili and soy sauce |
| | salt |

- ❖ Roast nuts in butter for 10 minutes, stirring often.
- ❖ Add sauce and seeds, cook 5 minutes.
- ❖ Sprinkle with salt and cool.

## Island Coconut Chips

- ❖ Extract coconut meat from a fresh coconut and cut into thin strips. A vegetable peeler works well for this.
- ❖ Spread chips on a cookie sheet and bake at 375° until chips begin to brown, about 10 minutes.

*Sprinkle with* Island Seasoning, Chapter 9

## Coconut Slices

A simple and inexpensive nibble is chilled coconut meat cut into bite sized pieces. It provides a nice tropical touch with sunset drinks and can be ready at short notice with minimal fuss.

# Dips and Spreads

## Aïoli

Carol~Yacht Elyxir

This dip can be used with vegetables, cold potatoes and as an addition to fish soup.

| | |
|---|---|
| 2 C | olive oil |
| 5 | egg yolks |
| 1 | lemon – juiced |
| 6 | garlic cloves |
| 1 t | salt |
| 1/2 t | sugar |

1/2 t mustard
pepper

❖ Puree all ingredients in a blender while slowly adding olive oil.

*Can be stored in the refrigerator for up to a month.*

## Quick Aïoli

Carol~Yacht Elyxir

1 C mayonnaise
5 garlic cloves – crushed
lemon juice – to taste
*red pepper – roasted
*roasted garlic

❖ Blend all ingredients together.

## Chutney and Cream Cheese Spread

Judi~Yacht Long Passages

1 block cream cheese
chutney or sweet relish

❖ Place cream cheese in a dish and cover with chutney.

*Serve with crackers.*

## Baba Ghanoush ~ Eggplant Dip

Anu~Yacht Kialoa II

This recipe, along with other Turkish recipes, was given to me by Anu, a professional sailing chef on both sailing and motor yachts around the world. Anu spent 6 years working as a guide in Turkey, after which she traded land life for the sea. Learning to speak Turkish she collected many wonderful recipes from the local people and she now feels more at home in the galley cooking Turkish food than her national dishes from the Netherlands.

When Anu wrote out her favourite dishes for me she also include this small paragraph, perhaps to inspire me to become more creative in my travel cooking.

*Because the Turks are very hospitable people, you will not be able to leave their homes before drinking the specially brewed çay tea or kahve coffee accompanied by home made tatli sweets and meze starters. If you are ever in Istanbul, you will enjoy an interesting visit to the imperial kitchens of the Topkapi Palace.*

*Turkish cuisine, often rated amongst the top three in the world, emerged during the time of the Ottoman Empire conquests across the Mediterranean. Here in these kitchens lavish dishes were created for the sole pleasure of the Sultan and his court. Chefs were employed under strict rules, resulting in a basic Ottoman cuisine that spread across the Mediterranean incorporating Chinese, Mongolian, Persian, Arab and Greek cuisine.*

| | |
|---|---|
| 4 | eggplants |
| 1/2 C | olive oil |
| 3 T | white wine vinegar or 2 T of tahini |
| 1 | egg yolk or 3 oz yogurt |
| 1 | lemon – juiced |
| 3 | garlic cloves – minced |
| | pinch of sugar |
| | S&P |

- ❖ Grill eggplants whole under a hot grill turning them at least once until their skins are split, blistered and soft. May take up to half an hour. An option is to roast them, *see Eggplants in Fruit and Vegetables.*
- ❖ Peel eggplants when they have cooled and blend in a food processor or mash.
- ❖ Add garlic, vinegar, lemon juice, sugar and egg yolk.
- ❖ Blend ingredients while slowly drizzling in olive oil, stop every now and then to check the consistency, it should be light and rather thin but you may choose to make it thicker.
- ❖ Adjust flavor with S&P.

*Serve slightly rounded and smoothed on a serving platter decorated with tomato wedges, black olives and parsley sprigs. This dip goes well witrh* Shepherd's Salad *and warm bread.*

## Quick Baba Ghanoush

- ❖ Peel eggplant and dice into cubes, sprinkle with salt, mix and let drain for an hour.

- ❖ Squeeze eggplant and steam in the pressure cooker for 3 minutes, eggplant should be very soft.
- ❖ Saute garlic in olive oil until brown, this gives baba ghanoush the smoky roasted flavor traditionally achieved when grilling the eggplant.
- ❖ Continue to make baba ghanoush by following the traditional directions above, substituting the prepared eggplant and garlic.

## Guacamole

| | |
|---|---|
| 2 | avocados |
| 3 T | lemon juice |
| 1 | garlic clove – crushed |
| several drops | chili sauce |
| | S&P |

- ❖ Blend all ingredients together.

## Hummus

Hummus is a Mediterranean dip or spread made from chickpeas. It can be flavored with pesto, roasted red peppers, sun-dried tomatoes, olives or cumin.

| | |
|---|---|
| 3 C | chickpeas – cooked or canned |
| 1/2 C | water |
| 1/2 C | olive oil |
| 1/4 C | vinegar or lemon juice |
| 1/4 C | sesame seeds – toasted |
| 8 | garlic cloves |
| 1 t | salt |
| | *substitite *Tahini* for vinegar and sesame seeds |

- ❖ Blend all ingredients together to the consistency of peanut butter and chill.

*Traditionally served rounded and smoothed on a flat tray, together with a dribble of olive oil and a garnish of paprika criss-crossed over the mound, finished with a sprinkling of parsley.*

*Serve with warmed pita pockets or tortillas, as a vegetable dip, or a spread on brown toast or crackers.*

## Olive Tapenade

| | |
|---|---|
| 25 | olives |
| 1/4 C | olive oil |
| 1/4 C | cilantro |
| 3 | garlic cloves – chopped |
| 2 | anchovy fillets or fish sauce |
| 2 T | lemon juice |
| 2 T | basil |
| 2 T | capers |
| 3 t | Dijon mustard |
| | salt |

❖ Blend all ingredients together.

## Sun~Dried Tomato Tapenade

| | |
|---|---|
| 1 C | sun-dried tomatoes |
| 1/3 C | capers |
| 3 | garlic cloves – chopped |
| 3 | anchovy fillets or fish sauce to taste |
| 2 T | olive oil |
| 2 T | cilantro |
| 1 T | basil |
| 2 t | vinegar |
| | ground pepper |

❖ Blend all ingredients together.

## Tahini Dip

| | |
|---|---|
| 1/2 C | tahini or sesame seeds – toasted |
| 1/4 C | lemon juice |
| 1/4 C | parsley |
| 1 | garlic clove |
| 3 T | water |
| 1/4 t | salt |

❖ Blend ingredients together, adding enough water to achieve the consistency of whipped cream.

❖ Cover and refrigerate

*Keeps up to one week.*

## Westri Dip

I first tasted this dip at a cruisers New Year's Eve party in Patagonia. It is more of a temperate climate dish, as baking it makes the boat too hot in the tropics unless you have a microwave.

| | |
|---|---|
| 1 C | Parmesan cheese |
| 1 C | mayonnaise |
| 1 C | canned artichokes, mushrooms or asparagus |

❖ Combine ingredients and bake one hour at 350°F or until golden brown.

*Serve warm as a dip with warm pita bread, crackers or vegetables.*

## Railroad Dip

Fran~Yacht Aka

Fran says this dish is super easy, and people just go crazy over it. They sit there smacking their lips saying,

"Hmmmm is it quiche?"

"Tastes like there's cream in it"

Very good hot or cold. You can add crab or shrimp but it definitely stands on it's own with no need to fluff it up.

| | |
|---|---|
| 2 C | cheese – grated |
| 2 C | mayonnaise |
| 1 1/2 C | minced onion |

❖ Combine ingredients.

*Serve with pita bread, crackers or vegetables.*

## Turkish Yogurt Dip

Anu~Yacht Kialoa II

This tangy yogurt dip goes well with Turkish food as both a dip and a dressing. I've also had it served as a side dish to chili beans and was surprised at the refreshing taste it added.

| | |
|---|---|
| 1 | garlic clove |
| 3 T | water |
| 1/4 t | salt |
| 1 C | yogurt – preferably thick and creamy |

1/2 T olive oil
*1 t cilantro

❖ Combine all ingredients except olive oil and chill.

*Just before serving, swirl oil over the top, garnish crosswise with paprika and fresh dill.*

## Vietnamese Dipping Sauce

2/3 C soy sauce
1/4 C rice wine or dry sherry
2 garlic cloves – crushed
2 T lime juice
1 t chili paste or chili pepper flakes
*grated carrot, cilantro or diced scallion

❖ Combine all ingredients.

*Serve with sushi, fish cakes or seafood.*

# Salsas

Made from fresh ingredients, salsas are a simple, low calorie addition to any meal enhancing the flavors of fish, poultry, meat and vegetables. Salsas are wonderful spread on crusty bread or served as a dip for crackers and vegatables.

## Grapefruit Salsa

2 grapefruit – chopped with membranes removed
1 orange – pieced
2 scallions – sliced
1 chili – minced
2 T mint – chopped

❖ Combine all ingredients.

## Hawaiian Salsa

| | |
|---|---|
| 1 C | fresh pineapple – cubed |
| 2 | tomatoes – cubed |
| 1/4 C | cilantro – chopped |
| 1/2 | Maui (sweet) onion – chopped |
| 1 | garlic clove – minced |
| 1 | chili pepper – minced |
| 1 t | coriander seed – crushed |
| 3/4 t | cumin |
| 1/2 t | salt |

❖ Combine all ingredients, chill and serve.

## Italian Salsa

| | |
|---|---|
| 5 | tomatoes – chopped |
| 1 | onion – chopped |
| 2 | garlic cloves – crushed |
| 2 T | basil – chopped |
| 3 t | chili pepper flakes |
| 1 t | lemon juice |
| | S&P |

❖ Combine all ingredients.

## Mexican Salsa Fresca

| | |
|---|---|
| 5 | tomatoes – chopped |
| 2 | jalapeño chilies – seeded and chopped |
| 1 | red onion – chopped |
| 3 T | cilantro – chopped |
| 2 | garlic cloves – crushed |
| 2 t | lime juice |
| | S&P |

❖ Combine all ingredients.

## Orange Salsa

3 oranges – chopped and membranes removed
1/2 C olives
lemon juice

❖ Combine all ingredients.

## Roasted Garlic Salsa

Roast a whole garlic head in the oven then squeeze the garlic out of the peel like paste. A quicker method – though it that does not provide the same taste – is to peel and chop the garlic then toss it in a pan with olive oil until brown.

5 tomatoes – chopped
2 onions – chopped
1/4 C cilantro – chopped
1 head roasted garlic
1 T tomato paste
fresh chili to taste

❖ Combine all ingredients.

## Tropical Salsa

Fran~Yacht Aka

1 papaya, 2 mangos or 1/4 C pineapple – chopped
1/4 C lemon or lime juice
1/4 C onion – grated
1 garlic clove – minced
chili powder or chilies to taste
cilantro
salt

❖ Combine all ingredients, chill and serve.

# Equatorial Meltdown

Cool bliss – the first I'd felt all day. An electric blue surrounds me as I sink deeper, feet first into the ocean, watching the light rays extented into an unknown galaxy and the dark-green hull glide by me like the mothership from *Star Wars*. I feel free in my own cool outer space wishing it would last forever.

Soon it's over and I'm back on deck to the hot blazing reality of crossing the Equator. I long for tomorrow when once again dad will slow the boat down just long enough for me to jump off the bow and catch the stern as *Swanhaven II* sails by. I never imagined that it could be this hot.

We have an invasion of fleas aboard. I'm covered in bites from head to toe. Heidi, our cat, is the culprit, but we have long since used up our one can of insect repellant. We had no fleas in Tahiti, but the Equator has caused them to hatch and multiply. Dad has resorted to drastic measures by submerging Heidi in a bucket of water to drown them. With each dunking, his arms emerge with more scratches from her sharp claws as she resists. She is now avoiding him. I can't watch these wild moments, and Heidi's Siamese cries are very haunting. I don't know who's winning – the fleas or Heidi.

In this heat it's hard to get excited about food. We have no refrigeration, and the provisions we got in Tahiti were not all that fresh. As a treat, in the Chinese supermarket in Papeete mum let

my brother David and I each choose a box of cereal as we gazed at expensive American brands lining the shelves. David choose Fruit Loops and I chose Alphabets.

On the appointed day, we eagerly opened our boxes of cereal. My Alphabets looked great, as I quickly tipped them out into a bowl and covered them in milk. But, when I raised my spoon to my mouth I didn't like the taste. I asked our American crew girl if she liked Alphabets and Kini replied, "Sure," but on tasting them she promptly announced they were stale. I was devastated.

Stuffed into plastic containers is our cheese, surrounded by cooking oil to stop it from molding. I have to pull hard at the big slimy block to release it from the tight suction the oil has created. It's like pulling your leg out of a mud hole when it's swallowed your gumboot. I place the slippery block on the chopping board and watch it smartly slide off and slowly skate around the counter-top to its own private tune. All I want is a small slice to eat with my cracker.

On night watch, when I reach into the jar of sweets, my hand closes around a huge sticky lump. The wine gums have all melted together, and in the morning their colors have merged, resembling the murky chunk I created one Christmas when I melted down my new crayon packet with a box of matches. Even the can of Coke I share with David holds no magic. The warm liquid tastes flat and sickly sweet as it lingers in my mouth.

We sight a ship, and we all dream of ice cream, imagining big freezers loaded with wonderful flavors. Maybe the ship is a "Mr Whippy" ice-cream truck of the high seas and will soon come steaming by playing it's jingle, a loudspeaker hailing that chocolate flakes are free today with a double cone. No such luck. But we catch a fish and David writes a log entry. He draws a picture of a shop with a neon sign flashing, "Fish and Ships."

Twenty days after leaving Tahiti, we arrive in Honolulu. We pull alongside the Texaco fuel dock in the Ala Wai Yacht Harbor with our boat looking smart and our Kiwi and yellow quarantine flags snapping in the trade-wind breeze.

"Aloha, Where you folks sail from?" asks the attendant.

"Tahiti," we reply.

"Well you just go on inside and help yourselves to a cold drink from the cooler," he offers. With the first slug of a fizzy tropical punch, meltdown images are wiped away and 20 days blend themselves into one to be stored away on a small meteor floating in a dark cool space inside my head.

# Finger Foods

## Falafels

Falafels are a Mediterranean patty that can be served with *Turkish Yogurt Dip* or in a warm pita pocket with tomatoes, bean sprouts, diced lettuce and yogurt or *Tahini Dressing.*

| | |
|---|---|
| 2 C | chickpeas – cooked |
| 1/3 C | water |
| 1/4 C | whole wheat bread crumbs |
| 1/4 C | parsley or cilantro – chopped |
| 1 | onion – chopped fine |
| 5 | garlic cloves – crushed |
| 1/4 T | chili pepper – chopped fine |
| 1 t | basil – chopped |
| 1/2 t | cumin |
| 1/2 t | ground turmeric |
| | S&P |
| | flour for coating |
| | oil for frying |

❖ Blend chickpeas until smooth, add remaining ingredients and mix well.

❖ Form mixture into 2" patties.

❖ Fry patties in hot oil until they are brown and crispy, drain on a paper towel.

*Serve falafels warm from the oven.*

## Tortilla Wrap

Mary~Yacht Kismet

This may seem a basic appetizer, but at a memorable cruisers dinner party hosted by Diane aboard *Impossible* one hot steamy night in Samoa it proved to be a delightful treat. I wrote it down to remind myself that life doesn't have to get too fancy.

tortillas
cream cheese
ham
green chilies – chopped
cilantro

❖ Spread tortilla with cream cheese, ham, chilies and cilantro.

❖ Wrap tightly, cut into rounds and arrange on a plate.

## Pita Chips

6 pita pockets
1/2 C butter
2 T parsley – chopped
2 T chives – chopped
4 garlic cloves – crushed
1 t lemon juice

- Cut pita bread into chip triangles.
- Blend above ingredients and spread onto chips.
- Bake at 350°F for 5 minutes until crispy, or toast in a frying pan.

## Turkish Zucchini Patties

Anu~Yacht Kialoa II

1/2 C flour
1/3 C parsley – chopped
2 zucchini – grated
1 onion – grated
1 egg
1 garlic clove – crushed
chili pepper – any kind
S&P
*1 C feta cheese – mashed

- Mix ingredients together.
- Heat enough olive oil (or 1/2 olive and 1/2 vegetable oil) in a deep skillet to float patties.
- Note: before frying the whole batch, first fry one tester, if patty does not hold together add more flour and possibly another egg, taste check the seasoning.
- Drop a fork full of batter into the oil and flatten with the fork, fit in as many patties as you can.
- Cook patties until golden on the bottom, about 3 minutes, turn and brown the other side.
- Remove when done and drain on paper towels, add new patties.

*To serve arrange patties on a large platter with* Turkish Yogurt Dip, *in the middle.*

## Peanut Patties

Excellent on their own or with sweet chili sauce.

1 C peanuts
1 C flour – self raising
1 onion
1/2 C milk
1/3 C coconut – grated
1 egg
4 garlic cloves – crushed
1 t each – cumin, coriander
chili to taste
sprinkle of salt when cooked

- Mix all dry ingredients, add egg and milk.
- Fry by spoonful.

*Serve hot.*

## Marinated Salmon ~ Gravlax

1 salmon fillet – skin on, scales removed
4 lemons – juiced
5 T olive oil
4 T coarse salt – not fine table salt
3 T sugar
ground pepper
parsley

- Place fish skin down on a shallow dish, sprinkle with lemon juice, salt, pepper and sugar.
- Cover with plastic wrap and marinate 12 hours in the fridge.
- Scrape off salt and pat with a paper towel.
- Cut diagonally in to thin slices, dress with olive oil, lemon juice and chopped parsley.

*Serve with bread.*

## Sushi

*Sushi* is the Japanese name given to seafood served with cooked, room temperature rice.

- The two most **common sushi** are *Maki* and *Nigiri*.

- Sushi is served with sliced preserved ginger and a **dipping sauce** of wasabi and soy sauce or try Vietnamese hot sauce.
- As you can use leftover rice with fresh seafood, sushi is a **versatile and economical** appetizer or meal.

## Sushi Rice

- For **2 C of rice** use 1/4 C rice wine vinegar.
- If **rice wine vinegar is unavailable** heat 1/4 C vinegar and dissolve 2 T sugar, add to rice.
- To use **leftover rice** from the day before, heat vinegar and stir in the rice until it is soft and moist.
- **Store rice** in a cool dark place covered, but not in the fridge as it will dry out.

## Maki Sushi

*Maki* sushi is seafood, vegetables and rice rolled in nori seaweed and sliced.

- Maki sushi contains a **three color** combination achieved by combining 3 fillings.

Ideas for fillings

thin omelet
cream cheese
sesame seeds – toasted
spam – Allie Boy's favorite

vegetables

avocado
julienne carrots
cucumber with skin on
spinach
dried mushrooms – soaked
scallions

seafood

raw tuna or other firm raw fish
smoked salmon
smoked fish
canned tuna
crab

lobster
caviar
salmon eggs
shrimp

## Nigiri Sushi

*Nigiri* sushi is seafood placed on an elongated rice ball spread with wasabi and sometimes belted with strip of nori.
It is less fussy to make than *Maki* sushi but does not look as impressive. I like to make both for a contrast in presentation.

Chapter 6

# Soups

# Cold Soups

## Gazpacho

| | |
|---|---|
| 2 C | stewed tomatoes – pureéd |
| 1 1/2 C | tomato sauce |
| 3/4 C | celery – chopped |
| 3/4 C | cucumber – chopped |
| 1/2 C | onion – chopped |
| 1/2 C | water |
| 1/4 C | green pepper – chopped |
| 1/4 C | red wine vinegar |
| 2 T | parsley – chopped |
| 2 T | olive oil |
| 1 t | Worcestershire sauce |
| 1/4 t | pepper |
| | garlic crushed |
| | *assorted seafood poached in white wine |

❖ Combine ingredients and chill several hours.

*Serve with a dollop of yogurt.*

# Bean and Grain Soups

## Spanish Chickpea and Spinach Soup

| | |
|---|---|
| 2 C | spinach – shredded or frozen |
| 1 C | chickpeas – soaked |
| 1 C | ham – diced |
| 1 | potato – chopped |
| 1 | slice bread |
| 2 | garlic cloves |
| 2 T | olive oil |
| | salt |
| | saffron |

❖ Drain chickpeas and cover with water, pressure-cook 15 minutes, or simmer 1 hour.

❖ Add potatoes, ham, salt and pressure-cook 5 minutes, or simmer 20 minutes, add saffron.

❖ Fry bread and garlic in oil, mash into a paste and add to chickpeas, this thickens and flavors the soup.

- ❖ In same pan sauté spinach in garlic and oil until soft, add to soup and simmer 3 minutes.

*Serve hot with a sprig of basil.*

## Italian Black Bean Soup

In Italy, it's customary to include the heel of a piece of Parmesan cheese to soups and stews, this adds a distinctive cheesy flavor that compliments the dish.

Although this classic soup is usually made with pasta and either rice or beans, I generally eliminate two of these ingredients, as I find yet another step inconvenient. I will, however, add any leftover rice, pasta or beans from a previous meal.

If I'm lazy or it's rough I sometimes use a can of red beans or chickpeas instead of cooking black beans and add rice or shell pasta with a cup of water.

Extra liquid can be soaked up with couscous to make a thicker stew.

| | |
|---|---|
| 6 C | water |
| 2 C | black beans – cooked |
| 2 C | cabbage – shredded |
| 3 | tomatoes |
| 2 | red peppers – diced |
| 2 | zucchini – diced |
| 2 | potatoes chopped |
| 1 | onion – chopped |
| 1 | celery stalk – diced |
| 1 | carrot – diced |
| 3 T | olive oil |
| 2 T | red wine |
| 2 | bay leaves |
| 1 t | sugar |
| 1 | garlic clove – chopped |
| | S&P |
| | *cooked chicken can be added at the end of cooking, allow it to heat through |

- ❖ Heat olive oil and sauté onion until brown.
- ❖ Add remaining ingredients and pressure-cook 10 minutes, or simmer 20 minutes until vegetables are tender, season to taste.

*Garnish with grated Parmesan cheese and parsley.*

## Caribbean Lentil Soup

| | |
|---|---|
| 4 C | water |
| 1 C | lentils |
| 1/2 C | parsley – chopped |
| 3 | potatoes – chopped |
| 2 | celery stalks – chopped |
| 2 | carrots – chopped |
| 1 | onion – chopped |
| 2 | scallions – chopped |
| 2 | bay leaves |
| 2 | garlic cloves – crushed |
| 1 | chili pepper – whole |
| 2 T | olive oil |
| 2 t | cider vinegar |
| | salt |

❖ Combine all ingredients, except vinegar and parsley, pressure-cook 10 minutes, or simmer 1 hour until lentils are soft.

❖ Mix in vinegar and parsley, remove bay leaves and chili pepper.

*Serve hot garnished with a swirl of yogurt.*

## Jamaican Split Pea Soup

| | |
|---|---|
| 4 C | boiling water |
| 1 C | split peas |
| 2 | scallions – chopped |
| 1 | onion – chopped |
| 2 | garlic cloves – 1 whole and 1 crushed |
| 1 | chili pepper – whole |
| 3 T | oil |
| 4 | all spice grains |
| 2 | bay leaves |
| 1 t | ground cumin |
| 1 t | curry powder |
| 1/2 t | chili pepper – seeded and chopped |
| 1/2 t | ginger – grated |
| 1/4 t | thyme |

❖ In pressure-cooker or saucepan place split peas, whole garlic clove, ginger, bay leaves, all spice, whole chili, scallions and curry powder, cover with water.

❖ Pressure-cook 15 minutes, or simmer 1 hour until split peas are tender, add thyme at end of cooking.

- Pour off excess liquid, discard chili and bay leaves, mash peas.
- Sauté onion, chopped chili and garlic until soft, mix in cumin.
- Add onion to split peas.

*Serve hot with* Yogurt Dressing.

## Mexican Split Pea Soup

Dyan~Yacht Ascension

8 C broth or water
1 C split green peas
4 potatoes – cubed
1 t oregano
1/2 t cumin

- Pressure-cook above ingredients on high 15 minutes, or simmer 1 hour.
- Add following and simmer 3 minutes.

1 1/2 C frozen corn
1 C cilantro – chopped
4 scallions – chopped
1 can green chilies – chopped
4 corn tortillas – toasted and cut into 1" pieces
3 T lime juice

*Serve hot garnished with cilantro.*

## Portuguese Sausage and Bean Soup

Patty~Hawaii

I met Patty in Hilo, Hawaii and on a visit to the boat she offered me this family recipe given to her by her mother. The Potugugese came to Hawaii as cowboys and sugarcane workers, and along with the ukulele, also introduced many new recipes. This one became a favorite among the locals. Portuguese sausages are large and spicy, and many butchers in Hawaii create their own specialty blend.

1 1/2 C kidney beans – soaked overnight
1 hamhock
1 Portuguese sausage – 12oz.
2 carrots – diced
2 potatoes – diced

| | |
|---|---|
| 1/2 | cabbage – sliced |
| 1 | celery stalk – sliced |
| 1 | onion – diced |
| 1 can | tomato sauce |
| | S&P |

- Cover hamhock with water and pressure-cook 10 minutes, or simmer 20 minutes.
- Sauté sausage and onion and add to hamhock along with beans, carrots, potatoes and tomato sauce.
- Pressure-cook 30 minutes, or simmer 2 hours.
- Add cabbage and simmer until cooked, season to taste.

*Serve with chopped basil.*

## White Bean and Eggplant Soup

| | |
|---|---|
| 6 C | vegetable broth |
| 1 C | white beans such as great northern – soaked over night |
| 1 C | broccoli florets |
| 1/4 C | parsley |
| 1 | eggplant – chopped |
| 2 | carrots – chopped |
| 3 | garlic cloves – chopped |
| 3 T | lemon juice |
| 2 T | olive oil |
| | S&P |

- Sauté vegetables for 5 minutes, add beans and broth, bring to a simmer.
- Pressure-cook 20 minutes, or simmer 1 hour.
- Purée soup and season to taste.

*Serve with grated Parmesan cheese and fresh chopped herbs.*

## White Bean and Pesto Soup

The tablespoon of pesto added when serving this versatile Mediterranean soup provides an elegant addition.

| | |
|---|---|
| 6 C | water |
| 1 1/2 C | fresh white haricot beans or cooked white |

beans such as navy or even chickpeas
1 C green beans – diced
3 tomatoes – chopped
2 potatoes – cubed
2 carrots – diced
1 onion – chopped
1 celery stalk – diced
2 T olive oil
S&P
pesto

❖ Sauté onion until soft and add remaining ingredients except pesto.

❖ Pressure-cook 10 minutes, or simmer 1 hour, season to taste.

*Serve each bowl with a tablespoon of petso and grated Parmesan cheese.*

## Chicken and Combo Grain Soup

Vicky Witch ~Cape Horn

8 C water or chicken broth
2 C brown rice, barley and split peas – com bined
2 chicken breasts – cut into strips
2 onions – chopped
4 garlic cloves – crushed
parsley, sage, thyme, and salt

❖ Pressure-cook combo grains in water 15 minutes, or simmer 1 hour until barley is tender.

❖ Add remaining ingredients and simmer until chicken is cooked.

*Garnish with* Yogurt Lime Dressing, *to add a pleasant refreshing taste.*

## Miso Soup

Carol~Yacht Lorraine

This simple soup is wonderful as as a quick warm-me-up and tasty low calorie treat.

I was first served this recipe in Port Townsend during a fly-by visit with my dearest friend Carol. She threw it together in no time at all, leaving us plenty of time to catch up on news. I was impressed! A hearty salad tossed with *Tahini Dressing* followed, before I sadly bid my farewell and made a dash for the ferry.

Later in New Zealand I purchased plastic packs of red miso. These I used across the Pacific and for our extensive expeditons in Alaska. The crew never tired of *Miso Soup* served at lunch and although the soup alone is not fulling enough for a hungry crew it certainly helps take the chill off an icy day.

| | |
|---|---|
| 4 C | water |
| 1 lb. | tofu – cubed |
| 4 T | miso paste |
| 4 T | brewers yeast |
| 2 T | dried seaweed |
| 4 | scallions – sliced |
| | *sliced mushrooms |

❖ Simmer ingredients for 5 minutes and serve.

## The Queen's English

We had rounded Cape Horn in the early morning, the tall headland an impressive sight in the gray light. Although it was the middle of summer, 30-knot winds and hailstorms were blasting around the Cape, and I opted to stay aboard and keep watch, while we were tied to the mooring buoy beneath the lighthouse and the crew visited ashore.

The three Chilean lighthouse keepers had received no visitors for three weeks and were eager for their mail and packages, which we were bringing. While the moorage was calm for a while, I decided to make Chicken and Combo Grain Soup for lunch and also bake the lighthouse keepers a Hawaiian Carrot Cake. I was busy with the mixture when a British voice came over the radio.

"Cape Horn lighthouse, Cape Horn lighthouse, Cape Horn lighthouse, this is the HMS *Endurance* calling".

No reply.

"Cape Horn lighthouse, Cape Horn lighthouse, Cape Horn lighthouse, this is the HMS *Endurance* calling."

No reply.

Thinking that the lighthouse keepers were being pretentious to such a British voice, I left my cooking and radioed the HMS *Endurance*, suggesting that they try calling the lighthouse in Spanish.

"Farro Carbo de Hornos, Farro Carbo de Hornos, Farro Carbo de Hornos, HMS *Endurance* se llama".

Still no reply.

It then occurred to me that I had been mistaken - the lighthouse keepers were not ignoring the English, but were greeting our crew and receiving their mail. In the middle of placing the cake in the oven, I radioed back the HMS *Endurance* and apologized for my mistake, advising them that the lighthouse keepers were engaged with our land party.

"Thank-you very much madam, and what vessel are you?" came the British voice.

"We're the yacht *Mahina Tiare* and our position is the mooring buoy stationed beneath the lighthouse," I answered.

Just then a loud rumbling occurred and I thought Oh No!!, we're adrift near the rocks.

A calm voice came over the radio and stated "Ah yes madam, quite right you are. We are the helicopter from the *Endurance*, on her way to Antarctica, and we can see quite clearly that you are in the bay and that your crew are ashore. Good day to you."

# Vegetable Soups

## Curried Carrot Soup

| | |
|---|---|
| 10 | carrots – diced |
| 4 C | water |
| 1/2 C | rice |
| 1/4 C | milk powder or cream |
| 1 | onion – chopped |
| 1 | celery stalk – chopped |
| 3 | garlic cloves – crushed |
| 2 T | butter |
| 1 T | ginger – grated |
| 1 t | curry paste |
| | S&P |

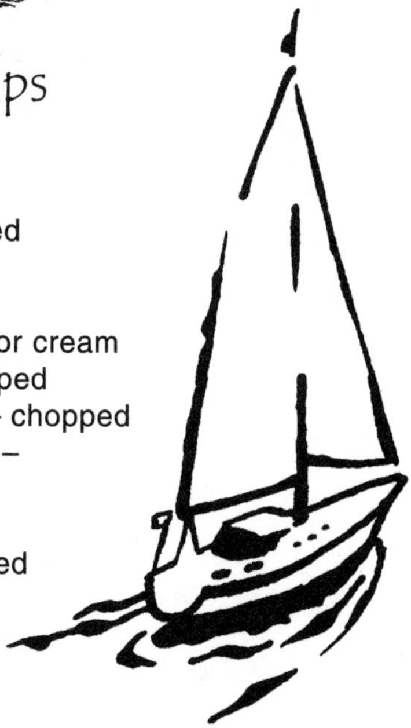

❖ Sauté onion, curry, garlic and ginger, add remaining ingredients.

❖ Pressure-cook 12 minutes, or simmer until carrots are soft.

❖ Blend together and season to taste.

*Serve garnished with dollop of chutney and fresh cilantro.*

## Irish Carrot Soup

Carol~Yacht Elyxir

| | |
|---|---|
| 10 | carrots – sliced |
| 4 C | vegetable or chicken broth |
| 1 | onion – chopped |
| 6 | garlic cloves – crushed |
| 1 T | lemon juice |
| 5 | whole cloves |
| | honey |

❖ Sauté carrots, onions, garlic, and cloves until onions are transparent.

❖ Add broth and pressure-cook 8 minutes, or simmer 15 minutes, remove cloves and mash.

❖ Add lemon juice and honey.

*Garnish with a drizzle of yogurt and a sprinkle of parsley.*

## Mushroom Soup

Jenn~Yacht Ocean Light II

| | |
|---|---|
| 2 C | mushrooms – sliced |
| 1 1/2 C | milk |
| 1 C | chicken stock – hot |
| 1/3 C | parsley |
| 2 T | onion – chopped |
| 2 T | flour |
| 1 T | butter |
| 1 t | tarragon |
| | S&P |

❖ Sauté onion for 2 minutes, add mushrooms and cook 3 minutes.

❖ Sprinkle in flour and stir in chicken broth.

❖ Bring to a boil, stir in milk and herbs, simmer 5 minutes, season to taste, *blend with hand blender.

*Serve garnished with sliced mushroom caps.*

## Pumpkin Lentil Soup

| | |
|---|---|
| 2 1/2 C | vegetable stock |
| 2 C | pumpkin |
| 1 C | lentils – soaked |
| 2 | onions – diced |
| 2 | potatoes – grated |
| 1 T | oil |
| 4 | garlic cloves – crushed |
| 1 t | ginger – grated |
| 1/2 t | each – cumin, coriander, and basil |
| | parsley |
| | S&P |

❖ Sauté onion and pumpkin until tender, approximately 5 minutes.

❖ Add spices, potatoes, lentils, and stock, pressure-cook 13 minutes, or simmer 90 minutes until lentils are tender.

*Serve with freshly baked bread or crackers.*

## Pumpkin Orange Soup

| | |
|---|---|
| 1 | pumpkin – cubed and skin removed |
| 4 C | vegetable or chicken broth |
| 1 C | orange juice |
| 2 | onions |
| 6 | garlic cloves – crushed |
| 1 t | cinnamon |
| 1/2 t | thyme |
| | * honey or sugar |
| | * cooked barley, rice, ham, bacon, ginger or curry |

❖ Sauté pumpkin, garlic and onions.

❖ Add broth, cinnamon and thyme, pressure-cook 10 minutes, or simmer 20 minutes until pumpkin is soft, mash.

❖ Add honey and S&P to taste.

*Garnish with a drizzle of yogurt and a sprinkle of parsley.*

## Curried Potato Soup

Carol~Yacht Elyxir

| | |
|---|---|
| 4 C | chicken broth |
| 1 C | orange juice |
| 5 | potatoes – chopped |
| 4 | carrots – chopped |
| 2 | onions – chopped |
| 2 | garlic cloves – crushed |
| 1 T | ginger – grated |
| 1 t | curry powder |
| | S&P |

- ❖ Sauté carrots, potatoes, onions, curry powder and ginger.
- ❖ Stir in chicken broth and pressure-cook 5 minutes, or simmer 15 minutes, mash.
- ❖ Add orange juice and heat through, season to taste.

*Garnish with cilantro and a spoon of* Mango Chutney.

## Peanut Potato Soup

| | |
|---|---|
| 4 C | water |
| 4 | carrots – chopped |
| 4 | potatoes – cubed |
| 2 | apples – chopped |
| 2 | celery stalks – chopped |
| 1 | onion – chopped |
| 1/4 C | peanut butter |
| 2 | garlic cloves – crushed |
| 3 T | oil or butter |
| 1/2 t | each – cumin, cinnamon and nutmeg |
| | S&P |
| | *chili of some form |

- ❖ Heat butter, sauté vegetables and apples.
- ❖ Add water and pressure-cook 5 minutes, or simmer 20 minutes until potatoes are tender, mash.
- ❖ Stir in peanut butter and spices.

*Garnish with chopped roasted peanuts.*

## Spinach and Parmesan Soup

| | |
|---|---|
| 4 C | spinach – chopped |
| 2 C | milk |
| 1 C | chicken broth |
| 1/4 C | Parmesan cheese – grated |
| 1/4 t | nutmeg |

- ❖ Heat broth and cook spinach, add milk and nutmeg, simmer 10 minutes.
- ❖ Add Parmesan and simmer 2 minutes, season to taste.

*Garnish with grated Parmesan.*

# Miscellaneous Soups

## Clam Chowder

| | |
|---|---|
| 2 C | clams – chopped and sautéed in their own nectar |
| 2 C | water |
| 1 can | evaporated milk |
| 5 | potatoes – cubed |
| 4 | bacon rashers – diced |
| 1 | onion – chopped |
| 1 | celery stalk – diced |
| 1 | carrot – sliced |
| 2 | garlic cloves – crushed |
| 1 t | Worcestershire sauce |
| | lemon juice |
| | chili pepper of some form |
| | S&P |

- ❖ Sauté bacon, onion, potatoes, celery, carrot and garlic.
- ❖ Add water, chili, Worcestershire sauce and S&P, simmer until potatoes are tender.
- ❖ Add clams, lemon juice and milk, stir well and heat.

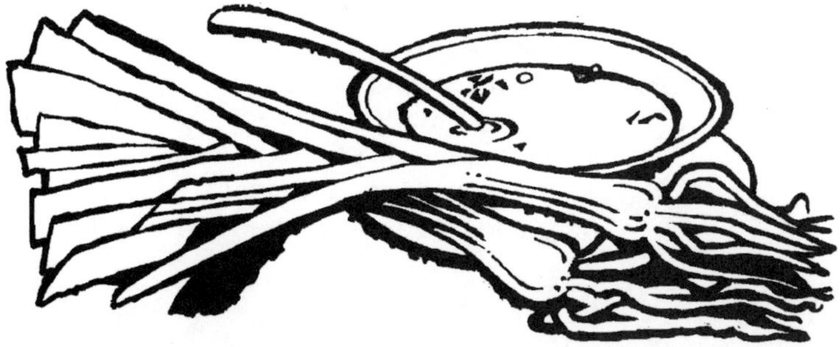

# New England Fish Chowder

| | |
|---|---|
| 2 C | milk |
| 2 C | water |
| 1 lb. | white fish |
| 1/2 C | white wine |
| 1/4 C | flour |
| 1/4 C | water |
| 2 | bacon rashers – diced |
| 1 | onion – chopped |
| 1 | bay leaf |
| 2 | whole allspice |
| 1 | garlic clove – crushed |
| | nutmeg |

- Sauté onion, garlic and bacon, add 2 C water, wine, bay leaf and allspice, bring to boil.
- Add fish, cover and simmer until fish flakes, about 10 minutes.
- Remove fish with slotted spoon and flake.
- Mix flour and 1/4 C water until smooth, gradually stir into soup, simmer until soup thickens.
- Stir in milk, return fish and stir over medium heat until heated through.
- Add nutmeg, season to taste, remove bay leaf and allspice before serving.

# Queen Charlotte Salmon Chowder

Jenn~Yacht Ocean Light II

| | |
|---|---|
| 1 1/2 C | salmon or 1 can, including juice |
| 1 can | evaporated milk or 2% milk |
| 1 can | creamed corn |
| 1 C | water |
| 1 C | chicken stock |
| 1/2 C | parsley – chopped |
| 4 | potatoes – diced |
| 3 | carrots – diced |
| 1 | onion – chopped |
| 1 | celery stalk – chopped |
| 1 | zucchini – diced |
| 1 | green pepper – chopped |
| 3 | garlic cloves – crushed |

| | |
|---|---|
| 2 t | butter |
| 1/2 t | ground pepper |
| 1/2 t | dill seed |

- Sauté onion, green pepper, celery and garlic for 3 minutes.
- Add potatoes, carrots, stock, water, pepper and dill.
- Pressure-cook 7 minutes, or simmer 20 minutes.
- Add zucchini and simmer 5 minutes, add salmon, milk and corn, heat through and stir in parsley just before serving.

*Serve hot with crusty bread.*

## Thai Chicken Soup

| | |
|---|---|
| 4 | chicken breast – sliced |
| 1 1/2 C | milk |
| 1 C | chicken broth |
| 1 can | coconut milk |
| 1 can | bamboo shoots |
| 1/2 C | sugar peas |
| 1 | onion – sliced |
| 3 | scallions – sliced |
| 3 | ginger slices |
| 3 T | fish sauce |
| 1/2 t | lemon zest |
| | chili of some form |
| | cilantro |

- Whisk broth and coconut milk together, add chicken, onions and ginger.
- Cook gently for 15 minutes, add lemon zest, chili, cilantro, scallions and vegetables, heat through.
- Add milk and simmer 10 minutes, stir in fish sauce.

*Garnish with a thin slice of lemon and sprig of cilantro.*

## Thai Fish Soup

Cow Bay Café~Prince Rupert, Canada

Adrienne uses fresh halibut for this soup but any firm white fish is suitable.

| | |
|---|---|
| 4 | fish fillets |
| 4 C | fish stock |

| | |
|---|---|
| 1 C | coconut milk |
| 1 C | clam nectar |
| 1 | onion - chopped |
| 1 T | vegetable oil |

Curry

| | |
|---|---|
| 2 | curry leaves |
| 1 t | paprika |
| 1 t | dried dill |
| 1/2 t | cayenne pepper |
| 1/2 t | cumin |
| 1/2 t | mustard |
| 1/4 t | turmeric |
| | grated ginger |

❖ Toast curry seasoning in dry frying pan to release flavor, add olive oil, onion and ginger, sauté.

❖ Add stock and nectar, bring to a boil, add pieced fish and simmer until nearly cooked.

❖ Stir in coconut milk and simmer 5 minutes, season to taste.

*Garnish with sliced lemon and serve hot with crusty bread.*

## Thai Salmon Soup

| | |
|---|---|
| 3 | salmon fillets – cubed |
| 3 C | chicken stock |
| 1 C | pineapple – cubed |
| 1/2 C | white wine |
| 1/4 C | red pepper – diced |
| 2 | scallions – sliced |
| 4 | garlic cloves – crushed |
| 3” | lemon grass – crushed |
| 2 | lime leaves – sliced |
| 1 T | cilantro – chopped |
| 1 T | vegetable oil |
| 1/2 t | salt |
| | *1 chili |

❖ Sauté garlic and chili in hot oil for 30 seconds to release flavors.

❖ Add red pepper, lemon grass, scallions, and lime leaves, sauté 30 seconds.

❖ Pour in stock and wine, bring to a boil.

- Add salmon and simmer 2 minutes.
- Reduce heat, add pineapple and simmer 5 minutes.

*Serve hot, garnished with cilantro.*

Chapter 7

# Salads and Salad Dressings

# Salads with Fruit

## Apple, Nut and Chicken Salad

| | |
|---|---|
| 2 C | cooked or canned chicken – pieced |
| 2 | apples |
| 1/2 C | Chinese cabbage – shredded |
| 1/2 C | peanuts – toasted |
| 1/2 C | bean sprouts |
| 2 T | lemon juice |

- ❖ Dice apples and sprinkle with lemon juice to prevent discoloring.
- ❖ Combine remaining ingredients.
- ❖ Chill and dress with *Coconut Peanut Dressing*.

## Green Papaya Salad

This salad can be made with any raw vegetables such as tomatoes, carrots, bell peppers, green beans etc.

| | |
|---|---|
| 1 | green papaya |
| 1 | onion – chopped |
| 3 T | coconut milk or salad oil |
| 2 T | lemon juice |
| | S&P |
| | *ginger or chili if desired |
| | *roasted peanuts – chopped |

- ❖ Peel and grate papaya, place in bowl of salted water and soak 1 hour, wash and drain.
- ❖ Add remaining ingredients, chill and serve.

## Green Papaya and Carrot Salad

| | |
|---|---|
| 2 C | green papaya – grated |
| 1 C | carrots – grated |
| 1/2 C | rice vinegar |
| 1/4 C | scallions – sliced |
| 2 t | honey |
| | ginger – grated |
| | Asian fish sauce or salt |

- ❖ Combine vinegar, honey and ginger.

- ❖ Stir in papaya, carrots and scallions.
- ❖ Add fish sauce to personal taste.

# Vegetable Salads

## Antipasto Salad

| | |
|---|---|
| 1 C | cauliflower florets |
| 1 can | black olives |
| 3 | small onions – chopped |
| 1 | carrot – diced |
| 1 | celery stalk – diced |
| 1 | red pepper – diced |
| 1/2 C | green beans |
| 1/2 C | water |
| 1/2 C | wine vinegar |
| 1/4 C | vegetable oil |
| 1 | garlic clove – crushed |
| 1 T | olive oil |
| 1 T | sugar |
| 1 t | oregano |
| | S&P |
| | *vegetables may be varied |

- ❖ Combine all ingredients, cover and simmer 5 minutes.
- ❖ Cool and refrigerate allowing a day or more to marinate before serving.

## Seeded Beet Salad

| | |
|---|---|
| 1 1/2 lb. | cooked beets or 2 large cans – sliced |
| 2 | green apples – sliced |
| 1/2 C | scallions – chopped |
| 2 T | red wine vinegar |
| 1 T | salad oil |
| 1/2 t | mustard seeds |
| 1/2 t | cumin seeds |
| | S&P |

- ❖ Toast seeds in a dry frying pan until they become fragrant.
- ❖ Combine seeds with remaining ingredients, adding the apple just before serving to maintain color contrast.

## Thai Broccoli Salad

Carol~Yacht Elyxir

5 C broccoli florets
3 T red pepper – chopped
3 T red onion – chopped
3 T rice vinegar or unflavored white vinegar
1 T sesame oil
2 t brown sugar
1 t chili pepper flakes
salt to taste

❖ Steam or parboil broccoli until al danté, rinse in cold water to halt cooking.

❖ Combine remaining ingredients and toss with broccoli just before serving.

*Garnish with toasted peanuts and/or raisins.*

## Broccoli and Bacon Salad

Carol~Yacht Elyxir

5 C broccoli florets
1/2 C olive oil
8 bacon rashers – cooked and crumbled
1 onion – chopped
3 T red wine vinegar

❖ Steam or parboil brocoli until al danté, rinse in cold water.

❖ Add remaining ingredients and toss.

*Garnish with toasted sunflower or pumpkin seeds.*

## Carrot Salad

3 C carrots – grated
1/2 C raisins
2 T olive oil
1 T honey
lemon juice
mint
S&P

*grated apple
*chopped nuts
*yogurt

❖ Combine all ingredients, chill and serve.

## Pickled Cucumbers

Affectionately known as bread and butter pickles, pickled cucumbers are a simple way of preserving cucumbers, especially when they start to turn bad. They keep well, are appealing in salads, and serve as a tasty snack with crackers and cheese.

| | |
|---|---|
| 1 C | vinegar – any kind |
| 1/2 C | white sugar |
| 3 | cumbers – sliced |
| 2 | onions – sliced |
| 1 T | salt |
| 1 t | celery seeds |

❖ Mix all ingredients together and place in a container.

*Chill and serve.*

## Cauliflower and Broccoli Salad

| | |
|---|---|
| 2 C | cauliflower florets |
| 2 C | broccoli florets |
| 1 C | sharp cheddar cheese – cubed |
| | mayonnaise |

❖ Mix all ingredients together.

*Chill and serve.*

## Cucumber and Yogurt Salad

| | |
|---|---|
| 3 | cucumbers – sliced |

❖ If you are preparing this salad in advance, arrange the cucumber slices in a colander and sprinkle with salt to allow the juices to drain.

❖ Mix cucumber slices with *Yogurt Garlic Dressing*.

## Eggplant and Tomato Salad

| | |
|---|---|
| 3 | eggplants – cubed |
| 2 | onions – sliced |
| 2 | red peppers – chopped |
| 1 can | whole tomatoes |
| 5 | garlic cloves – crushed |
| 3 T | olive oil |
| 2 T | lemon juice |
| 3/4 t | ground turmeric |
| | salt |
| | pinch of sugar |
| | cilantro – chopped |

- ❖ Sauté eggplant in half the olive oil until golden, drain on paper towel.
- ❖ In remaining oil sauté onions, garlic, peppers, tomatoes and turmeric.
- ❖ Simmer mixture until it thickens slightly.
- ❖ Add eggplant, reduce heat and simmer about 6 minutes.
- ❖ Stir in lemon juice and salt, cool.

*Garnish with cilantro just before serving with* Yogurt Lime Dressing.

## Turkish Potato Salad

Anu~Yacht Kialoa II

| | |
|---|---|
| 4 | potatoes – cubed |
| 3 | eggs – hard boiled, peeled and quartered |
| 1/2 C | red cabbage – shredded |
| 1/3 C | fresh parsley |
| 1/3 C | Greek black olives |
| 1/4 C | olive oil |
| 1 T | mayonnaise |
| 1 T | ground cumin |
| | lemon juice |

- ❖ Boil potatoes in salted water, or chicken broth for more flavor, until tender, rinse under cold water to stop further cooking, cool.
- ❖ When the potatoes are cool, mix in cabbage, eggs, parsley, olives and cumin, chill.
- ❖ Just before serving add olive oil, lemon juice, mayonnaise and S&P.

## Minted Potato Salad

Carol~Yacht Elyxir

| | |
|---|---|
| 4 C | potatoes – small or cubed |
| 1 C | peas |
| 1/4 C | sour cream or natural yogurt |
| 2 | garlic cloves – crushed |
| 4 T | cider vinegar |
| 2 T | sugar |
| | mint leaves – chopped |
| | S&P |

❖ Cook potatoes until tender, drain and cool.

❖ Mix all ingredients together and chill.

*Garnish with a sprig of mint before serving.*

## French Potato Salad

| | |
|---|---|
| 4 | potatoes – cubed and cooked |
| 1 C | celery – chopped |
| 1/2 C | olive oil |
| 1/4 C | cider vinegar |
| 1/4 C | parsley |
| 2 | carrots – grated |
| 2 | scallions – chopped |
| 1 | onion – chopped |
| 1 | green pepper – sliced |
| 1 | garlic clove – crushed |
| 2 T | Dijon mustard |
| 1/2 t | oregano |
| | chili of some form |
| | S&P |

❖ Blend oil, vinegar, salt, oregano, mustard and garlic until smooth, pour over hot potatoes and marinate until potatoes are cool.

❖ Add remaining ingredients, mix well and season to taste.

*Serve chilled on shredded lettuce.*

## Mediterranean Potato Salad

| | |
|---|---|
| 10 | new potatoes – cooked |
| 1 C | green beans – sliced and cooked |
| 1 can | tuna – drained |
| Dressing | |
| 1/2 C | olive oil |
| 1 can | anchovies |
| 3 | shallots – chopped |
| 2 T | lemon juice |
| 1 T | capers |
| 1 T | parsley |

- ❖ Heat oil and sauté shallots for 2 minutes, add remaining dressing ingredients and continue sautéing for 3 minutes.
- ❖ Mix dressing into potatoes, beans and tuna.

## Shepherd's Salad

Anu~Yacht Kialoa II

| | |
|---|---|
| 100 g | feta cheese |
| 12 | Greek olives |
| 2 | tomatoes |
| 1 | red onion |
| 1 | cucumber |
| 1 | green pepper |
| 1/4 C | fresh parsley – chopped |
| | lemon juice or white wine vinegar |
| | olive oil |
| | S&P |

- ❖ Cut cheese, tomatoes, cucumber and green pepper into 1" cubes, finely slice the onion and add olives and parsley.
- ❖ Chill and toss salad with lemon juice, olive oil and S&P just before serving.

*Garnish with lemon wedges.*

## Tomato and Citrus Salad

| | |
|---|---|
| 6 | tomatoes – sliced into wedges |
| 1/2 C | celery leaves – chopped |
| 1 | onion – sliced |

Dressing

| | |
|---|---|
| 1 T | cider vinegar |
| 1 T | oil |
| 1 T | brown sugar |
| 1 T | citrus zest |

# Coleslaws

## Asian Coleslaw

| | |
|---|---|
| 2 C | cabbage – shredded |
| 2 | oranges – segmented with membranes removed |
| 1 | cucumber – sliced |
| 1 | avocado – sliced |
| 2 T | sesame seeds – toasted |

Dressing

| | |
|---|---|
| 3 T | rice wine vinegar |
| 3 T | soy sauce |
| 1 T | sesame oil |
| 1 t | sugar |
| | ground pepper |

## Apricot and Onion Coleslaw

| | |
|---|---|
| 2 C | broccoli florets |
| 3 C | cabbage – shredded |
| 5 | dried apricots – sliced |
| 1 t | caraway seeds |

Dressing

| | |
|---|---|
| 1 | onion – chopped |
| 1 | garlic clove – crushed |
| 2 T | sugar |
| 2 T | vinegar |
| 2 T | oil |
| | S&P |

## Cara's Coleslaw

| | |
|---|---|
| 1 1/2 C | cabbage – shredded |
| 1/4 C | red cabbage – shredded |
| 1/4 C | carrot – grated |
| 2 T | raisins |
| 1 T | sunflower seeds |
| 1 T | mayonnaise |
| 1 T | pecans – chopped |
| 2 t | cider vinegar |
| 1 t | mustard |
| | sprinkle of caraway seeds |
| | pinch celery seeds |

❖ Mix all ingredients together and chill.

*Serve garnished with toasted pecans.*

## Chili Coleslaw

| | |
|---|---|
| 3 C | cabbage – sliced |
| 1 C | bean sprouts |
| 1/4 C | mint leaves – chopped |
| 2 | shallots – sliced |
| 1 | red pepper – liced |

Dressing

| | |
|---|---|
| 2 T | sweet chili sauce |
| 1 T | oil |
| 1 T | vinegar |

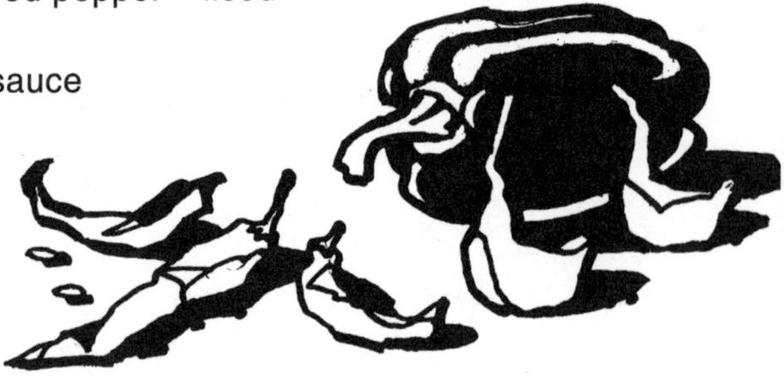

## Pineapple Coleslaw

| | |
|---|---|
| 3 C | red cabbage – shredded |
| 1/2 C | pineapple – crushed |
| 1/2 C | raisins or prunes – chopped |
| 3 | celery stalks – sliced |
| 2 T | parsley |

Dressing

| | |
|---|---|
| 2 T | cider vinegar |
| 1 T | oil |
| 1 T | sugar |

## Jamaican Coleslaw

Gary the Greek~Friday Harbor

3 C cabbage – shredded

Dressing

1 C honey roasted peanuts – chopped, in a pinch you can use peanut butter
1/4 C rice wine vinegar
2 limes – juice and zest
chili of some form
cilantro – chopped
ginger – grated
*coconut flakes

# Grain and Pasta Salads

## Couscous Salad

3 C couscous – cooked
1/2 C corn – frozen or canned
1/2 C peas – frozen or canned
1/2 C raisins
2 scallions – chopped
1 carrot – grated
parsley

❖ Combine all ingredients.

*Serve chilled with your favorite salad dressing.*

## Chickpea Salad

Simple and casual, this salad originates in North Africa though the addition of chili easily modifies it to Asian cuisine.

2 C chickpeas – cooked
3/4 C scallions or red onion – chopped
2 tomatoes – diced
cilantro – chopped
*some form of chili for an Asian flavor

❖ Toss all ingredients together.

*Serve chilled with* Toasted Cumin Vinaigrette.

## Egyptian Lentil Salad

| | |
|---|---|
| 1 C | lentils |
| 4 | scallions – sliced |
| | lemon juice |
| 1 t | cumin |
| | parsley or mint – chopped |
| | S&P |

- Cook lentils until tender, drain.
- Mix hot lentils with remaining ingredients, this allows the lentils to absorb the dressing.

*Serve chilled.*

## Minted Lentil Salad

| | |
|---|---|
| 1 1/2 C | bean sprouts |
| 1 C | lentils |
| 1/2 C | mint leaves – chopped |
| 1/4 C | red onion – minced |
| 1/4 C | orange juice |
| 2 T | olive oil |
| 1 T | balsamic vinegar |
| 1 t | orange zest |
| 1 t | salt |
| | ground pepper |

- Cook lentils until tender, drain.
- Combine lentils with remaining ingredients and toss well.

*Serve chilled.*

## Chinese Chicken Noodle Salad

Carol~Yacht Elyxir

| | | |
|---|---|---|
| 500g | 2-minute noodles or linguine | |
| 2 | chicken breasts – grilled and sliced, or 1 can | |
| a selection: | salad vegetables of your choice | |
| | cabbage | green beans |
| | carrots | snow peas |
| | red peppers | broccoli |
| | green onions | fresh cilantro – chopped |

- Cook noodles, rinse in cold water and drain.
- Thinly slice the vegetables and slightly blanch those you don't want crunchy such as carrots, green beans and broccoli.
- Mix noodles and vegetables together, scatter chicken on top.

*Sprinkle with toasted sesame seeds and drizzle with* Peanut Dressing.

## Crunchy Chicken Noodle Salad

Elliot~Magellan Straits

| | |
|---|---|
| 3 C | cabbage – shredded |
| 1 | chicken breast – cooked and sliced |
| 1 pkg. | 2 minute noodles – with noodles broken |
| 2 | scallions – sliced |
| 2 T | sesame seeds – toasted |
| 2 T | almonds – sliced |
| | S&P |

- Mix all ingredients together.
- Dress with your favorite dressing, or mix sugar, vinegar, and oil with the noodle spice packet.

## Indonesian Rice Salad

Leila~Yacht Reveille

This salad feeds many and is always a hit at potlucks. It is the perfect use for leftover rice and a versatile way to stretch salad greens. We generally make it aboard once a week and depending on what salad ingredients we have at hand it is often varied. I never alter the dressing and the rice I most often use is jasmine rice, however brown rice makes a healthier salad.

| | |
|---|---|
| 2 C | rice – cooked |
| any combination | chopped vegetables: |
| | bell peppers |
| | bok choy |
| | ...bage |
| | ...sprouts |
| | ...sley |

scallions
a selection long lasting foods:
nuts – toasted
coconut – grated
corn – canned or frozen
dates – chopped
pineapple – crushed
peas
pumpkin, sunflower or sesame seeds
raisins
sesame seeds
water chestnut slices

❖ Mix all items together with rice and chill.

*Just before serving dress with* Indonesian Dressing.

## Taboule Wheat Salad

Middle East

I've found that fresh parsley keeps extremely well (see herbs), so I often enjoy this salad at sea. It can be made with dried herbs equally well. Cracked wheat is not common worldwide, so I generally stock up with it when I can. I was delighted to find it in southern Chile. Though slightly unprocessed with husks throughout, it still made a wholesome, healthy salad. I discovered that I needed to add hot water instead of cold to soften the wheat, and substitute cilantro for parsley. Sometimes I add sliced radishes to add extra color.

| | |
|---|---|
| 1 C | bulgar (cracked wheat) |
| 1 C | water |
| 1 C | tomatoes – chopped |
| 1 C | parsley– chopped |
| 1/4 C | olive oil |
| 1/4 C | lemon juice |
| 4 | scallions – sliced |
| 1 t | fresh mint – chopped |
| 1 | garlic clove – crushed |
| | S&P |
| | *chili pepper of some form |

❖ Place wheat in a bowl and cover with water, let stand 30 min.

❖ Drain if necessary, add remaining ingredients and mix well.

*Chill and serve.*

## Autumn Taboule Salad

Cow Bay Café~Prince Rupert

| | |
|---|---|
| 1 C | bulgar |
| 1 C | water |
| 1/2 C | wild rice – cooked |
| 1/2 C | raisins |
| 1/2 C | red pepper – diced |
| 1/2 C | corn |
| 1/2 C | cucumber – diced |
| 1/4 C | parsley – chopped |
| 1 | lemon – juiced |

❖ Place wheat in bowl and cover with water, let stand 30 minutes.

❖ Drain if necessary, add remaining ingredients and mix well.

*Chill and serve.*

## Tucsan Bean and Tuna Salad

| | |
|---|---|
| 2 C | white beans – cooked |
| 1 can | tuna – drained and flaked |
| 1/3 C | black olives – chopped |
| 1/4 C | parsley – chopped |
| 5 | sun-dried tomatoes – sliced |
| 3 T | vinegar – balsamic |
| 2 T | olive oil |
| 1 T | pesto |
| | ground pepper |
| | *marinated artichoke hearts |

❖ Mix beans, tuna, tomatoes, olives and parsley.

❖ Blend pesto, vinegar and olive oil, pour over salad.

*Season with pepper and serve chilled.*

# Seafood Salads

## Hawaiian Poke

| | |
|---|---|
| 1 lb. | fresh tuna – cubed |
| 1/4 C | red onion – minced |
| 2 | tomatoes – chopped |
| 2 | scallions – sliced |

| | |
|---|---|
| 1 | garlic clove – crushed |
| 2 T | soy sauce |
| 1 T | sesame seeds – toasted |
| 2 t | coarse salt |
| 1 t | dried chili pepper |
| 1 t | grated ginger |

- ❖ Combine salt, ginger, garlic and chili, add tuna and coat well.
- ❖ Stir in remaining ingredients, cover and refrigerate 2 hours.

*Serve on a small bed of salad greens.*

## Poisson Cru ~Tahitian Marinated Fish

| | |
|---|---|
| 2 lb. | fresh fish |
| 1 C | coconut milk |
| | limes or lemons |
| | Tabasco or chili peppers – chopped |
| | ginger – grated |
| | garlic – crushed |
| | tomatoes – chopped |
| | carrots – grated |
| | onions – chopped |
| | scallions – sliced |
| | *any vegetables you think go well |
| | S&P |

- ❖ Cut fish into strips or small bite size pieces.
- ❖ Squeeze enough juice to cover fish and marinate for an hour until the fish turns white.
- ❖ Drain juice and combine fish with remaining ingredients.

*Serve chilled on a bed of shredded lettuce.*

## Marinated Cracked Crab

Cara~M/V St Elias

| | |
|---|---|
| 3 | Dungeness crabs – cleaned, cooked and cracked |
| 1/4 C | red wine vinegar |
| 1/4 C | olive oil |
| 5 | garlic cloves – crushed |

2 T lemon juice
1 t chili pepper flakes
fresh herbs – basil, rosemary, chives, oregano, parsley or whatever you have
S&P

❖ Combine all ingredients and marinate for 2 hours.

*Serve chilled over a bed of lettuce.*

## Seared Peppered Tuna Salad

3 tuna fillets -- 1" thick
3 T olive oil
1 T green peppercorns
1 T black peppercorns
1 T red peppercorns

❖ Grind peppercorns and oil together to form a paste.

❖ Spread paste over tuna and chill 3 hours.

❖ Barbecue, grill, broil, or sear tuna in a hot dry skillet, about 1 minute each side.

❖ Wrap tuna in plastic and chill 2 hours, slice thin.

*Serve tuna on top of greens and drizzle with* Chinese Dressing.

# Dressings

## Salad Vinaigrette

This classic recipe can be changed endlessly, it is always refreshing, and keeps well in the cupboard. I usually make it the day before leaving on a passage so that I can use fresh parsley and then not have to worry about messing with it at sea. The longer it sits the better the flavors develop. I mix it in a quart-size squeeze bottle that I can shake to release the dressing before serving.

1 C olive oil
1/3 C red wine vinegar
1/4 C chopped parsley
2 T balsamic vinegar
1 T capers
3 garlic cloves – crushed
2 t Dijon mustard

1 t honey
S&P
*2 T balsamic vinegar

❖ Combine all ingredients in a bottle and shake well, adjust ingredients to taste

Variations

*use white wine or cider vinegar instead of red

*add tarragon, basil, oregano, or rosemary

*use lemon juice instead of vinegar or use half-and- half

## Blue Cheese Dressing

1 C blue cheese
1/4 C milk
1 T sour cream or yogurt

❖ Blend all ingredients together and let sit 1 hour to thicken.

## Caesar Dressing

Carol~Yacht Elyxir

1/2 C olive oil
1/3 C Parmesan cheese – grated
3 T sour cream or yogurt
2 T lemon juice
1 T Worcestershire sauce
1 T Dijon mustard
1 garlic clove – crushed
pepper

❖ Blend all ingredients together.

## Chutney Dressing

Carol~Yacht Elyxir

1/3 C olive oil
1/4 C red wine vinegar

2 garlic cloves – crushed
3 T mango chutney
1 T honey
2 t mustard
*chili sauce

❖ Blend all ingredients together.

## Cumin Vinaigrette

2 garlic cloves – crushed
3 T olive oil
3 T lemon juice
1 t cumin
cumin
S&P

❖ *Toast cumin in small pan until fragrant, about 30 seconds.

❖ Blend all ingredients together.

## Peanut Dressing

1/4 C peanut oil, peanut butter or choppped nuts
3 T sesame oil
2 T cider or rice wine vinegar
2 T soy sauce
2 T basil or cilantro – chopped
2 T honey or brown sugar
1 T lemon juice
1 t chili sauce
garlic and ginger – crushed
S&P

❖ Blend ingredients together until smooth.

## Chinese Dressing

❖ Make *Peanut Dressing* using olive oil and add:

2 t mustard

## Indonesian Dressing

❖ Make *Peanut Dressing* and add:

1/2 C orange juice

## Thai Dressing

❖ Make *Peanut Dressing* and add:

1/4 C coconut milk

## Kiwi Vinaigrette

1/2 C salad oil
2 kiwifruit – peeled and chopped
1 garlic clove – chopped
3 T white wine vinegar
2 t Dijon mustard
1 t ginger – grated
chili to taste
S&P

❖ Blend all ingredients together.

*Serve on grilled chicken salad.*

## Lemon Tahini Dressing

Carol~Yacht Lorraine

1/4 C water
1/4 C tahini
1/4 C olive oil
2 T lemon juice
2 T soy sauce
*celery and onion – chopped

❖ Blend all ingredients together.

*Serve on salad greens or vegetables.*

## Miso Dressing

Jenn~Yacht Ocean Light II

1/4 C olive oil
1/4 C vegetable oil

1/8 C balsamic or rice vinegar
2 T sherry
1 T miso
3 garlic cloves – minced
S&P

❖ Blend all ingredients together and store in a bottle.

*Serve on salad greens or vegetables.*

## Papaya Seed Dressing

The seeds of the papaya have an elaborate peppery taste that enhance this dressing and give an added zip to any salad.

1/4 C balsamic vinegar
1 T honey
1 T papaya seeds
1 T poppy seeds
1 T lemon juice
2 garlic cloves – crushed
1/2 t cumin
S&P

❖ Blend all ingredients together and serve with salad.

## Sesame Dressing

1/2 C salad oil
1/4 C lemon juice
1/8 C sesame oil
2 garlic cloves – crushed
2 scallions – chopped
3 T sesame seeds – toasted
1 T honey
1/2 t salt

❖ Blend all ingredients together saving 1 T of sesame seeds to toss in at the end.

## Tofu Dressing

Leila~Yacht Reveille

1 box tofu or feta cheese
1/4 C olive oil
1/4 C vinegar

1 T honey
1 T tarragon
1 garlic clove – crushed
pepper

❖ Blend all ingredients together.

## Wasabi Salad Dressing

1/2 C salad oil
3 T rice wine vinegar
2 t wasabi

❖ Mix all ingredients together.

## Wasabi Seafood Dressing

This dressing is exquisite with cold fish or seafood.

1/2 C mayonnaise
1 T wasabi paste
2 t rice wine vinegar or lemon/lime juice
1 t ginger – grated
1/2 t garlic – crushed
*1/2 t sesame oil or sesame chili oil

❖ Mix all ingredients together and serve chilled.

## Yogurt Garlic Dressing

This refreshing dressing is often mixed with chopped cucumbers and served as an accompaniment to Mediterranean dishes.

1 C yogurt
2 garlic cloves – crushed
2 T olive oil
1 T chopped mint

❖ Blend ingredients together.

## Yogurt Lime Dressing

1 C yogurt
2 limes juiced
1 t coriander
1/2 t salt
*mint – chopped
*onion – chopped

❖ Blend ingredients together.

Chapter 8

# Fruits and Vegetables

# Beets

## Cooking Tips for Beets

- ❖ Do not peel beets until they are cooked or they will lose their color.
- ❖ To cook beets until tender, pressure-cook 20 minutes or simmer 45 minutes.

## Beet and Potato Salad with Lemon

From Ethiopia, this salad is a delightful marriage of colors and flavors.

| | |
|---|---|
| 1 lb. | red skinned potatoes – cooked and chopped |
| 1 lb. | beets – cooked and chopped |
| 1/4 C | lemon juice |
| 1/2 | onion – chopped |
| 3 T | vegetable oil |
| 1 | jalapeño chili – seeded and minced |
| | S&P |

❖ Combine all ingredients.

*Serve warm or at room temperature.*

## Moroccan Beets

| | |
|---|---|
| 2 C | beets – chopped |
| 1 T | olive oil |
| 1 T | lemon juice |
| | cilantro – chopped |
| | S&P |

❖ Mix all ingredients together.

*Serve chilled.*

## White Beets

| | |
|---|---|
| 2 C | beets – chopped |
| 1/2 C | yogurt |
| 2 T | mayonnaise |

2 t horseradish
1/2 t Dijon mustard
chives – chopped

❖ Mix all ingredients together.

*Serve either warm or cold.*

# Cabbage

## Bubble and Squeak

This old English standby for stretching leftovers was always a favorite when I was growing up sailing. My earliest memories of this dish go back to when I was little and loved it so much that I named my two pet mice Bubble and Squeak.

cabbage – shredded
potatoes – cooked and sliced

❖ Fry cabbage in pan and when al denté, add potatoes and heat through.

*an egg can be added to hold it together

*Serve with ketchup or chili sauce.*

Fran from the yacht *Aka* has another variation of *Bubble and Squeak* using mashed potatoes:

❖ Make mounds of mashed potato and throw everything into it; peas, cabbage, mince, carrots, onion etc.

❖ Sauté patties in large frying pan.

*This is great on a passage, as, once it's on your plate, it doesn't move.*

## Coconut Cabbage

Carol~Yacht Elyxir

4 C cabbage – shredded
1/2 C coconut – grated
2 green chilies – chopped
2 T oil
1 T Dijon mustard

1 garlic clove – crushed
1/4 t cumin
1/4 t turmeric

- ❖ Sauté onion, add all ingredients, cover and cook until done.

## Cabbage Pancakes

Carol~Yacht Elyxir

4 C cabbage – shredded
1 onion – diced
1 green pepper – diced
3 eggs
2 T flour
1 T milk
parsley – chopped
salt to taste

- ❖ Sauté onion and green peppers.
- ❖ Combine eggs, flour and milk, add remaining ingredients and mix well.
- ❖ Spoon mixture into frying pan, like a pancake, and cook until done.

## Cabbage Peking

Carol~Yacht Elyxir

4 C cabbage – shredded
1 onion – sliced
1/4 C rice vinegar
1 T honey
1 T salad oil
1 T ginger – grated
soy sauce

- ❖ Sauté onion, ginger and cabbage 2 minutes.
- ❖ Stir in vinegar, honey and soy sauce.
- ❖ Sprinkle with sesame seeds.

*Serve hot or cold.*

## Sweet and Sour Red Cabbage

| | |
|---|---|
| 1/2 | red cabbage – shredded |
| 1/4 C | raisins |
| 1 | onion – chopped |
| 2 | garlic clove – crushed |
| 2 T | vegetable oil |
| 2 T | apple cider vinegar |
| 2 T | honey |

- ❖ Saute onion and garlic, add cabbage and toss quickly to coat.
- ❖ Splash cabbage with vinegar, add honey and raisins, toss and cover.
- ❖ Steam until al denté.

*Serve hot.*

## Versatile Cabbage

Carol~Yacht Elyxir

| | |
|---|---|
| 1/2 | cabbage - shredded |
| 1 | onion - chopped |
| 1 t | vegetable oil |
| | salt |

- ❖ Sauté onion in the oil, add cabbage and cover.
- ❖ Steam over low heat until al denté.
- ❖ Can add a dash of water to help steam.

Variations

*Use butter instead of oil and add a small dash of nutmeg.
*Sprinkle with grated cheese.
*Mix with cooked pasta and add 1 T caraway seeds.
*Mix with 3 C mashed potatoes, 1 C grated cheese, and bake for 30 minutes in medium oven.

# Cauliflower

## Mustard Cauliflower

Carol~Yacht Elyxir

| | |
|---|---|
| 4 C | cauliflower florets |
| 2 T | vegetable oil |

| | |
|---|---|
| 2 t | mustard seeds |
| 2 t | ginger - grated |
| 2 t | lemon juice |
| 1/2 t | turmeric |
| | cilantro |
| | salt |

- ❖ Toast mustard seeds in a dry pan until they begin to pop.
- ❖ Add ginger and turmeric, sauté for 30 seconds.
- ❖ Add cauliflower, stir to coat, splash with 1/2 C water, cover and steam until al denté.
- ❖ Stir in lemon juice and season with S&P.

*Garnish with fresh cilantro.*

# Carrots

## Moroccan Carrots

Carol~Yacht Elyxir

| | |
|---|---|
| 4 | carrots - sliced |
| 2 | garlic cloves –- crushed |
| 2 T | whole cloves |
| 2 T | whole cumin |
| 2 T | olive oil |
| 2 T | lemon juice |
| | parsley - chopped |
| | salt |

- ❖ In enough water to cover carrots, add garlic, cloves, and cumin, bring to a boil.
- ❖ Add carrots and cook until al denté.
- ❖ Drain carrots and toss with oil, lemon juice, salt and parsley.

*Serve cool.*

# Eggplant

## Purging Eggplant

Eggplant is often purged to remove some of the bitterness and make it less absorbent.

- ❖ Slice or cube eggplant and place in a colander.
- ❖ Sprinkle with salt and let drain 30 minutes.

## Roasted Eggplant

The roasted pulp of the eggplant is used on dips and spreads, *see Baba Gonash.*

- ❖ Place whole, oil coated, eggplant in roasting pan, pierce the skin in a few places.
- ❖ Roast or grill until skin is blackened and wrinkled.
- ❖ Peel off skin.

## Braised Eggplant

Carol~Yacht Elyxir

| | |
|---|---|
| 3 | eggplants |
| 4 T | olive oil |
| 2 T | lemon juice |
| | garlic – crushed |
| | orgeano |
| | salt |

- ❖ Slice eggplants crosswise and sprinkle both sides with salt, when "sweaty" wipe off liquid.
- ❖ In a very hot skillet, braise eggplant until golden and tender, drain on a paper towel and salt.
- ❖ Dress with lemon juice, garlic, oregano and chill.

## Eggplant and Tomato Casserole

Carol~Yacht Lorraine

| | |
|---|---|
| 2 | eggplants – sliced |
| 1 C | cheese – grated |
| 1 C | red wine |
| 1 | onion – chopped |
| 1 can | tomato puree |

| | |
|---|---|
| 1/2 C | bread or cracker crumbs |
| 1/2 C | mushrooms – sliced |
| 1/4 C | celery – chopped |
| 2 | egg yolks – beaten |
| | olive oil |

- ❖ Dip eggplant slices in eggs and bread crumbs, brown in olive oil.
- ❖ Layer baking dish with tomato puree, eggplant and vegetables.
- ❖ Cover with cheese and bake 15 minutes.

## Italian Eggplant Casserole

| | |
|---|---|
| 2 | eggplants – sliced |
| 3 | onions – chopped |
| 1 can | stewed tomatoes |
| 1 C | red wine |
| 1 C | cheese – grated |
| 1/4 C | oil |
| 3 | garlic cloves – crushed |
| | S&P |

- ❖ Sauté eggplant until soft and brown, drain on a paper towel.
- ❖ Sauté onion and garlic, add tomatoes and wine, simmer 5 minutes.
- ❖ Layer baking dish with eggplant, tomatoes and cheese.
- ❖ Bake 1 hour.

## Ratatouille

| | |
|---|---|
| 2 | eggplants – cubed and purged |
| 3 | zucchini – chopped |
| 2 | green peppers – chopped |
| 2 | tomatoes – chopped |
| 1 | onion – chopped |
| 2 | garlic cloves – crushed |
| 2 T | parsley – chopped |

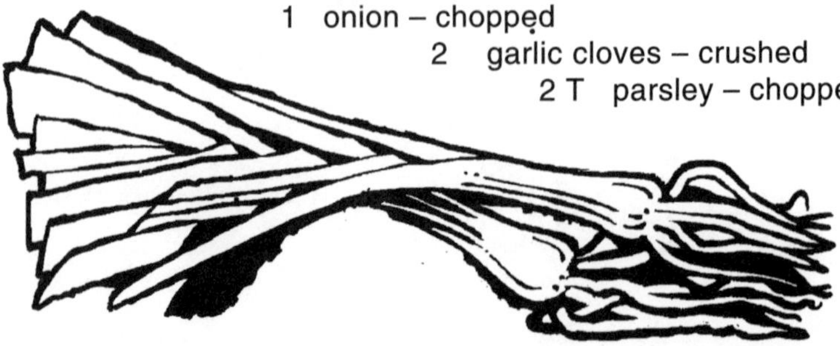

2 T basil – chopped
1 T tomato paste
1 t thyme
1/2 t sugar
S&P
*1 C coconut milk may be added for a tropical flavor

- ❖ Sauté eggplant with peppers and zucchini until brown, drain on a paper towel.
- ❖ Sauté onion, add tomatoes and seasoning, simmer 15 minutes.
- ❖ Add eggplant, heat through and serve.

## Sicilian Caponata

2 eggplants – cubed
3 tomatoes – chopped
2 celery stalks – chopped
1 onion – chopped
10 green olives
3 T wine vinegar
2 T cocoa powder
2 T capers
1 T sugar
2 bay leaves
1 dried chili
olive oil
thyme
S&P

- ❖ Sauté eggplant in hot olive oil until soft, add remaining ingredients and simmer 15 minutes.

*Serve warm garnished with parsley and toasted almonds.*

# Leeks

## Curried Leeks

Carol~Yacht Elyxir

3 C leeks – chopped
1/2 T butter
1 t cumin seeds

| | |
|---|---|
| 1 t | turmeric |
| 1 t | ginger – grated |
| 1/2 t | *Garam Masala* |

- ❖ Sauté cumin seeds in butter.
- ❖ Add all remaining ingredients except Garam Masala, cover and cook until tender.
- ❖ Stir in *Garam Masala* and serve.

# Papaya

## Green Papaya Curry

| | |
|---|---|
| 2 | green papaya – peeled and diced |
| 1/2 C | coconut milk |
| 2 T | butter |
| 1 | onion – diced |
| 2 | garlic cloves – crushed |
| 2 | green chilies |
| 2 t | ginger – grated |
| 1 t | curry powder |
| | S&P |

- ❖ Sauté onion, garlic and ginger in butter.
- ❖ Add chilies, curry powder and S&P, cook paste until golden, about 5 minutes.
- ❖ Stir in the coconut milk and add papaya.
- ❖ Cook 30 minutes stirring occasionally, add more coconut milk if curry dries out.

# Peppers: Green, Red and Yellow

## Roasted Peppers

Many Mediterranean dishes include roasted peppers. To achieve this distinct flavor follow these directions:

- ❖ Roast, grill or turn whole pepper over a flame until skin is blacken and blistered.

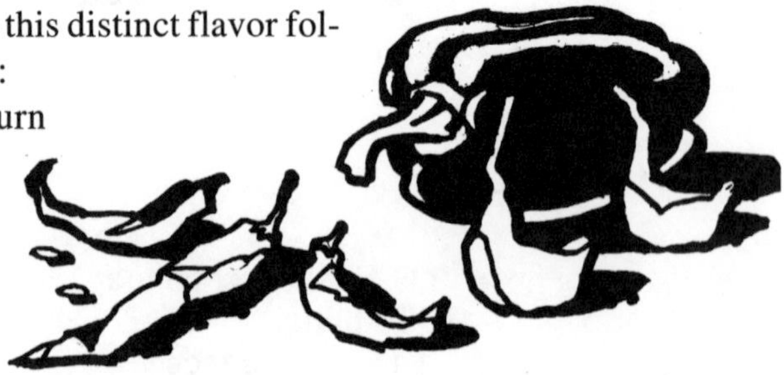

- ❖ Place roasted pepper in a paper bag to cool for 10 minutes.
- ❖ Peel the skin off, slice the pepper open and scrape out the seeds and ribs.

# Potatoes

## Curried Potatoes

Carol~Yacht Elyxir

| | |
|---|---|
| 3 C | potatoes – chopped |
| 2 C | peas or beans |
| 1/2 C | water |
| 3 | tomatoes – chopped |
| 1 | onion – chopped |
| 2 | garlic cloves – crushed |
| 2 T | vegetable oil |
| 1 T | ginger – grated |
| 1 t | cumin |
| 1/4 t | chilies |

- ❖ Sauté garlic, ginger and onion in oil, stir in spices and tomatoes.
- ❖ Add peas, potatoes and water, cover and simmer until potatoes are cooked.

*Garnish with fresh cilantro.*

## Hash Browns

1 potato – per person

- ❖ Grate potatoes and rinse in a sieve with salt water.
- ❖ Fry in oil.

## Irish Potato Pancakes ~ Fadge

Commodore Alex

It was a sunny day in B.C., Canada, and we were tied up at the Prince Rupert Yacht and Rowing Club after our arrival from Hawaii. John and I were busy scrutinizing our varnish work, wondering if the August weather would let us place a touch-up coat on the toerails. Alex was next door working away on his boat, and overhearing our conversation, offered a magnifying glass for our inspection.

"Sure thanks, as this is the only thing in life I have to worry about." I replied.

Alex laughed, and I explained that I was officially handing over the job of varnishing to John, as I had to continue writing a book. I'd caught his interest.

"What is your book about? Alex asked.

"If you'll give me your favorite recipe you'll know" I replied

"It's Irish fadge, and its great for brunch when you're out cruising." came the reply.

| | |
|---|---|
| 6 | potatoes – boiled and mashed |
| 1/2 C | flour |
| 2 | scallions – chopped |
| | S&P |

- ❖ Combine all ingredients and shape mixture into pancakes.
- ❖ Sauté pancakes until golden brown.

*Serve hot with Canadian bacon, scrambled eggs and fresh fruit.*

## Mexican Potatoes

| | |
|---|---|
| 6 | potatoes – sliced |
| 2 C | cheese – grated |
| 1/2 C | olives – sliced |
| 2 | tomatoes – chopped |
| 1 | onion – chopped |
| 3 T | olive oil |
| | chili of some form |
| | S&P |

- ❖ Layer a baking dish with potatoes, onion, chili and tomato, sprinkle with olive oil.
- ❖ Cover with another layer of potatoes, drizzle with olive oil and top with cheese.
- ❖ Bake 45 minutes at 425° until potatoes are cooked, sprinkle with cilantro.

*Serve with salsa, sour cream or guacamole.*

## Potato and Zucchini BBQ

Barbara~Tahiti 98

5 potatoes – sliced
5 zucchini – sliced
4 onions – sliced
Italian herds – basil, rosemary and oregano
butter or olive oil

- ❖ Place all ingredients on a large sheet of aluminum foil, sprinkle with Italian herbs and S&P, with knobs of butter.
- ❖ Wrap foil into a tight package and place on a corner of the barbecue, cook vegetables until tender, about 20 minutes.

## Spanish Potatoes

Dr Michel~Southern Ocean

This is delicious way to dress up leftover potatoes.

4 C potatoes – cooked and cubed
1/4 C olive oil
5 garlic cloves – crushed
2 T paprika
2 T wine vinegar
salt

- ❖ Sauté potatoes in half the oil.
- ❖ In a small pan sauté garlic in remaining oil stir in paprika and vinegar, pour over warm potatoes.

# Taro Leaf

## Taro Leaf

Grown in the Caribbean and Pacific, the cooked leaves of the taro plant can easily be substituted for spinach. The desired leaf should be young and tender, take caution in choosing the plant variety as some contain calcium oxalate resulting in an itchy mouth and throat. When cooked, the leaves can be frozen in plastic bags for later use in quiches, pastas or green curry.

1 1/2 lb. young taro leaves – no bigger than 16"

- ❖ Wash leaves.
- ❖ Cut out the middle stalk, pinch off the tip of the leaf and coarsely shred the leaf.
- ❖ Simmer leaves in water for 20 minutes.
- ❖ Drain and mash.

## Coconut Creamed Taro Leaf

South Pacific

Baking powder is used in this recipe to remove the "sting" from the taro leaf and to preserve the green color.

| | |
|---|---|
| 1 1/2 lb | young taro leaves |
| 1/2 C | coconut milk |
| 1 | onion – chopped |
| 3 T | butter |
| pinch | baking powder |
| | S&P |

- ❖ Cook taro leaves following the directions above, squeeze out excess liquid.
- ❖ Sauté onion in butter, add coconut milk, taro leaves and baking powder, heat through.
- ❖ Season to taste.

# Zucchini

## Zucchini Provçencal

| | |
|---|---|
| 6 | zucchini – sliced |
| 4 | tomatoes – chopped |
| 1 | onion – sliced |
| 1 T | olive oil |
| 2 | garlic cloves – crushed |
| | basil |
| | S&P |

- ❖ Sauté onion and garlic, add zucchini and cook 3 minutes.
- ❖ Add tomatoes and simmer 10 minutes.

# Vegetables

## Fijian Vegetable Curry

2 C coconut milk
1 C vegetable stock
1 C *Curry Paste*
1 C pumpkin – cubed and par boiled
1 C green beans – sliced
1 C cauliflower florets
2 carrots – sliced
2 onions – chopped
2 potatoes – cubed and par boiled
1 eggplant – chopped
1 green pepper – chopped
2 T butter
1 T mustard seeds
2 t chili pepper – chopped
basil

- ❖ Toast mustard seeds in a dry frying pan until they pop, add butter and onions, cook until soft.
- ❖ Add green pepper, curry and chili, cook 3 minutes.
- ❖ Add remaining vegetables, stir in stock and 1 C coconut milk, cook vegetables until al danté.

*Serve on rice with remaining coconut milk drizzled on top, garnish with a sprinkle of chopped basil.*

Chapter 9

# Seasonings Marinades and Sauces

# Herb Mixes

## Italian Herb Mix

I make up an Italian herb mix in a 2-cup sized container and use it in most of my dishes requiring herbs. At sea it's a lot easier to shake one seasoning into a dish than find, open, close and stow each herb. At first I thought that by consolidating my herbs, food might get a little boring, as every dish would result in the same flavor, but with the addition of fresh herbs and or pesto, a dish can easily take on a different flair.

I renew my dried herbs at every major provisioning stop and continually add to the Italian herb mix to keep it fresh and interesting. French and Italian dried herbs are far superior to American brands, and I always stock up on them when I'm cruising in French territories.

These herbs mixed together make a great blend that is quick to use.

1/4 C basil
1/4 C oregano
1/8 C rosemary
1/8 C savory
1/8 C sage
1/8 C thyme

❖ Combine all ingredients and store in a cool place.

# Spice Mixes

## Cajun Spice

1 T paprika
2 t garlic powder
1 t cayenne pepper
1 t ground pepper
1/2 t salt
1/2 t oregano
1/2 t thyme

❖ Combine all ingredients and store in a cool place.

## Curry Powder

| | |
|---|---|
| 2 T | ground coriander |
| 1 T | turmeric |
| 1 T | mustard seeds |
| 1 T | ground cumin |
| 2 t | cinnamon |
| 1 t | ground cardamom |
| 1 t | fenugreek |
| 1 t | chili powder |
| 1 t | ground black pepper |
| 1 t | ginger |

❖ Mix all ingredients together with hand blender for 4 minutes.

## Curry Paste

| | |
|---|---|
| 1 C | stewed tomatoes |
| 1/4 C | coconut milk |
| 1 | onion – chopped |
| 2 | lemons – juice and zest |
| 2 T | *Garam Masala* |
| 2 T | curry powder |
| 1 T | soy sauce |
| 6 | garlic cloves – crushed |
| 2 t | turmeric |
| 1 t | ginger – grated |
| 1 t | chili peppers – chopped |
| 1 t | mustard seeds |

❖ Blend all ingredients together until chunky.

*Keeps refrigerated for a week, or frozen for several months.*

## Moroccan Spice

Cow Bay Café~Prince Rupert, Canada

| | |
|---|---|
| 1/2 C | fennel seeds |
| 1/4 C | coriander seeds |
| 2 t | cumin |
| 2 t | whole cloves |
| 1 t | cardamom |

❖ Toast spices together in a frying pan to release their flavor.

❖ Grind spices to the consistency of medium ground coffee.

## Thai Green Curry Paste

Green curry is wonderful with fish, vegetables and chicken, *see Thai Fish Green Curry.*

| | |
|---|---|
| 1/2 C | coconut cream |
| 1 | onion – chopped |
| 1 | green pepper – chopped |
| 1 | lemon – juice and zest |
| 5 | young lemon or lime leaves, or lemon grass |
| 2 | garlic cloves – crushed |
| 2 T | cilantro – chopped |
| 1 T | ginger – grated |
| 2 t | brown sugar |
| 1 t | fish sauce |
| 1 t | turmeric |
| 1 t | cumin |
| 1 t | salt |
| 1 t | ground pepper |
| 1/2 t | coriander |
| 1/2 t | cloves |
| 1/2 t | nutmeg |
| | chili of some form to taste |

❖ Blend all ingredients together until smooth.

## Thai Red Curry Paste

| | |
|---|---|
| 4 | chilies – chopped |
| 3 | garlic cloves – crushed |
| 5 | young lime or lemon leaves |
| 1 | lime – juice and zest |
| 1 | lemon – juice and zest |
| 2 | scallions – chopped |
| 1 | bunch – cilantro chopped |
| 1 T | ginger – grated |
| 2 t | paprika |
| 2 t | peanut oil |
| 1 t | fish sauce |
| 1 t | cumin seeds – toasted and ground |
| 1 t | nutmeg |
| | S&P |

❖ Blend all ingredients together until smooth.

## Garam Masala

| | |
|---|---|
| 1/4 C | ground coriander |
| 2 T | cumin |
| 1/2 t | ground black pepper |
| 1/2 t | cardamom seeds |
| 1/2 t | cinnamon |
| 1/4 t | black pepper |
| 1/4 t | ground cloves |
| 1/4 t | nutmeg |

❖ Mix all ingredients together and store in airtight container.

## Island Seasoning

Island Seasoning is excellent on fried bananas, grilled chicken or fish, curries and veggies.

| | |
|---|---|
| 1 T each | allspice, nutmeg and cloves |
| 1/2 T each | cinnamon and mace |
| 1 t each | thyme and pepper |

❖ Combine all ingredients and store in a cool place.

## Mustard

| | |
|---|---|
| 2/3 C | wine vinegar |
| 1/2 C | yellow mustard seeds |
| 3 T | honey or brown sugar |
| 1 t | salt |
| 1/4 t | cinnamon |

❖ Soak mustard seeds in vinegar for 36 hours.

❖ Blend all ingredients together until smooth, add extra vinegar if the mustard is too thick.

*Mustard will keep for a year in sterile, sealed jars.*

## Taco Seasoning

| | |
|---|---|
| 1 T | oregano |
| 1 T | cilantro |
| 1 T | paprika |
| 1 T | cumin |

1 garlic clove
2 t lime juice
2 t chili pepper flakes
sugar
S&P

# Fish Marinades

## Asian Fish Marinade

2 T soy sauce
1 T peanut oil
1 t brown sugar
S&P

- ❖ Blend all ingredients together.
- ❖ Rub fish with S&P, brush with marinade.
- ❖ Grill or broil fish until just cooked.

*Serve with* Asian Relish.

## Fish in Mustard Marinade

Carolyn~Tahiti 98

1/4 C Dijon mustard
1/4 C olive oil
1/4 C lime juice
1/4 C orange juice
2 scallions – chopped
3 garlic gloves – minced

- ❖ Marinate fish for 15 minutes then poach in marinade.

## Jamaican Fish Marinade

1/3 C brown sugar
1/4 C dark rum
2 T olive oil
2 T orange juice
1 T lime juice
1 T ginger – grated
1 T garlic – crushed

1 t diced fresh or dried chilies
1/4 t allspice

- Blend all ingredients together.
- Marinate fish 2 hours then poach in marinade.

### Thai Fish Marinade

1 T brandy
2 t oyster sauce
2 t soy sauce
3 cilantro sprigs
2 garlic gloves – crushed
2 whole black peppers – ground

- Mash all ingredients together to form a paste.
- Spread paste onto fish and barbecue, broil or poach until done.

## Meat Marinades

### Citrus and Ginger Chicken Marinade

1/2 C orange juice
1/4 C lemon juice
2 T sugar
2 T mint – chopped
2 T ginger – grated
2 T oil
S&P

- Combine all ingredients together and marinate chicken overnight.
- Grill, poach or barbecue chicken until done.

### Teriyaki Marinade

1/2 C soy sauce
1/2 C water
1/4 C sherry
1/4 C sugar
2 garlic cloves – crushed

1 scallion – chopped
1 T ginger – grated

❖ Combine all ingredients and marinate meat for 2 hours.
❖ Grill, poach or barbecue meat until done.

# Sauces

## Apple Sauce

3 apples – peeled and chopped
1 T water
1 T butter
2 cloves
lemon juice
sugar

❖ Simmer all ingredients until apples are cooked, beat with a fork until smooth.
❖ Add sugar to taste.

## Black Bean Sauce

Jenn~Yacht Ocean Light II

1 C water
1 onion – chopped
5 garlic cloves – crushed
2 T honey
2 T sherry
2 T fermented black beans – chopped
1 T soy sauce
1 T peanut oil
2 t cornstarch – mixed with 1 T cold water
1 t fish sauce
*1 t ginger
*chili pepper flakes

❖ Sauté onion, garlic, and back beans in hot oil for 1 minute.
❖ Add water, soy sauce, fish sauce, sherry and honey, simmer 5 minutes.
❖ Drizzle in corn starch mixture and stir over a low heat until sauce thickens, about 1 minute.

## Thai Sweet and Sour Sauce

2/3 C water
2/3 C sugar
1/2 C rice wine vinegar
3 T chili paste
2 garlic cloves – crushed
cilantro

❖ Combine all ingredients to form sauce.

❖ Add to stir fried meat and/or vegetables.

## Barbecue Sauce

1 C ketchup
2 T Dijon mustard
2 T vinegar or sherry
2 T maple syrup
1 T Worcestershire sauce
1 garlic clove – crushed
chili of some form

❖ Blend all ingredients together.

## Mango Barbecue Sauce

2 mangos – pureéd
1/4 C sherry
3 cloves garlic – crushed
2 T tomato paste
1 T Worcestershire sauce
1 T oil
1 T lime juice
2 t ginger – grated
2 t brown sugar
2 t vinegar
2 t Dijon mustard
1 t Sambal Oelek
S&P

❖ Sauté garlic and ginger in oil for 30 seconds, add sherry and simmer 2 minutes.

- ❖ Add remaining ingredients and continue to simmer 10 minutes.
- ❖ Marinate ribs, chicken or shrimp in sauce, bake or barbecue, brushing with sauce until done.

## Peanut Sauce

| | |
|---|---|
| 1/2 C | water |
| 1/2 C | peanut butter |
| 3 T | soy sauce or teriyaki sauce |
| 1 T | lemon juice |
| 1 T | oil (not olive) |
| 1 | garlic clove – mashed |
| 2 t | sesame oil |
| 2 t | brown sugar |
| 1 t | chili pepper flakes |

- ❖ Brown garlic and chili pepper in oil 1 minute.
- ❖ Add remaining ingredients and simmer until smooth.

## Tarragon Mustard Sauce

| | |
|---|---|
| 2 T | butter – melted |
| 2 T | Dijon mustard |
| 1 T | honey |
| 1 T | lemon juice |
| 1 T | tarragon – chopped |
| 2 | scallions – chopped |
| | ground pepper |

- ❖ Blend all ingredients together until smooth.

*Serve with fish baked in wine.*

## Tartar Sauce

| | |
|---|---|
| 1/2 C | mayonnaise |
| 2 T | dill pickles – chopped |
| 2 T | capers |
| 2 T | chives or scallions – chopped |
| 1 t | lime or lemon juice |

- ❖ Combine all ingredients, chill and serve.

# Vegetable Sauces

## Baked Honey Glaze

This sweet glaze is delightful on a variety of roastable vegetables such as sweet potato, carrots, parsnip, yam, pumpkin and potatoes.

| | |
|---|---|
| 4 C | vegetables – chunked |
| 2 T | honey |
| 1 T | vinegar |
| 1 T | butter |
| | pepper |

- ❖ Combine all ingredients in a baking dish and bake 25 minutes.

## Mustard Cheese Sauce

This wonderful tangy cheese sauce gives a new life to steamed cauliflower, carrots, broccoli, spinach or cabbage.

| | |
|---|---|
| 1 C | milk |
| 1/4 C | cheese – grated |
| 2 T | butter |
| 2 T | flour |
| 2 T | Dijon mustard |
| | ground pepper |

- ❖ Melt butter, stir in flour and cook until frothy.
- ❖ Slowly stir in milk until mixture boils and thickens.
- ❖ Remove from heat, add cheese, mustard and S&P.

# Vegetable Dressings

## Grilled Vegetable Dressing

| | |
|---|---|
| 1/2 C | olive oil |
| 3 T | salt |
| 3 T | brown sugar |
| 2 T | paprika |
| 1 1/2 T | ground black pepper |
| 1 | garlic clove – crushed |
| 1 1/2 t | cayenne pepper |
| | basil |

- ❖ Mix spices together and moisten with oil until you reach the consistency of paint.
- ❖ Brush seasoning onto sliced vegetables and grill both sides, approximately 8 minutes.

## Lemon Vegetable Dressing

3 T olive oil
2 T bell pepper – diced
1 T lemon juice
1 T lemon zest
1/2 salt

- ❖ Mix all ingredients together and serve over steamed vegetables.

Chapter 10

# Beans and Grains

# Beans

Readily found worldwide, in many varieties, long lasting, and cheap, beans are an excellent source of protein. Beans combine well with tomatoes, onions, cheese and garlic making them a simple addition to any galley, especially in bouncy conditions when nourishing one-pot meals are needed most.

## Cooking Time for Beans

| Beans | Soak Time | Stove-top Time | Pressure Cooker Time |
|---|---|---|---|
| Black beans | 8 hrs | 1 hr | 15 min |
| Chick Peas | 8 hrs | 1 hr | 15 min |
| Kidney beans | 8 hrs | 3 hrs | 25 min |
| Lima beans | 8 hrs | 30 min | 10 min |
| Navy beans | 8 hrs | 3 hrs | 30 min |
| Northern beans | 8 hrs | 2 1/2 hrs | 20 min |
| Pea beans | 8 hrs | 3 hrs | 25 min |
| Pinto beans | 8 hrs | 2 hrs | 15 min |
| Soy beans | 8 hrs | 3 hrs | 35 min |
| Split peas | none | 2 1/2 hrs | 25 min |
| White beans | 8 hrs | 3 hrs | 15 min |

## Tips on Cooking Beans

- **Soak beans** for 8 hours, generally overnight, in water.
- **Discard** any beans that float, as they are bad.
- **A quicker option** to soaking beans is to blanch them for 3 minutes then let them rest 1 hour tightly covered.
- Use **3 cups** of fresh water to cook one cup of beans.

- **1 cup of beans** will increase to 2 1/4 cups during cooking.
- **Don't salt beans** until they are cooked as the skin becomes tough.
- **Cook beans until tender** anywhere from 1 1/2 hours to 3 hours stove top time.
- **Cooking time for beans varies** as the older they are the longer they take to cook.
- To **test if beans are cooked** place a few on a spoon and gently blow on them. If the skin peels back they're done.

## Eco Burgers

Nicholas~Tahiti 98

Nicholas created these burgers to use up the leftover refried beans we had from the previous night's dinner.

| | |
|---|---|
| 3 C | couscous |
| 2 C | refried beans |
| 1 C | salted peanuts - chopped |
| 1 | onion – chopped |
| 1 | carrots – grated |
| 1 | egg |
| 2 | garlic cloves – crushed |
| 1 T | sesame seeds |
| | S&P |

- Combine all ingredients in a bowl and shape into patties.
- Fry in olive oil until golden.

*Serve with tossed garden salad.*

## Baked Beans

| | |
|---|---|
| 4 C | water |
| 1 can | tomatoes |
| 1 C | bacon – sliced |
| 1/2 C | navy beans |
| 1/4 C | tomato sauce |
| 1/4 C | brown sugar |
| 1 | onion – chopped |
| 1 | green pepper – chopped |

1 celery stalk – chopped
3 T Dijon mustard
salt

- ❖ Place beans in 2 C water and pressure cook 5 minutes, or simmer 15 minutes, drain.
- ❖ Mix all ingredients together and pressure cook 20 minutes, or bake covered 1 1/2 hours
- ❖ Simmer uncovered 5 minutes to thicken.

## Chili Beans

2 C black, red or kidney beans – cooked
1 can whole peeled tomatoes
1 can tomato paste
1 onion – chopped
1 green pepper – chopped
1 celery stalk – chopped
4 garlic cloves – chopped
2 T Dijon mustard
1 T chili pepper – chopped
2 t cumin
1 t lemon juice
fresh basil and oregano
S&P
*1/4 C bulgar wheat
*3 T barbecue sauce
*1 small can of Mexican salsa or enchilada sauce may replace chili
*1 apple – chopped
*5 bacon rashers – chopped

- ❖ Combine all ingredients and pressure-cook 10 minutes, or simmer about 25 minutes.
- ❖ Continue to simmer if possible for another 15 minutes to allow flavors to develop.

*Serve garnished with cilantro, grated cheese, yogurt dressing, or* Pink Onion Relish.

## Portuguese Sausage and Beans

2 C red kidney beans – cooked
2 C spicy sausage or salami – sliced
1 can stewed tomatoes
1 onion – chopped
1 green pepper – chopped
2 celery stalks – sliced
3 garlic cloves – crushed
2 T basil – chopped
chili of some form
S&P

❖ Sauté sausage until browned, add onion, pepper and celery, cook 3 min.

❖ Add beans, tomatoes and seasoning.

❖ Pressure cook 10 minutes, or simmer 20 minutes.

*Serve over rice.*

## Pumpkin and Bean Stew

2 C pumpkin – cubed
2 C white beans – cooked
1 C water
1/2 C scallions – chopped
2 carrots – chopped
2 apples – chopped
8 mushrooms
ginger – grated
soy sauce

❖ Combine all ingredients and pressure-cook 10 minutes, or simmer 20 minutes.

# Who's Coming to Dinner?

It was my turn to be cook, and I was mentally going through our lockers contemplating what to prepare for dinner. We were sailing north on a cold afternoon through the labyrinth of Patagonia's archipelago, it had been three days since our last contact with civilization, a radio call giving the required identification information while passing a remote light house.

Sunlight rays were streaming from the sky, turning the steel water blue and basting the distant hillside in a mellow light. Briefly a white shape appeared inside a beam of light, and I wondered if an angel had landed from heaven. All thoughts of food vanished as I realized it was a sailboat. Excitement broke out onboard and John called on the radio giving our position. A reply came stating that they were the yacht *Chiloe* on their way south. In his elation at sighting another vessel, John asked them to consider stopping for the day to join us for dinner. "Yes" came the reply and I was quickly down to two dinner options rice and beans, or spaghetti.

As their white sail grew larger I began to question how big was *Chiloe* and how many were onboard. I called on the radio asking how many to expect for dinner. "There's thirteen of us and a dog" came the reply. Yikes!!!! I panicked; not only did I have our crew of six to feed but 13 more, too. It's amazing how quickly the enchantment of the prospect of company becomes daunting, even though our crew kept reassuring me that beans and rice would be fine for dinner - again.

Five minutes later a providential crackle came across on the radio. "This is the 32'-yacht *Chiloe* and Charlie and I will be happy to join you for dinner, we'll bring the beers!"

Shrimp stir-fry and jasmine rice was my menu choice followed by apple cobbler.

## Couscous

Originally from North Africa, couscous is fine milled wheat only requiring hot water and 5 minutes to prepare. It is the perfect onboard dish, especially in heavy weather. I often add couscous at the end of cooking stews and soups to absorb the juices and thicken the dish making it a hearty and interesting one-pot meal, *see Italian Black Bean Soup.*

Couscous is safer to prepare in rough conditions than rice or pasta as you can boil the hot water in an enclosed kettle, place it in the thermos and use it when you need to prepare the couscous, thus eliminating more pots on the stove requiring attention.

Traditionally couscous was served at the end of the week to use up all the vegetables before market day on Saturday. Served in a large round dish, the grain is piled into a mound with a depression at the top. Chicken or meat is placed in the hollow with the vegetables on top or around the side.

Inexpensive and available worldwide couscous keeps well in an airtight, waterproof, container.

## Tips on Cooking Couscous

- ❖ Add 2 cups of boiling water to 2 cups of couscous and let stand 5 minutes. Makes 4 cups.
- ❖ Couscous can be dressed with almonds, raisins, dates, herbs, or sun-dried tomatoes.

## Almond Couscous

| | |
|---|---|
| 1 1/2 C | couscous |
| 1 1/2 C | vegetable broth |
| 1/4 C | raisins |
| 2 | zucchini – diced |
| 1 | onion – diced |
| 3 T | slivered almonds – toasted |
| 1 T | butter |
| 1 T | cilantro |
| 1 T | mint |
| 1/4 t | cumin |
| S&P | |

- ❖ Sauté onion and zucchini, heat broth and butter, add couscous and let stand 5 minutes.
- ❖ Toss in remaining ingredients and season to taste.

## Vegetable and Date Couscous

| | |
|---|---|
| 1 1/2 C | vegetable broth |
| 1 1/2 C | couscous |
| 1 | onion – diced |
| 1 | red pepper – diced |
| 1 | zucchini – diced |
| 1/2 C | dates – diced |
| 1/4 C | coriander – chopped |
| 4 T | olive oil |
| 1/2 T | paprika |
| 1 t | cumin |
| | salt |
| | coriander |
| | *chicken – cooked and diced |

- ❖ Sauté onion, add zucchini and red pepper, cook 2 minutes.
- ❖ Bring broth to a boil, add all ingredients.
- ❖ Remove from heat, cover and let stand 5 minutes.
- ❖ Add coriander and fluff with a fork.

# Lentils

Inexpensive, long-lasting, nutritious, nourishing and simple, lentils are a staple provision and I enjoy using them a couple of times throughout a passage. They obtain a sophisticated taste when seasoned with spices and herbs, while enhancing vegetables, poultry, seafood, and meats.

## Tips on Cooking Lentils

| Lentil | Soak Time | Stove-top Time | Pressure Cooker Time |
|---|---|---|---|
| Large green/brown | 1 hr- optional | 1 1/2 hrs | 25 min |
| red | 25 min-optional | 25 min | 10 min |

- **One cup** of lentils equals 2 1/2 cups cooked.
- **Red lentil**s disintegrate when cooked.

## Jamaican Curried Lentils

| | |
|---|---|
| 3 C | water |
| 1 1/2 C | lentils |
| 1 can | pineapple – chopped |
| 1 | onion – chopped |
| 2 | garlic cloves – crushed |
| 2 T | oil |
| 2 T | curry powder |
| | S&P |

- Sauté onion and garlic, add curry, lentils, pineapple and water.
- Pressure-cook 10 minutes, or simmer 25 minutes until lentils are soft.

## Lentil Loaf

Lynne~Yacht Kirwin

| | |
|---|---|
| 1 C | lentils |
| 1 C | rice |
| 1 C | bread crumbs |
| 1/2 C | vegetable broth |
| 1 | onion – chopped |
| 1 | green pepper – diced |
| 2 | eggs – beaten |
| 2 t | soy sauce |
| 2 t | vinegar |
| 3 | garlic cloves – crushed |
| 1/2 t | sage and thyme |
| | sesame seeds |

- Cook lentils and rice together.
- Combine all ingredients except sesame seeds, add more breadcrumbs if mixture is too moist.
- Place mixture in an oiled bread pan and sprinkle with sesame seeds.

- Bake 350°F for 30 minutes covered with foil then uncovered for 10 minutes.
- Let sit 15 minutes before slicing.

*Serve with salad.*

## Mediterranean Lentil Stew

Dr Michel~Southern Ocean

| | |
|---|---|
| 4 C | water |
| 1 1/2 C | lentils |
| 3 | tomatoes – chopped |
| 2 | onions – chopped |
| 2 | carrots – diced |
| 2 | celery stalks – sliced |
| 4 | garlic cloves – peeled but left whole |
| 2 T | butter |
| 2 T | brown sugar |
| 1 T | vinegar or lemon juice |
| 2 | bay leaves |
| | French Herbs de Provençe – rosemary, oregano and basil |
| | S&P |
| | *pre cooked roasted chicken or canned chicken |
| | *cooked shell pasta |

- Sauté vegetables, add water and heat.
- Add lentils, S&P and bay leaves.
- Pressure-cook 10 minutes, or simmer 1 1/2 hours.
- Add sugar, vinegar, spices and herbs.

*Serve on brown rice with grated cheese and a twist of lemon.*

## Fijian Lentil Stew

| | |
|---|---|
| 1/2 lb. | chicken, beef or lamb – cubed |
| 1 1/2 C | lentils |
| 3 C | water |
| 1 C | spinach, peas or green beans |

1/2 C raisins
2 carrots – chopped
1 onion – chopped
3 garlic cloves – chopped
2 t ginger – grated
1 t cumin seeds
1/2 t cinnamon
1/4 t allspice
S&P
*1 C coconut milk

- ❖ Sauté onions, add spices, lentils, meat, carrots, water and raisins.
- ❖ Pressure-cook 10 minutes, or simmer 30 minutes.
- ❖ Add vegetable greens and simmer 5 minutes.

## Middle Eastern Lentil Stew

Dyan~Yacht Ascension

3 C water
1/2 C barley
1/2 C lentils
1/2 C brown rice
1/2 C raisins or currants
1/2 C mint – chopped
2 onions – chopped
2 garlic cloves – chopped
2 T olive oil
1 T vinegar
1 t cumin
2 t sugar
1/2 t cardamom
S&P

- ❖ Sauté onions and garlic, add remaining ingredients except S&P, mint and raisins.
- ❖ Pressure-cook 15 minutes, or simmer 40 minutes.
- ❖ Toss in raisins and mint, season to taste.

# Rice

Jambalaya, risotto, pilaf, narsi goreng, sushi and biriyani are names of distinguished rice dishes from across the Northern Hemisphere. Originating in India, rice traveled throughout the trade routes and became integrated into local dishes. As varied as the dishes themselves, so are the cooking methods of each particular variety of rice. From short grain to long grain, arborio, basmati, black, brown, carolina, jasmine, patana, sticky and wild, the choices are endless. As an all-round favorite rice, I use basmati and stock up in large quantities when available. Basmati rice stores well in plastic sealed containers and doesn't require rinsing.

## Tips on Cooking Rice

- Allow **2 cups of water** for every **cup of rice.**
- One cup of uncooked rice yields **3 cups of cooked** rice.
- For **four people** I cook 1 1/2 cups of rice in 3 cups of water.
  - Bring water to a boil, add the rice and cover with a lid.
  - Cook on low heat 15 minutes until tender.

  *Let rice stand 5 minutes before serving.*

## Cooking Time for Rice

| Rice Variety | Stovetop Cooking | Pressure Cooker |
|---|---|---|
| White Rice | 20 minutes | 7 minutes |
| Brown Rice | 45 minutes | 15 minutes |

## Cardamom Rice

Carol~Yacht Elyxir

| | |
|---|---|
| 3 C | vegetable or chicken broth |
| 1 1/2 C | rice |
| 1/2 C | raisins |
| 1 T | butter |
| 1 | bay leaf |
| 1 t | curry powder |
| 1 t | cardamom |
| 1/4 t | cumin |

❖ Sauté rice in butter, add remaining ingredients except broth and cook 1 minute.

❖ Add broth and cook until rice is done.

## Coconut Rice

From Burma, this dish is a pleasant accompaniment to a main course.

| | |
|---|---|
| 3 C | water |
| 1 1/2 C | rice |
| 3/4 C | coconut milk |
| 1 | onion – sliced |

❖ Place all ingredients in a saucepan and cook until rice is done.

## Indian Curry Pilaf

| | |
|---|---|
| 3 C | chicken broth |
| 1 1/2 C | rice |
| 1/2 C | raisins |
| 3 T | vegetable oil |
| 1 1/2 T | soy sauce |
| 1/2 t | turmeric |
| 1/2 t | curry powder |

❖ Sauté curry and turmeric in oil for 30 seconds.

❖ Add rice and cook 5 minutes.

❖ Stir in broth, soy sauce and raisins, heat until boiling, cover and cook until rice is done.

## Jambalaya

| | |
|---|---|
| 2 C | water |
| 2 C | shrimp |
| 1 C | spicy sausage – sliced |
| 1 C | baked ham – diced |
| 3/4 C | rice |
| 1 can | stewed tomatoes |
| 2 | celery stalks – diced |
| 1 | onion – quartered |
| 3 | garlic cloves – crushed |
| 2 T | oil |
| 1 | bay leaf |
| 1 t | each – oregano and thyme |

- Sauté sausage and ham for 2 minutes, remove meat from pan.
- Add garlic, onions and celery to pan, sauté 3 minutes.
- Combine all ingredients, except shrimp and bring to a boil, stirring occasionally.
- Cover and pressure-cook 10 minutes, or simmer 30 minutes.
- Stir in shrimp, cover, let sit 5 minutes to allow rice to absorb the liquid.

## Paella

Vicki Witch

Paella is generally a dish for a crowd. Each Boxing Day, John and I sail to Stuart Island in the San Juan Islands to join friends Bob and Carol at their beach house for an island get-together. Paella is the traditional dish, for this gathering, with everyone bringing their favorite seafood to add to the paella pan, thus the resulting dish is a surprise from year-to-year.

This recipe to serve 6-8 people is from my good friend Vicki, an excellent cook who has joined us on a number of extreme expeditions including rounding Cape Horn.

| | |
|---|---|
| 4 C | water or chicken broth |
| 1 lb. | shrimp |
| 1 lb. | baby clams |
| 2 C | rice |
| 1/2 C | parsley – chopped |

| | |
|---|---|
| 1/2 C | peas |
| 2 | spicy sausages – chopped |
| 2 | chicken breasts – cubed |
| 3 | tomatoes – chopped |
| 1 | green pepper – chopped |
| 6 | scallions – sliced |
| 3 | garlic cloves – crushed |
| 1 t | honey |
| 1 | bay leaf |
| | butter and olive oil |
| | oregano |
| | saffron |
| | S&P |

- ❖ Sauté chicken and sausage in a casserole dish that can be used over direct heat.
- ❖ Add scallions, garlic, green pepper and tomatoes, sauté 3 minutes.
- ❖ Add rice and saffron, stir 5 minutes, pour in 2 C broth, add honey and bay leaf, bring to simmer.
- ❖ Cover and bake for 30 minutes, or simmer 25 minutes.
- ❖ Add 1 C broth and arrange shrimp on top, cover and cook 10 minutes.
- ❖ Add last 1 C broth, push calms into rice, cook covered 10 minutes until clams open.
- ❖ Add peas and toss.

*Serve garnished with lemon wedges.*

## Spanish Tomato Pilaf

| | |
|---|---|
| 3 C | vegetable broth |
| 1 1/2 C | rice |
| 2 | tomatoes – chopped |
| 4 T | butter |
| 1 t | tomato paste |
| | S&P |

- ❖ Stir tomatoes, butter and S&P over moderate heat for 5 minutes, mash tomatoes with spoon.
- ❖ Add stock and tomato paste, cook 5 minutes.
- ❖ Stir in rice, cover and cook until rice is done.

## Mexican Rice

| | |
|---|---|
| 4 | chicken breasts |
| 3 C | water |
| 1 1/2 C | rice |
| 1 C | peas |
| 1 | onion – chopped |
| 1 | carrot – diced |
| 1 | red pepper – chopped |
| 2 T | olive oil |
| 2 T | lemon juice |
| 2 | mint sprigs |
| | S&P |

- Simmer chicken in water for 10 minutes, cover and let stand 10 minutes, remove chicken and shred into bite size pieces, reserve stock.
- Sauté onion, add carrots and rice, brown 3 minutes.
- Stir in chicken stock and lemon juice, bring to a boil then turn heat to medium-low.
- Add chicken, mint, and red pepper, cover and cook 15 minutes.
- Add peas near end of cooking, remove mint.

*Garnish with fresh mint leaves and serve with salsa.*

## Narsi Goreng

Carol~Yacht Elyxir

An Indonesian "national dish," narsi goreng is an ornately garnished fried rice studded with vegetables and meat, dressed with a flavorful sweet soy sauce.

| | |
|---|---|
| 4 C | cooked rice |
| 1 C | chicken or shrimp – cooked |
| 1/2 C | cabbage – shredded |
| 1 | green pepper – chopped |
| 1 | celery stalk – chopped |
| 2 | scallions – chopped |
| 1 | carrot – grated |
| 1 | onion – finely chopped |
| 1/4 C | coconut milk, yogurt or sour cream |
| 3 | garlic cloves – crushed |

| | |
|---|---|
| 2 T | oil |
| 2 T | lemon juice |
| 2 T | sweet soy sauce |
| 1/2 t | each – cardamom, turmeric and chili pepper flakes |
| | ginger – grated |
| | S&P |

❖ Sauté onion, garlic and spices.

❖ Add meat, lemon juice, soy sauce and vegetables, sauté 3 minutes.

❖ Stir in rice and coconut milk, heat through.

*Garnish with chopped tomatoes or omelet strips.*

Chapter 11

# Pasta

## Tips on Cooking Pasta

- I generally allow **3 oz of pasta per person** for a hungry crew.
- When it's **rough at sea** it is safer to cook pasta in the pressure cooker with the lid on but no weight.
- Add a dash of **cooking oil** to the pasta water to stop the pasta from sticking together.
- To stop cooked **pasta from sticking**, don't totally drain the pasta or run it under cold water.

## Italian Cheeses that go well with Pasta

- **Mozzarella:** is a mild stringy cheese used on pizza. You may substitute 1/2 cheddar and 1/2 packaged Parmesan.
- **Parmesan:** is a hard, long lasting cheese often available pre-grated, though it is best served freshly grated from a block. The rind from a block of Parmesan is called the heel and it goes well in soups and stews.
- **Ricotta:** is a mild soft cheese that can be made from milk and vinegar, *see Cheese.*

## Garlic Pasta

| | |
|---|---|
| 1 lb. | pasta – cooked |
| 1/4 C | olive oil |
| 4 | garlic cloves – crushed |
| 1 | chili – minced |
| | S&P |
| | mint and parsley |

- Sauté garlic, chili and a generous grinding of black pepper in half the olive oil until it begins to turn golden.
- Stir garlic into hot drained pasta, add remaining oil, mint and parsley, season to taste.

## Pea Pasta

| | |
|---|---|
| 1 lb. | pasta shells – cooked |
| 3 C | peas |

| | |
|---|---|
| 1 C | white wine |
| 1 | onion – chopped |
| 3 | garlic cloves – crushed |
| 2 T | olive oil |
| | basil |
| | S&P |
| | *bacon |

- Sauté onion and garlic until soft, add peas and white wine, heat through.
- Mix with pasta.

*Serve hot with grated Parmesan cheese.*

## Russian Pasta "Haluski"

Fran~Yacht Aka

| | |
|---|---|
| 2 C | cabbage – sliced |
| 1 C | pasta – cooked |
| 1/3 C | olive oil |
| 1 | onion – sliced |
| 3 | garlic cloves – crushed |
| | S&P |
| | *spicy sausage |

- Sauté cabbage, onion and garlic in olive oil, cover pan and steam until soft.
- Toss vegetables with pasta and season to taste.

## Shellfish and Spinach Pasta

| | |
|---|---|
| 1 lb. | pasta |
| 1 lb. | clams |
| 1/2 lb. | mussels |
| 2 C | mushrooms – halved |
| 2 C | spinach |
| 1 C | white wine |
| 1/4 C | stock |
| 6 | garlic cloves – sliced |
| 3 | scallions – chopped |
| 3 T | parsley – chopped |
| 2 T | olive oil |
| 2 T | butter |

1 T chili pepper flakes
1/2 t salt

- Sauté garlic, chili and scallions in oil and butter for 30 seconds.
- Add mussels and clams, cook 2 minutes.
- Stir in wine, stock, spinach and mushrooms, cook until shellfish open, about 5 minutes.
- Toss shellfish, parsley and hot pasta together.

## Vegetable Lasagna ~Speedy

2 C spinach or cabbage – shredded
1 C broccoli or cauliflower florets
1 C beans or zucchini
1 C cheese – grated
3 potatoes – cubed
2 t butter
1 onion

- Sauté onion and garlic until soft.
- Boil enough water to hold all remaining ingredients, add potatoes and cook 10 minutes.
- Add broccoli, beans and spinach, toss in pasta and cook 8 minutes.
- Layer drained pasta and vegetables and in a baking dish with onion and cheese.
- Bake in hot oven until cheese melts, about 10 minutes.

## Basil Chicken and Olive Pasta

1 lb. pasta – cooked
4 chicken breasts – diced
2 tomatoes – diced
1 onion – diced
1/2 C green pepper – roasted
1/2 C mushrooms – sliced
1/4 C white wine
1/4 C black olives
6 T olive oil
2 T butter

2 T herbs to taste – basil (pesto), oregano and thyme
1 T capers
2 garlic cloves – crushed
S&P

- Sauté chicken in butter 3 minutes, add garlic and onion, cook 2 minutes.
- Add tomatoes, green pepper and mushrooms, stir until vegetables cook.
- Add wine, olives, herbs and capers, heat through.

*Serve over hot pasta.*

## Sesame Pasta

Page~Yacht Ever After

1 lb. pasta – cooked
4 scallions – chopped
1 red pepper – chopped
4 T sesame seeds
2 T sesame oil
hot sauce to taste
fresh ginger to taste

- Toss all ingredients together.

*Serve either hot or cold.*

## Walnut Pasta

1 lb. pasta – cooked
1 1/2 C walnuts – chopped
2/3 C Parmesan cheese – grated
1/2 C olive oil
1/4 C basil – chopped
5 garlic cloves – crushed
3 T olive oil
S&P

- Sauté garlic and walnuts until lightly toasted, about 5 minutes.

*Toss all ingredients together.*

## Zucchini and Mozzarella Pasta

1 lb. pasta – cooked
4 C zucchini – sliced and sautéed
1 C mozzarella cheese – cubed
1/2 C olive oil
1/2 C Parmesan cheese – grated
2 eggs – beaten
S&P

❖ Stir mozzarella into hot pasta, add remaining ingredients, stirring to set eggs.

*Serve with Parmesan cheese and ground pepper.*

## Pancakes, Popcorn and Pasta

February 18 1990
Yacht Maiden – 1998-90 Whitbread Around the World Race
Latitude: 58° 39' S
Longitude: 118° 03' E

I now know it will possible to for me to write my journal entries even if I take up caving. Once again I'm squashed up into my bunk writing on my stomach. With my head touching the bunk above me where Detroit Dawn (Riley) rests, this leaves little to be desired. I dare not wiggle too much for fear I'll wake her. Our generator has died, we have no power, so I'm writing by flashlight.

I hear water sloshing around the floor like an underground river. The side of the hull is dripping to such and extent that I wouldn't be surprised to see stalagmites and stalactites forming as the water is slowly breaking down the insulating foam, turning it into an alternative substance. Outside the raging continues.

Today has been one of both amusement and fear. This wretched weather is still here, it's been like this for 4 days now, apparently the whole fleet is experiencing this low. Our winds haven't dropped below 40 knots with the reduced visibility, and *Maiden* is rocketing along at 15 knots. With spray for miles, we take turns standing 15-minute bow watches, on the look out for more icebergs. Rumor has it that behind us *La Poste* is experiencing a little letup in the conditions – phew, so hopefully this won't be Day 5 of this stuff.

Lying here in bed, I tend to forget all to quickly the bone-chilling situation on deck – how the cold just bites into me after the first hour. I become so weary of the smallest of matters, bracing against the frequent lashings of chilling spray with hunched shoulders and clenched teeth. A movement such as lifting a hand sends the freezing water inside my gloves running down my palm and up the length of my arm. I'm tired of the cold.

Michèle lies on the bunk below mine. She's out of action since this morning when we were struck by a major rogue wave. It swept both Tanja and I down the deck, piling us on top of each other like driftwood, along with the dorade. Michèle who was steering, was no where to be seen; she'd been compressed into the steering cockpit well, a bent and broken wheel testimony to the wave's force and the strength that Michèle held on. We feared she'd broken her back, but thankfully it is only muscle damage. Food is our biggest distraction. Yesterday was half way on this 6,000 mile leg from New Zealand to Uruguay, around Cape Horn. I produced the fruitcake nanna had baked for us.... well, only half of it, as the whole cake was too heavy to bring. It was fantastic and we ate the lot. Nanna cried when she gave it to me, it was the first time I'd seen tears in her eyes. I miss her.

Breakfast today was pancakes. It's hard on Jo to cook pancakes for 11 of us, but she knows we love them so – they are such a welcoming comfort food. Popcorn was the main dish for lunch, a total overdose, followed by carrots and New Zealand tasty cheddar cheese. Jo's evening menu plan is freeze-dried smoked fish, but I'm the only one who likes it so it doesn't warrant the gas to cook it. Pasta is the choice of the majority and it gets smothered according to individual pallets. Parmesan cheese, mayonnaise, pepper, ketchup, hot sauce, butter and sugar all find their home in various dishes. I passed on the pasta; I'm bored with it and ate a chocolate bar instead. So much for my diet.

I wonder what's for breakfast?

# Pasta Sauces

## Greek Artichoke Sauce

| | |
|---|---|
| 2 C | artichoke hearts |
| 3/4 C | feta cheese – cubed |
| 1/4 C | Greek black olives |
| 4 | tomatoes – diced |
| 1 T | olive oil |

- ❖ Sauté artichokes, olives and tomatoes.
- ❖ Add feta cheese and heat.

*Serve over cooked pasta.*

## Carbonara

| | |
|---|---|
| 1 C | sour cream |
| 1 C | mushrooms – sliced |
| 8 | bacon rashers |
| 1 | onion – chopped |
| 1 | egg yolk |
| 2 | garlic cloves – crushed |
| 2 T | olive oil |
| | parsley |
| | pepper |
| | *1/4 t chili pepper flakes |
| | *tomato – chopped |
| | *smoked salmon |

- ❖ Sauté bacon, garlic and onion, add mushrooms and cook 3 minutes.
- ❖ Beat sour cream and egg yolk together, add to mushrooms and stir until sauce thickens.

*Pour over cooked pasta and garnish with parsley.*

## Caponata ~ Eggplant Sauce

| | |
|---|---|
| 1 | eggplant – cubed and purged |
| 2 | yellow peppers – roasted and sliced |
| 1 can | stewed tomatoes – drained and chopped |
| 1/2 C | black olives |

1/2 C pine nuts – roasted
1/4 C red wine
1 onion – chopped
4 anchovy fillets – chopped
3 garlic cloves – crushed
2 T olive oil
2 T capers
basil
S&P
Parmesan cheese

- ❖ Sauté garlic, eggplant, onion, tomatoes and anchovies for 10 minutes.
- ❖ Add capers, olives, peppers, wine and basil, cover and cook 10 minutes, season to taste.
- ❖ Serve with pasta or as a pizza topping.

*Garnish with basil leaves, pine nuts and grated Parmesan cheese.*

## Olive and Caper Sauce

1 can stewed tomatoes
1 C black olives – chopped if large
4 T capers
2 T olive oil
4 anchovy fillets – chopped
3 garlic cloves – crushed
parsley
basil

- ❖ Sauté garlic and anchovies until they nearly melt.
- ❖ Stir in tomatoes, olives and capers, cook 5 minutes.

*Serve mixed with hot pasta and garnish with chopped parsley.*

## Smoked Chicken Sauce

1 1/4 C cream
1 smoked chicken breast – sliced
1 onion
3 T butter
1 T lemon juice
1 egg yoke

2 garlic cloves – crushed
parsley
S&P
*can replace chicken with smoked salmon

❖ Saute onion and garlic.

❖ Add combined cream and egg yolk, heat until thick.

❖ Stir in lemon juice, add chicken, and heat through.

*Serve on pasta and garnish with parsley.*

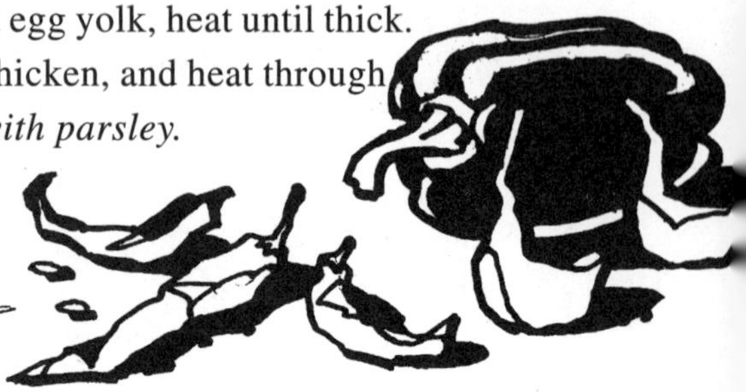

## Spaghetti Sauce

1 can stewed tomatoes
1 can tomato paste
2 C mushrooms – halved
1/2 C red wine
1/4 C olives
2 carrots – grated
1 onion – chopped
1 zucchini – diced
1 green pepper – diced
3 garlic cloves – crushed
2 T olive oil
2 T capers
2 T oregano – chopped
2 T basil – chopped
2 t thyme – chopped
S&P

❖ Sauté onion and garlic.

❖ Add remaining ingredients and simmer 15 minutes.

*Serve over hot pasta with grated Parmesan cheese.*

## Sun~Dried Tomato and Basil Sauce

Ginny~Fiji

2 C sun-dried tomatoes – chopped and soaked in oil
2 C water
2 C cream

| | |
|---|---|
| 1/2 C | basil – chopped |
| 1 | onion – chopped |
| | S&P |

- ❖ Sauté onion, add remaining ingredients and bring sauce to a simmer.
- ❖ Continue to simmer until liquid is reduced by half.

*Serve mixed with hot pasta and garnish with parsley.*

## Tomato and Caper Sauce

| | |
|---|---|
| 1 can | stewed tomatoes |
| 1 can | tomato paste |
| 1 C | red wine |
| 1 | carrot – grated |
| 1 | celery stalk – sliced |
| 1 | onion – chopped |
| 1 | red pepper – chopped |
| 1 | zucchini – sliced |
| 3 | garlic cloves – crushed |
| 3 T | capers |
| 2 T | olive oil |
| | basil, oregano, thyme and parsley |
| | S&P |
| | *Italian sausage |

- ❖ Sauté garlic, carrot, celery, onion, red pepper and zucchini.
- ❖ Add wine, stewed tomatoes and tomato paste, simmer 15 minutes.
- ❖ Stir in capers and herbs, season to taste.

*Serve over hot pasta with grated Parmesan cheese.*

## Uncooked Tomato Sauce

| | |
|---|---|
| 2 lb. | sweet tomatoes – peeled, seeded and chopped |
| 2 C | basil – chopped |
| 1/3 C | olive oil |
| 3 | garlic cloves – crushed |
| 2 t | balsamic vinegar |
| | S&P |

*grated Parmesan cheese to pass around the table

❖ Mix all ingredients together and let stand for one hour for flavors to develop.

*Serve mixed with hot pasta and garnish with basil leaves.*

## Tuna and Tomato Sauce

| | |
|---|---|
| 1 can | stewed tomatoes – drained |
| 2 C | tuna – cooked and flaked, or canned |
| 1 C | mushrooms – sliced |
| 1 | onion – chopped |
| 2 T | capers |
| 1 T | olive oil |
| 3 | garlic cloves – crushed |
| | S&P |
| | *chili pepper of some form |

❖ Sauté garlic, onion, chili and mushrooms.

❖ Add tomatoes and simmer 10 minutes.

❖ Add tuna and capers, simmer another 10 minutes.

*Serve on hot pasta and garnish with chopped parsley.*

## Niçoise Tuna Sauce

| | |
|---|---|
| 1/3 C | Niçoise olives – pitted and chopped |
| 1/4 C | olive oil |
| 2 | scallions – chopped |
| 2 | garlic cloves – chopped |
| 2 T | parsley – chopped |
| 3 t | capers |
| | lemon juice |
| | S&P |

❖ Sauté garlic, scallions and capers.

❖ Add remaining ingredients.

*Serve over hot pasta.*

## Walnut Sauce

| | |
|---|---|
| 1 1/2 C | walnuts – chopped and toasted |
| 1/2 C | Parmesan cheese – grated |
| 1/2 C | olive oil |
| 1/2 C | cream |
| 4 T | butter |
| 1 | garlic clove – crushed |
| | salt |

❖ Combine olive oil, butter and nuts, toss in cheese and cream then salt to taste.

*Serve mixed with stuffed pasta.*

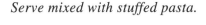

## Pesto

Pesto is a thick, uncooked, blended sauce made with Parmesan cheese, olive oil and white nuts, such as almonds, pine nuts, macadamias or cahews. Pesto goes especially well mixed with hot pasta or as a dressing for vegetables, fish or chicken. Basil pesto keeps well in the fridge and can be used to flavor dishes that require fresh basil.

## Basil Pesto

Brian~Raivavae 98

Upon arriving in Raivavae, French Polynesia from New Zealand I noticed a huge basil bush on the end of the wharf. After picking a few basil sprigs I encouraged Brian to prepare basil-pesto fettuccine for our dinner party with guests that night. I had no pine-nuts, so substituted sesame seeds. I also rather underestimated the quantity of basil we required and throughout the preparation of this dish we had to send crew sprinting down the wharf in relays for more leaves.

| | |
|---|---|
| 1 C | basil leaves – chopped |
| 1/2 C | olive oil |

1/2 C Parmesan cheese – grated
2 onions – sliced
5 garlic gloves – crushed
4 T pine-nuts – toasted
salt

❖ Blend all ingredients together.

## Black Olive Pesto

1 1/2 C black olives – pitted
1/2 C olive oil
4 garlic cloves – crushed
4 anchovy fillets
lemon zest

❖ Blend all ingredients together.

## Roasted Red Pepper Pesto

2 red peppers – roasted and peeled or sautéed in oil
1/2 C pine-nuts – toasted
1/2 C tomatoes – chopped
1/2 C Parmesan cheese – grated
1/2 C olive oil
4 garlic cloves – crushed
S&P
lemon juice
basil or parsley
*chili of some form

❖ Blend all ingredients together.

*If serving on pasta leave out the Parmesan cheese and serve it on the side.*

## Spinach Pesto

2 C spinach leaves – chopped
1 C basil leaves – chopped
1 C Parmesan cheese – grated

1/2 C olive oil
2 garlic cloves – minced
black pepper

- Mix spinach, basil and garlic together, slowly add olive oil.
- Stir in cheese and season to taste.

## Sun-Dried Tomato Pesto

1 C sun-dried tomatoes – chopped
1/2 C basil – chopped
1/2 C black olives – sliced
1/2 C olive oil
3 T lemon zest
3 garlic cloves
ground pepper

- Blend all ingredients together.
- Let stand an hour for flavor to develop.

*Serve mixed in hot pasta.*

## Tuna and Walnut Pesto

2 C tuna – cooked and flaked, or canned
3/4 C olive oil
1/2 C walnuts
2 T lemon zest
1 t Worchestershire sauce
parsley
basil
S&P

- Blend all ingredients together while gradually adding olive oil.

# 2~minute Noodles

## Noodle Omelets

Fran~Yacht Aka

1 pkg. 2 min noodles

5 eggs – beaten
vegetables of your choice – chopped
seasonings of your choice

- ❖ Cook noodles with enclosed packet, while noodles are cooking you may add vegetables to soften them.
- ❖ Mix all ingredients together and cook like omelets, you can make either or one large one or smaller ones.

*Serve hot or cold.*

## Thai Vegetable Noodles

Carol~Yacht Elyxir

| | |
|---|---|
| 2 pkg. | 2 minute noodles – cooked |
| 3/4 C | water |
| 3/4 C | coconut milk |
| 2 | carrots – julienne |
| 2 | zucchini – julienne |
| 3 | scallions – sliced |
| 4 | garlic gloves – crushed |
| 2 T | Thai red curry paste |
| 1 T | soy sauce |
| 1 T | olive oil |
| 3 t | ginger – grated |
| 1 t | sesame oil |

- ❖ Sauté ginger and garlic until just sizzling.
- ❖ Add vegetables and stir-fry until al denté, remove to bowl.
- ❖ Add water, coconut milk, soy sauce and curry, reduce sauce for 5 minutes while stirring.
- ❖ Combine noodles, curry sauce and vegetables.

*Garnish with chopped roasted peanuts and mint, basil or cilantro.*

Chapter 12

# Eggs and Poultry

# Eggs

## Tips on Cooking Eggs

- Use **water** instead of milk to mix omelets, as milk will make them tough.
- Do not **salt** eggs until cooked.

## Frittata

| | |
|---|---|
| 5 | eggs |
| 3 C | vegetables – grated carrots, zucchini, potatoes and mushrooms |
| 1/4 C | Parmesan cheese – grated |
| 1/4 C | butter |
| 2 | onions – chopped |
| 2 T | water |
| | S&P |
| | *spicy sausage |

- Sauté onions, add vegetables and cook until tender.
- Beat eggs, water and cheese together, pour over vegetables and cook until set.
- Sprinkle with Parmesan cheese and grill until golden.

*Cut into wedges and serve hot.*

## Marmit's Egg Bake

| | |
|---|---|
| 7 | eggs |
| 1 1/2 C | cheese – grated |
| 1 C | mushrooms – sliced |
| 1 C | sausage or bacon – chopped |
| 1 C | potato – grated |
| 1 C | cottage cheese |
| 2 | scallions – chopped |
| | parsley |
| | chili to taste |
| | S&P |

- Sauté bacon or sausage, add mushrooms and potato, cook until tender.
- Spread vegetables into greased baking dish.

- Beat eggs, chili, S&P, scallions and cheese together, mix in with vegetables.
- Sprinkle with parsley and grated cheese.
- Bake 35 minutes at 350°F.

## Macaroni Frittata

| | |
|---|---|
| 6 | eggs |
| 1 1/2 C | macaroni – cooked |
| 1 C each | frozen corn, peas and green beans |
| 1 C | cheddar cheese |
| 3/4 C | milk |
| 1/4 C | Parmesan cheese – grated |
| 1 | onion – chopped |
| 1 | tomato – chopped |
| 1 | red pepper – chopped |
| 1 | zucchini – chopped |
| 2 | garlic cloves – crushed |
| 1 T | vegetable oil |
| | basil – chopped |
| | oregano – chopped |
| | S&P |

- Combine macaroni, Parmesan cheese and 2 eggs, spread over a greased baking dish.
- Sauté onion and garlic 3 minutes, add remaining vegetables and cook until soft, spread over macaroni.
- Beat remaining eggs, milk and herbs together, stir in cheese and pour over vegetables
- Bake 25 minutes at 350°F.

## Mediterranean Omelet

| | |
|---|---|
| 1 C | feta or ricotta cheese – crumbled |
| 1/4 C | parsley – chopped |
| 8 | eggs |
| 5 | scallions – sliced |
| 3 T | olive oil |
| | mint |
| | S&P |

❖ Beat all ingredients together except oil.

❖ Heat 2 t oil in frying pan, pour in egg and cook on low for 10 minutes.

❖ Drizzle with remaining oil and grill until golden.

*Cut into wedges and serve hot or cold.*

## Popeye's Scramble

Melissa~Yacht Sula

| | |
|---|---|
| 8 | eggs |
| 2 C | spinach – chopped |
| 2 C | mozzarella cheese |
| 1/2 C | bacon – cooked |
| | S&P |

❖ Beat eggs together, stir in spinach and bacon, season to taste.

❖ Pour egg into pan to form either one large omelet or 4 individual ones.

❖ Add cheese when egg is half way through being cooked.

## Quiche

Base

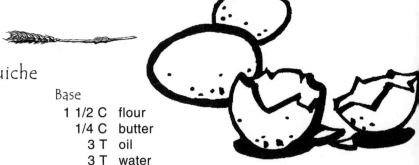

| | |
|---|---|
| 1 1/2 C | flour |
| 1/4 C | butter |
| 3 T | oil |
| 3 T | water |
| 1 t | sugar |

❖ Rub butter, oil and sugar into flour with finger tips until mixture reaches an even consistency.

❖ Add water and mix to make a dough.

❖ Press mixture into a baking dish.

Filling

| | |
|---|---|
| 4 | eggs |
| 1 C | cheese – cubed, try Brie or feta cheese |
| 3/4 C | milk |
| 1 | onion – sautéed |
| 1 | tomato – sliced |

Italian or French herbs – basil, parsley, oregano and thyme
S&P
any combination: your choice of – cooked asparagus, mush rooms, spinach, green pepper, peas, corn, Greek olives, ham, cooked crab, smoked salmon, sautéed bacon, sun-dried tomatoes or pesto

- Beat eggs and milk together, stir in herbs, season to taste.
- Arrange remaining ingredients in base, pour in egg mixture and lay tomato slices on top.
- Bake 40 minutes until egg has set.

*Serve with tossed green salad.*

## Tex~Mex Huevos Rancheros

Mac~who is boatless

2 C refried beans
1/2 C sour cream
1/4 C salsa
1 green pepper – sliced
chili sauce
scallions

- Simmer beans, sour cream, salsa and pepper together in large skillet.
- Break eggs on top, cover and cook until eggs set.

*Serve with grated cheese and hot sauce.*

# Chicken

## Pressure Cooker Times for Chicken

| Weight | Chicken Size | Time to Cook | Liquid Required |
|---|---|---|---|
| 3 lb. | chicken - whole | 20 minutes | 1 C |
| 2 lb. | chicken- pieces | 10 minutes | 3/4 C |

## Babootie

Amy~San Francisco

At home on the water or hosting a dinner party, Amy is a dear friend and a long treasured mentor in my sailing life. In my early sailing career she fueled my thoughts with her wild stories of Sydney-Hobart yacht races and sailing around Cape Horn. I first tasted this South African dish many years ago and was delighted when I heard from Amy that she had served it at a dinner party last week. This tried and true recipe has travelled the test of time, like an old friend.

| | |
|---|---|
| 2 lb. | chicken pieces |
| 1 can | tomatoes – chopped |
| 1 C | dried apricots – chopped |
| 1/2 C | slivered almonds |
| 2 | bananas – sliced |
| 2 | onions –chopped |
| 1 | apple – peeled and diced |
| 2 | garlic cloves – crushed |
| 2 T | curry powder |
| | tomato juice as needed to thin |

- ❖ Brown onion, garlic, curry and chicken.
- ❖ Add remaining ingredients and simmer, gently stirring until cooked.

*Serve with rice, chutney and beer!*

## Caribbean Banana Chicken

| | |
|---|---|
| 4 | chicken breasts |
| 1/2 C | white wine |

Banana Sauce

| | |
|---|---|
| 1 C | coconut milk |
| 2 | bananas – chunked |
| 1 | onion – chopped |
| 1 | lime – juice and zest |
| 2 | garlic cloves – crushed |
| 1 T | butter |
| 1 t | ginger – grated |
| 1/2 t | chili |
| | S&P |

- ❖ Sauté onion, garlic, ginger and chili, add bananas and cook 3 minutes.
- ❖ Stir in coconut milk and lemon juice, simmer 10 minutes, season with S&P.
- ❖ Sauté chicken breasts for 5 minutes, add wine and cook until chicken is nearly done.
- ❖ Add banana sauce and cook until chicken is done.

*Garnish with parsley and serve with rice and vegetables.*

## Cape Horn Chicken

Vicki Witch

| | |
|---|---|
| 4 | chicken breasts |
| 2 C | cooked grain or beans – rice, lima beans, or chickpeas |
| 1 can | stewed tomatoes |
| 1 C | corn |
| 3 | potatoes – chopped |
| 1 | carrot – choppped |
| 1 | onion – choppped |
| 1 | celery stalk – chopped |
| 2 | bay leaves |
| 3 | garlic cloves – chopped |
| 2 T | Worcestershire sauce |
| 1/2 t | thyme |
| | chili of some form |
| | parsley |
| | S&P |

- ❖ Sauté chicken, add onions and garlic, stir in remaining ingredients except beans, corn and parsley.
- ❖ Pressure-cook 10 minutes, or simmer 40 minutes.
- ❖ Stir in beans, corn and parsley.

## Citrus and Garlic Chicken

| | |
|---|---|
| 4 | chicken breasts – cut into large pieces |
| 1 C | white wine |
| 1/3 C | juice–lemon, lime, orange or mixed |

10 garlic cloves – unpeeled
3 T olive oil
1 T whole pepper corns
basil
S&P

- Combine all ingredients in pressure-cooker or large pot.
- Pressure-cook 10 minutes, or simmer covered 45 minutes.
- Remove lid and place pot on high heat for 10 minutes to reduce liquid by half.

*Garnish with a slice of lemon and serve with potatoes and salad.*

## Chicken Cacciatore

4 chicken breasts
2/3 C white wine
1 can stewed tomatoes
6 mushrooms – sliced
1 onion – chopped
1 green pepper – chopped
1 celery stalk – chopped
4 garlic cloves – chopped
4 T olive oil
2 bay leaves
1 t oregano
1/2 t thyme
citrus zest
chili of some form
S&P
parsley

- Sauté onion and garlic, add chicken and brown, add remaining ingredients.
- Pressure-cook 5 minutes, or simmer 15 minutes.

*Serve on pasta, rice or couscous.*

## Greek Black Olive Chicken

4 chicken breasts
1 can stewed tomatoes
1 can tomato paste

| | |
|---|---|
| 2 C | Greek black olives |
| 2 C | red wine |
| 5 | mushrooms – sliced |
| 1 | carrot – grated |
| 1 | zucchini – sliced |
| 3 | garlic cloves – chopped |
| 2 T | capers |
| 2 T | Italian herbs |

- Marinate chicken in red wine.
- Sauté chicken, add garlic and onions, cook 3 minutes.
- Add remaining ingredients including red wine marinade and pressure-cook 7 minutes, or simmer 15 minutes.

*Serve on rice, pasta or couscous and garnish with grated Parmesan cheese.*

## Italian Green Olive Chicken

| | |
|---|---|
| 4 | chicken breasts |
| 1/2 C | green olives |
| 1/4 C | white wine |
| 3 | tomatoes |
| 2 | garlic cloves – crushed |
| 2 T | butter |
| 2 T | Italian herbs |

- Sauté chicken in skillet until brown, add butter, garlic and tomatoes, cook 3 minutes.
- Mix in wine, olives, and herbs and cook 5 minutes.

*Serve on pasta or rice with garden salad.*

## Jamaican Chicken

| | |
|---|---|
| 4 | chicken breasts |
| 1/2 C | white wine |

Jamaican Sauce

| | |
|---|---|
| 3 | oranges – peeled and segmented with membrane removed |
| 1 | onion – sliced |
| 3 | garlic cloves – crushed |
| 4 T | raisins |
| 3 T | ginger – sliced |

6 allspice berries
2 t oil

- ❖ Sauté ginger in oil for 3 seconds, add onions, raisins, oranges, garlic and spice, simmer 10 minutes.
- ❖ Sauté chicken breasts for 5 minutes, add wine and cook until chicken is nearly done.
- ❖ Purée Jamaican sauce, add to chicken and cook until done.

*Serve with wild rice and tossed salad.*

## Lemon Yogurt Chicken

4 chicken breasts
1 C yogurt
1/4 C onion – diced
1/4 C mayonnaise
4 T Parmesan cheese
2 T Dijon mustard
2 T flour
2 T lemon juice
dried oregano
paprika
Worcestershire sauce
Tabasco sauce

- ❖ Place chicken in baking dish, drizzle with lemon juice and sprinkle with Tabasco.
- ❖ Mix yogurt and flour, add mayonnaise, mustard, Worcestershire sauce, oregano and onions.
- ❖ Spread yogurt over chicken, sprinkle with cheese and paprika.
- ❖ Bake 30 minutes until cooked.

*Garnish with parsley and serve with rice and salad.*

## Lemon Mustard Chicken

4 chicken breasts
1/4 C Dijon Mustard
1 lemon – juice and zest
1 T olive oil
chili pepper
S&P

- ❖ Place chicken in a baking dish.
- ❖ Combine remaining ingredients and spread over chicken.
- ❖ Bake 25 minutes until cooked.

*Garnish with lemon slices and parsley, serve with rice with salad.*

## Mango Chicken

4 chicken breasts
1 1/2 C mango – peeled and diced
1/2 C chicken stock
2 limes - juiced
2 garlic cloves – crushed
3 T brown sugar
1 T ginger – grated
1/2 t cinnamon
1/4 t cloves
1 chili – diced
grated coconut for topping
*can replace mango with papaya

- ❖ Place chicken in a baking dish.
- ❖ Combine remaining ingredients and spread over the chicken.
- ❖ Bake 25 minutes until cooked.

*Garnish with mango slices and parsley, serve with rice and salad.*

## Mediterranean Chicken

4 chicken breasts

Sauce

1/2 C sun-dried tomatoes
10 Greek olives
2T basil

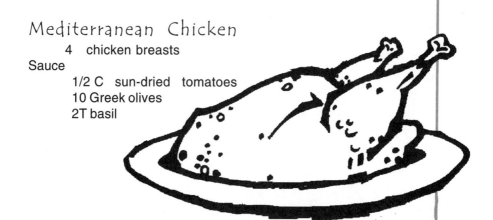

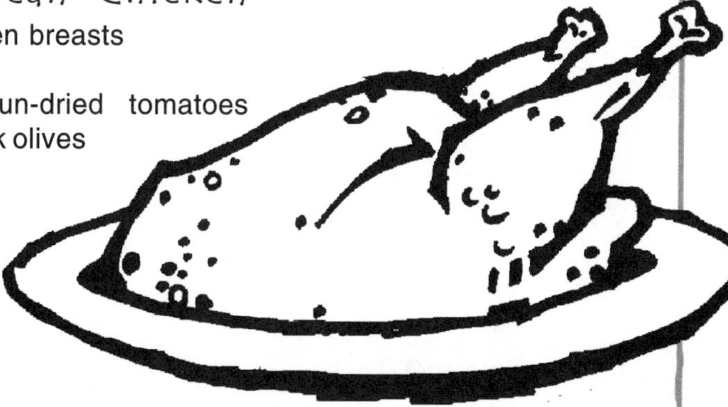

2 T parsley
3 garlic cloves
1 T Dijon mustard
1 T balsamic vinegar
2 t capers
2 t olive oil
S&P

- ❖ Purée sauce ingredients together to form a thick paste, reserve 2 T of paste.
- ❖ Coat chicken breasts with paste and refrigerate 4 hours.
- ❖ Mix reserved paste with yogurt or sour cream to serve with chicken.
- ❖ Grill, bake or sauté chicken.

*Serve with wild rice and tossed salad.*

## Orange Ginger Chicken

4 chicken breasts

Sauce

1/2 C orange juice
3 T tomato paste
2 T brown sugar
1 T ginger – grated
1 t mixed spice
1 t cinnamon
S&P

- ❖ Combine all sauce ingredients to form a paste.
- ❖ Place chicken in baking dish and cover with sauce.
- ❖ Bake 25 minutes until cooked.

*Garnish with orange slices and parsley and serve with rice with salad.*

## Tahitian Fruit Chicken

6 chicken pieces or one whole chicken
1 C coconut milk

Marinade

- 1/2 C coconut milk
- 1/2 C white wine
- 1 onion – chopped
- 1 lime – juice and zest
- 2 garlic cloves – crushed
- 2 t soy sauce
- 2 t honey
- 1 chili – chopped

Tropical Fruit

- 4 pineapple rings
- 4 papaya slices
- 4 mango slices
- 2 bananas sliced lengthwise
- 1 T butter
- 1 T lemon juice
- 2 t brown sugar
- 1 t cinnamon

❖ Combine marinade ingredients and marinate chicken for a few hours.

❖ Remove chicken from marinade and roast in 15 minutes.

❖ Cover chicken with fruit and marinade, bake another 15 minutes until chicken is cooked.

❖ Remove fruit and chicken to serving dish, keep warm.

❖ Pour pan juices into a saucepan and bring to a boil, add 1 C coconut milk and heat through, serve with chicken and fruit.

*Garnish with basil and toasted coconut, serve with rice and salad.*

## Tandoori Chicken

- 6 chicken pieces – skin removed
- 1/2 C lemon juice
- 1 onion – chopped
- 3 garlic cloves crushed
- 2 T paprika
- 1 T ginger – grated
- 1 T curry powder
- 1 T Garam Marsala
- 1 t brown sugar
- chili of some form
- S&P

- ❖ Slice chicken with small cuts to allow spices to penetrate.
- ❖ Combine marinade spices and rub into chicken, marinate overnight.
- ❖ Roast chicken with marinade in butter, turning to coat with juices, until done, about 20 minutes.

*Serve with rice and vegetables.*

Chapter 13

# Fish and Seafood

# Fish

## Fish with Mango Sauce

| | |
|---|---|
| 4 | fish filets |
| 1 C | orange juice |
| 1/4 C | coconut cream |
| 1/4 C | coconut – grated |
| 2 | mangos – peeled and chopped |
| 1 | lime – juiced |
| 2 T | honey |
| 2 T | butter |
| 1 T | chutney |
| 1 t | cinnamon |
| S&P | |

- ❖ Layer fish in a buttered baking dish, dot with butter and sprinkle with S&P.
- ❖ Combine all remaining ingredients except coconut and coconut cream, spread over fish.
- ❖ Pour coconut cream over the mango and sprinkle with coconut.
- ❖ Bake fish until done.

*Serve with rice and salad.*

## Fish Cakes

My mum Lesley~Yacht Taitoa

cooked fish
mashed potatoes
S&P
*sliced onions, parsley or garlic

- ❖ Combine fish and potatoes, season to taste.
- ❖ Shape fish into cakes and sauté until brown.

*Serve with favourite dipping sauce.*

## Thai Fish Cakes

Dorothy~Yacht Adagio

This recipe makes 14 fish patties enough to feed six people. Extra mixture can be formed into patties and frozen.

| | |
|---|---|
| 2 lb. | white fish fillets |
| 2 | onions – sliced |
| 2 | eggs |
| 5 | garlic cloves – crushed |
| 4 T | oil |
| 4 T | fish sauce |
| 2 T | ginger minced |
| 2 T | hot chili sauce or fresh chopped chilis |
| 2 t | flour |
| | chopped cilantro |
| | S&P |

- Heat 2 T of oil in a large skillet, sauté fish, onion, garlic, chili's (sauce) and ginger, stirring and chopping fish until just cooked.
- Sprinkle flour over fish and stir in.
- Combine remaining ingredients, add fish and mix well.
- Heat 1 T oil in skillet, form fish into patties and cook until brown.

*Serve with sweet chili sauce or your favorite chutney.*

## Fish with Enchilada Sauce

Dee~M/V Penguin

| | |
|---|---|
| 1 lb. | fish – cubed |
| 1 | onion – chopped |
| 2 T | olive oil |

Sauce

| | |
|---|---|
| 1 C | hot water |
| 1 C | tomato puree |
| 1 can | green chilies |
| 1 | garlic clove – crushed |
| 1 t | oregano |
| 1/2 t | cumin |
| | S&P |

- Mix all sauce ingredients together in a sauce pan and simmer 10 minutes.
- Sauté fish and onion in olive oil, add to sauce.

*Serve on rice or tortillas.*

## Fish with Italian Tomato Sauce

| | |
|---|---|
| 4 | fish fillets |
| 1/3 C | olive oil |
| 1/3 C | red wine |
| 1 can | stewed tomatoes |
| 4 | scallions – chopped |
| 4 | garlic cloves – crushed |
| 3 T | capers |
| 1 t | oregano |
| | parsley |
| | S&P |

- ❖ Sauté scallions and garlic, add wine, tomatoes, oregano and S&P simmer 5 minutes.
- ❖ Taste, if sauce is bitter add some sugar, mix in capers.
- ❖ Place fish into sauce and simmer until cooked.
- ❖ Sprinkle with parsley.

*Serve with rice, pasta or couscous.*

## Fish with Orange Sauce

| | |
|---|---|
| 4 | fish fillets |

Orange Sauce

| | |
|---|---|
| 1/4 C | mayonnaise |
| 1 | orange – juice and zest |
| 2 | garlic cloves – crushed |
| 2 T | yogurt |
| 1 T | chives – chopped |

- ❖ Combine sauce ingredients.
- ❖ Sauté fish in half sauce, turns over, add remaining sauce and cook until done.

*Garnish with fresh chopped dill and serve with potatoes and salad.*

## Smoked Fish with Parsley Sauce

This recipe also works well with smoked chicken. Cut smoked chicken into serving size pieces and follow the instructions below.

| | |
|---|---|
| 4 C | smoked fish – flaked |
| 1 1/2 C | milk |

2 T butter
2 T flour
2 T parsley – chopped
S&P

- ❖ Melt butter in pan, stir in flour and cook until frothy.
- ❖ Slowly add milk, stirring until mixture boils and thickens.
- ❖ Add fish, parsley and S&P, heat through.

## Garlic and Lemon Fish

4 salmon steaks

Lemon Sauce

1 lemon – juice and zest
3 T olive oil
3 T butter – melted
2 T garlic – chopped
1 t fresh tarragon

- ❖ Combine sauce ingredients.
- ❖ Brush one side of salmon with sauce and BBQ or sauté 5 minutes.
- ❖ Turn fish over and brush second side with remaining mixture, cook 5 minutes more.

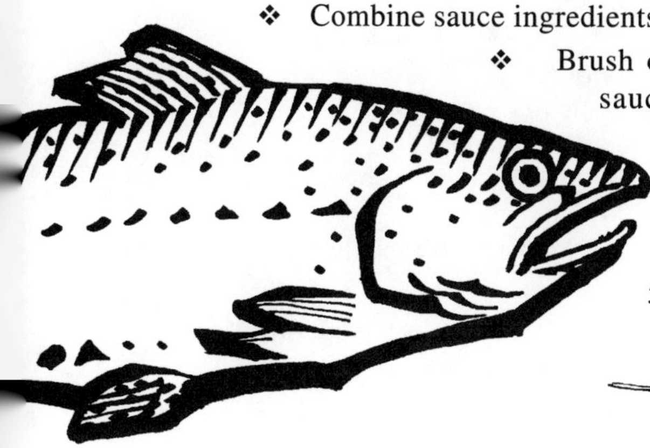

## Ginger Salmon

Jenn – Yacht Ocean Light II

4 salmon steaks
1/3 C maple syrup
1 T ginger – grated

- ❖ Marinate salmon in syrup and ginger for 2 hours.
- ❖ Bake in oven until cooked.

## Greek Baked Fish

4 fish fillets
3 C spinach
1 C Greek black olives
1 onion – diced
1 lemon – sliced
basil – chopped
olive oil
S&P

- Combine olives, basil and onion.
- Layer spinach, fish and olives in a baking dish.
- Drizzle with olive oil, place a top layer of spinach and garnish with lemon slices.
- Bake 20 minutes or until fish is cooked.

## Fish with Sun-Dried Tomato Pesto

4 fish fillets

Pesto

1/4 C olive oil
8 garlic cloves – chopped
4 t parsley – chopped
3 t sun-dried tomatoes – chopped
1 t salt

- Mash salt and garlic into a paste, add parsley, tomatoes and olive oil.
- Place pesto in fridge and let flavors develop overnight.
- Slice fish with length wise slits and spread with pesto.
- Barbecue or bake fish until done.

## Swedish Baked Fish

Elisabeth~Sweden

4 fish fillets
1 C grated cheese
1 C whipped cream
1 tube pink caviar
fresh dill

- ❖ Layer fish in a baking dish.
- ❖ Cover with grated cheese and caviar.
- ❖ Spread a layer of cream over the fish and sprinkle with dill.
- ❖ Bake 20 minutes or until fish is done.

## Thai Fish Green Curry

| | |
|---|---|
| 4 | fish fillets – cut into pieces |
| 2 C | coconut cream |
| 1 C | snow peas or spinach |
| 1 batch | *Green Curry Paste* |
| 2 | onions – sliced |
| 2 T | oil |
| 2 T | cilantro or basil |
| | *can substitute chicken for fish |

- ❖ Sauté onions, add curry and cook 3 minutes.
- ❖ Add 1 1/2 C coconut cream and simmer 15 minutes.
- ❖ Add fish, peas and remaining coconut milk, check seasoning, perhaps add extra chili.

*Garnish with chopped basil and serve with rice.*

## Fish with Thai Dressing

| | |
|---|---|
| 4 | fish fillets |
| Dressing | |
| 1/2 C | cilantro |
| 1 | red onion – chopped |
| 2 T | sherry |
| 1 T | ginger – grated |
| 1 T | soy sauce |
| 2 t | brown sugarb |
| | lemon juice |
| | chili of some form to taste |

- ❖ Blend dressing ingredients together.
- ❖ Sauté fish on one side, turn over, add dressing and cook until done.

# A Slice of Life

We'd raced across the Atlantic from England to the Caribbean on the qualifying race for the Whitbread Around the World Race – a team of girls on *Maiden*, our refitted 58-foot sloop. Having finished my rigging projects for the day, I thought I'd go check out the shipyard near English Harbour, Antigua, where we were moored. I entered Carib Marine, a small store with the basics, and wandered aimlessly around the shelves. There was nothing I particularly needed, but it was just interesting to look. As I passed by one stand, a flash of color caught my eye: fishing lures.

The lures weren't made up, just a random selection of parts that reminded me how great it is to catch fish while out on the ocean. Thinking of our return voyage to England, I realized that since we weren't racing back maybe I could fish if conditions were right. I purchased a handful of bits with which I could create lures and stowed them away onboard.

On my off-watch after leaving Antigua, I assembled a couple of lures. Having never fished the Atlantic, I wasn't too sure what to expect, and after an hour of working wire, hooks and lures, I thought I had a rig that might catch us a fish.

I set the lure behind the boat with the nylon cord I normally used for rerunning halyards. Sailing conditions were good, our boat speed was around 10 knots with the spinnaker holding nicely in the breeze. We had reggae playing on the stereo, and I settled down in the shade of the mainsail to study my French lessons.

Conversation from the on-watch drifted over. I'd never heard talk of fishing onboard before, but now everyone was an expert.

"Don't you have to been doing four knots to catch a fish?" Louise remarked.

"There's too much line out," announced Nancy.

"Blue lures work better than green," proclaimed Marie-Claude.

"Shall I cook the fish in butter and garlic?" Jo, the optimist, asked.

These comments were new to me, but no one was asking me directly what *I* thought.

After an hour, I went below to rest, the fishing lure skipping merrily behind the boat. Later, coming up on deck ready for my watch, I looked expectantly behind for the lure, but there was nothing there. Checking along the deck, I noticed my line still twined about its stick, the middle cleated off as I had left it – but the end waving in the breeze. The on-deck conversation marched on as usual: boys and dieting, but not a word of fishing.

My line had been sliced. I'd hooked a fish alright, but the on-watch had decided that fresh fish was not worth blood and death on the aft deck.

Beans anyone?

## Indian Fish Tikka

| | |
|---|---|
| 4 | fish fillets, you may also use chicken |
| 1/2 C | yogurt |
| 1/2 C | sweet chili sauce |
| 1 | onion – chopped |
| 1 | lime – juice and zest |
| 1 T | ginger – grated |
| 2 t | coriander |
| 2 t | soy sauce |
| 1 t | honey |
| 1 t | cumin |
| 2 | garlic cloves – crushed |
| 1/2 T | ground pepper |
| salt | |

❖ Combine all ingredients and marinate fish for 4 hours.

❖ Barbecue, grill or sear fish in hot dry frying pan.

*Garnish with lemon slices and cilantro, serve with rice and salad*

## Fish with Japanese Miso Dressing

| | |
|---|---|
| 4 | fish fillets, preferably salmon |
| 4 T | miso |
| 2 T | sherry |
| 1 T | olive oil |

1 T ginger – grated
1 t sugar
*2 T sesame seeds – toasted

- In a saucepan heat miso, sugar, sherry, oil and ginger.
- Brush fish with miso dressing and barbecue, grill or sauté until cooked.

*Garnish with sesame seeds and serve with tossed salad and rice.*

# Shellfish

## Clam Sauce

Cara–M/V St Elias

1 can clams – if using fresh clams or mussels add more wine and simmer until clams open
6 T shallots – chopped
4 T olive oil
4 T butter
3 T white wine
6 garlic cloves – chopped
2 t lemon juice
*sun-dried tomatoes
*parsley, basil or tarragon – chopped

- Sauté garlic and shallots in oil and butter until soft.
- Add clam juice, wine and lemon juice, simmer 5 minutes.
- Add calms and heat through.

*Serve with pasta or rice and salad.*

## Mussels Marinière

24 mussels – large
1 onion – chopped
1/2 water
1/2 white wine
2 T parsley – chopped
*bacon – chopped

- Bring onions, water, wine and parsley to a boil.
- Add mussels and simmer until they open, about 3 minutes.

## Italian Mussels

| | |
|---|---|
| 24 | mussels – large |
| Sauce | |
| 1 can | stewed tomatoes |
| 1 can | tomato paste |
| 1/2 C | white wine |
| 1 | onion – chopped |
| 2 T | olive oil |
| 1 T | mustard |
| 1 T | parsley |
| 1 | garlic clove – crushed |
| 2 t | flour |

- ❖ Sauté onion, add remaining ingredients and bring to a boil.
- ❖ Add the mussels and remove as they open.

*Serve with crusty herbed bread.*

## Casino Oysters

| | |
|---|---|
| 6 | oysters – per person |
| 1/2 C | celery – chopped |
| 1/4 C | onion – chopped |
| 1/4 C | green pepper – chopped |
| 8 | bacon strips – chopped |
| 2 T | Worcestershire sauce |
| 2 t | lemon juice |
| | chili sauce |

- ❖ Sauté celery, onion, green pepper and bacon.
- ❖ Add Worcestershire sauce, tobasco and lemon juice.
- ❖ Pour sauce over oysters in half shell and sprinkle with Parmesan cheese.
- ❖ Bake 10 minutes at 400°F, or grill 10 minutes until oysters are heated through.

*Serve from the shell.*

## Scallops in Lime

| | |
|---|---|
| 1/2 lb. | scallops |
| 2 T | cilantro – chopped |

2 T olive oil
1 T soy sauce
2 garlic cloves – crushed
1 t lime juice
pepper

❖ Heat olive oil in skillet until almost smoking.

❖ Add soy sauce and scallops, cook until browned, about 2 minutes.

❖ Turn scallops over and cook until opaque, approximately 2 minutes.

❖ Add cilantro, garlic and lime juice, season with pepper and toss to combine.

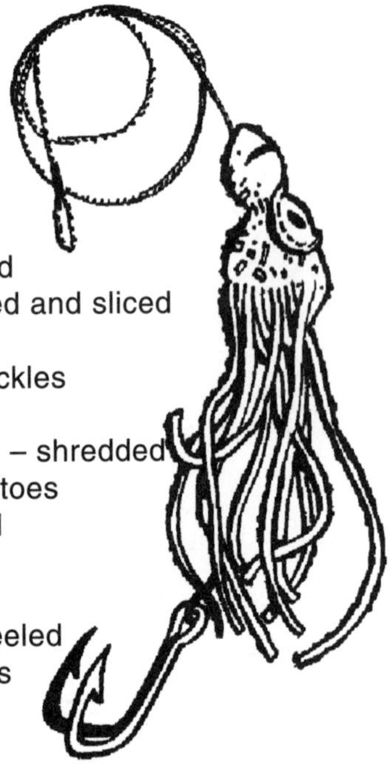

## Italian Fish Stew

1 lb. fish
1 lb. shrimp – unpeeled
1/2 lb. calamari – cleaned and sliced
1/2 lb. scallops
12 baby clams or cockles
12 mussels
3 C fresh basil leaves – shredded
1 can Italian plum tomatoes
2 onions – chopped
1/4 C white wine
1/4 C olive oil
3 garlic cloves – peeled
1/2 t chili pepper flakes
S&P

❖ Sauté onions and garlic.

❖ Add pepper flakes, tomatoes and wine, simmer 5 minutes.

❖ Add the seafood in layers depending on individual cooking time, place squid on the bottom and firm fish next, top with scallops, shrimp, and clams last.

❖ Simmer until seafood is cooked, about 15 minutes.

❖ Add basil and salt to taste.

*Serve in individual bowls with toasted bread or couscous on the bottom to absorb the broth.*

## West Coast Seafood Stew

Jan~Bottoms Up

| | |
|---|---|
| 1/2 lb. | white fish – cubed |
| 25 | shrimp – shelled |
| 20 | mussels |
| 1 | can tomatoes |
| 1 | can clam juice |
| 1/2 C | dry vermouth of dry white wine |
| 2 | onions – chopped |
| 1 | yellow pepper – diced |
| 5 | garlic cloves – crushed |
| 3 T | tomato paste |
| 3 T | parsley – chopped |
| 2 T | flour |
| 1 t | *Italian Herbs* |
| 1/4 t | chili pepper flakes |
| | S&P |

- ❖ Combine shrimp, fish, garlic and olive oil.
- ❖ Sauté onion and bell pepper until tender, stir in flour and tomato paste.
- ❖ Add clam juice and cook 3 minutes.
- ❖ Stir in tomatoes, herbs, red pepper flakes and S&P, simmer 8 minutes.
- ❖ While sauce is simmering bring vermouth to a boil, toss in mussels and steam covered until they open.
- ❖ Add shrimp and fish to sauce, simmer 5 minutes.
- ❖ Add mussels along with cooking liquid and simmer until all ingredients are cooked.

*Sprinkle with parsley and serve with crusty bread and tossed garden salad.*

# Calamari and Octopus

## Preparing Fresh Calamari

- ❖ Carefully **pull the calamari apart** by twisting and tugging head and tentacles away from the body, remove the cuttlebone.
- ❖ **Pull off the skin** membrane covering the body and throw away.

- **Turn the calmari inside out** and rinse, slice the body into rings.
- **Slice the tentacles form the head** below the eyes and pull out the beak form the center, throw away everything except the tentacles.
- **Slice the tentacles** in to rings.

## Preparing Freshly Caught Octopus

- **Turn head upside down** and sever the muscles that hold the viscera.
- **Turn head inside** out and remove and dark ink sacs.
- **Beat the octopus against the rocks** with a large wooden spoon or smooth piece of wood for 10 minutes, or whack the whole carcass against the rocks about 75 times.
- Every so often stop and **scrub the carcass** until it foams, rinse in the ocean, repeat it stops foaming.

## Marinated Giant Clam, Calamari or Octopus

| | |
|---|---|
| 1 | giant clam, or equivalent calamari or octopus strips |
| 1 | onion – chopped |
| 1/4 C | soy sauce |
| 1 T | lime juice |
| 2 | garlic cloves – crushed |
| 2 | chilies – chopped |
| 1 T | ginger – grated |

- Boil clam meat 10 minutes.
- Add clam to remaining ingredients and marinate 2 hours.
- Cover and simmer on low for 30 minutes, stirring occasionally.

## Italian Calamari

| | |
|---|---|
| 1 lb. | squid – cut into rings |
| 2 C | spinach |
| 1 C | white wine |
| 1/2 C | mushrooms |
| 1/2 C | parsley – chopped |

2 tomatoes
1 onion – chopped
1 celery stalk – chopped
1 T olive oil
1 garlic clove – crushed
chili of some form

❖ Sauté onion, garlic, chili and celery, add squid and sauté 10 minutes.

❖ Add remaining ingredients and pressure-cook 15 minutes, or simmer 1 hour.

*Serve warm with crusty Italian herb bread.*

## Provençal Octopus

2 lb. octopus – cleaned and tenderized
5 C red wine
2 C tomatoes – chopped
1 onion – chopped
2 T olive oil
1 T sugar
3 garlic cloves – chopped
3 parsley stalks
thyme
S&P

❖ Sauté onion and octopus, add tomatoes, wine and enough water to cover the octopus.

❖ Add remaining ingredients and pressure-cook 20 minutes, or simmer 1 hour until tender.

*Serve hot or cold garnished with chopped parsley.*

## Fijian Curried Octopus

2 lb. octopus cooked and sliced
2 C coconut cream
1 onion – chopped
1 lemon – juice and zest
2 garlic cloves – crushed
1 batch *Curry Paste*

| | |
|---|---|
| 2 t | tomato paste |
| 1 t | ginger – grated |
| 1 t | chilies – chopped |
| 3 T | basil |
| | S&P |
| | *can replace octopus with shrimp |

- Sauté onion, add garlic, ginger, chili and curry, cook 2 minutes.
- Add tomato puree, lemon juice and octopus, simmer 10 minutes.
- Stir in coconut cream, basil and S&P, heat through.

*Serve on rice with Mango Salsa, see Chapter 13.*

# Shrimp and Prawns

## Boiled Shrimp and Prawnns

- Bring a pot of salt water, or 1/4 C salt added to fresh water to a boil.
- Add shrimp and boil for 4-8 minutes until shrimp turn pink, depending on the size.
- Do not over cook or the shrimp will not be firm.
- Cool, pinch of head and tail, peel off shell.
- Remove dark entail tract form the back with a sharp knife, rinse.

*Serve with a dip or in a salad.*

## Shrimps in White Wine

Jenn~Yacht Ocean Light II

| | |
|---|---|
| 2 lb. | raw shrimps |
| 1/2 C | white wine |
| 1/4 C | olive oil |
| 6 | garlic cloves – chopped |
| 3 | bay leaves |
| 1 t | oregano |
| 1 t | rosemary |
| | ground pepper |

- Sauté shrimps in herbs for 3 minutes.

- Reduce heat, add wine and gently cook until shrimps are done, about 3 minutes.

*Serve with a dip or in a salad.*

## Shrimp Benedict

Theresa~Yacht Vega

| | |
|---|---|
| 1/2 C | cream cheese |
| 1/2 C | mozzarella or Parmesan cheese |
| 1/4 C | milk |
| 1 | onion – diced |
| 1 | red pepper – diced |
| 1 | zucchini – sliced |
| 5 | asparagus stalks – sliced |
| 2 T | butter |

- Sauté onion, add pepper, zucchini and asparagus, cook 3 minutes.
- Stir in cream cheese, add cheese and milk, mix to make a sauce.
- Add shrimp and heat through.

*Serve with pasta, rice or toasted sour dough bread.*

## Bahaman Shrimp

Dee~M/V Penguin

| | |
|---|---|
| 1 1/2 lb. | raw shrimp |
| 1 | green pepper – sliced |
| 1 | tomato – chopped |
| 1/2 C | cream |
| 1/2 C | shredded coconut |
| 1/3 C | scallions – sliced |
| 4 T | butter |
| 2 T | rum |
| 1 T | Dijon mustard |
| | ground black pepper |

- Sauté scallions and green pepper in butter.
- Add shrimp and black pepper, cook until shrimp turn pink.
- Combine cream, mustard, coconut and tomato, add to shrimp and heat.

*To serve, flambé shrimp with rum and serve with rice with salad.*

## Lemon Prawns

1 lb. raw prawns
6 T butter
1 scallion – chopped
5 garlic cloves – crushed
2 T lemon juice
1 T olive oil
lemon zest
chili of some form
parsley
salt

- ❖ Melt butter, add onion, oil, garlic and lemon juice, cook until bubbly.
- ❖ Add prawns and cook, stirring, until prawns turn pink.
- ❖ Stir in parsley, lemon zest and chili.

*Serve warm garnished with lemon wedges.*

## Shrimp in Cream Sauce

Dee~M/V Penguin

1 lb. shrimp or scallops
1 can crushed tomatoes
1/2 C white wine
1/2 C cream
8 shallots – diced
8 scallions – diced
3 T olive oil
3 T butter
2 T sugar
2 T basil – chopped
2 garlic cloves – crushed
2 t tarragon
1/2 t thyme

- ❖ Sauté shrimp in oil and butter, set aside.
- ❖ Sauté herbs and garlic, add tomatoes and wine, cook on high heat until it thickens, about 4 minutes.
- ❖ Stir in cream and sugar, simmer 30 seconds.
- ❖ Add shrimp and season with S&P.
- ❖ Pour over pasta or rice.

*Garnish with avocado and serve with salad.*

## Prawn Curry

Jenn~Yacht Ocean Light II

| | |
|---|---|
| 1 lb. | Prawns |
| 1 C | sour cream |
| 1/2 C | chicken broth |
| 3 | tomatoes – chopped |
| 1 | avocado – chopped |
| 1 | onion – chopped |
| 3 T | butter |
| 3 T | flour |
| 2 T | lemon juice |
| 1/2 T | curry |

- Toss avocado and tomatoes with lemon juice.
- Melt butter add curry and onion, sauté 3 minutes.
- Stir in flour and broth and bring to a boil.
- Add sour cream, fold in tomatoes, shrimp and avocado.
- Simmer until prawns are cooked.

*Serve with rice and green salad.*

## The Trade Off

Quite often it is possible to trade for local foods. You need to educate yourself on what it is you are trading for to be sure that you will use the food and not let it go to waste.

We arrived in Puerto Eden, a small town of 400 people south of the English Narrows in the Chilean Fiords. Its a busy little place, built on a soggy island with no roads, only a meandering wooden boardwalk wrapping around the waterfront.

We had been told that the shellfish in Chile had red tide poisoning, but the locals ignore the warnings and continue to harvest the mussels and clams. Piles of shells littered the foreshore, and smoldering fires smoked the strings of shellfish hanging in small shacks. The township survives on the seafood industry, sending its produce to the towns of Puerto Montt in the north and Punta Arenas in the south.

No sooner had we anchored off town than a bright-yellow 20-foot boat approached with a small boy of about 12 years standing at the oars. In the bottom of his boat was a large pot crawling with various sizes of centolla crab. He motioned to his mouth that he wanted food, and with our limited Spanish we understood that he wanted flour and rice. I invited him onboard and gave him two bags of rice, but we were out of flour. When I opened our canned locker, he gasped in amazement, and I gestured for him to choose some cans of his liking. I also gave him a boat hat as a farewell present and as a thank you for his effort to bringing us the crab.

It was Barry's turn to cook, and he proceeded to boil up the two large buckets of crabs. We certainly learned the hard way, for it took us all evening to extract the meat from the small spiky crabs.

Next time, the crew decided, we'd only go for the Big Ones! The following day we visited the village's only store, and noticing the bare shelves, we understood the young boy's wonder as he gazed at our provisions.

# Crab and Lobster

## Tips on Cooking Crab or Lobster

Bring a large pot of salt water to a boil.

- ❖ Add the crab or lobster and simmer for about 8 minutes per pound.
- ❖ Immerse the cooked crab or lobster in cold water to arrest the cooking process.

*Let cool then eat.*

## Crab with Black Bean Sauce

Jenn~Yacht Ocean Light II

Jenn serves fresh Dungeness crab with *Black Bean Sauce* as a dip for a healthier alternative to butter or mayonnaise.

*A side dish of basmati rice completes the meal.*

# Stretch Lobster

Fran~Yacht Aka

I'm afraid that you have to use a can of cream of something in this dish but at least the lobster, fish etc. is fresh unless you cheat and use canned. Stretch lobster goes a long way and it's easy to increase the amount at the last minute.

- 1 C cooked lobster, crab, shrimp or even chicken
- 1 can cream of something soup
- 1 can mild chili
- 1 T fresh parsley or dried mixed herbs, whatever you can get your hands on
- 1 t paprika – color only
- tarragon to taste – foo-foo according to Fran, but it makes the dish

❖ Heat all ingredients together.

*Serve over rice.*

Chapter 14

# Beef, Lamb and Pork

## Pressure-Cooking Times for Meat

| Weight | Meat | Time | Liquid Required |
|---|---|---|---|
| 2 lb. | beef – cubed | 10 minutes | 1 C |
| 3 lb. | beef – pot roast | 35 minutes | 1 1/2 C |
| 2 lb. | lamb – cubed | 10 minutes | 1 C |
| 3 lb. | lamb – leg | 35 minutes | 1 1/2 C |
| 2 lb. | pork – cubed | 10 minutes | 1 C |
| 2 lb. | pork – ribs | 20 minutes | 1 1/2 C |
| 3 lb. | pork – leg | 40 minutes | 1 1/2 C |

# Beef

## Curried Beef

Carol~Yacht Elyxir

| | |
|---|---|
| 1 lb. | beef – cubed |
| 1 C | tomatoes – chopped |
| 1/2 C | water |
| 1/2 C | peas |
| 1 | zucchini – sliced |
| 1 | carrot – sliced |
| 1 | onion – chopped |
| 4 T | yogurt |
| 3 T | butter |
| 2 | garlic cloves – crushed |
| 2 t | curry paste |
| 1 | cinnamon stick |
| | chili of some form |

- ❖ Sauté onions, chili and garlic with curry, add meat and brown.
- ❖ Add tomatoes, water, cinnamon and vegetables.
- ❖ Pressure-cook 15 minutes, or simmer 45 minutes.
- ❖ Add yogurt just before serving.

*Serve on rice with Yogurt Dressing*

## Provençal Beef Stew

| | |
|---|---|
| 2 lb. | beef – cubed |
| 3 C | red wine |
| 1 C | mushrooms |
| 1/2 C | olives |
| 5 | pickling onions – chopped |
| 4 | bacon strips – chopped |
| 2 | carrots – chopped |
| 4 | garlic cloves – crushed |
| 1 t | thyme |
| 1/4 t | rosemary |
| | orange zest |
| | S&P |
| | parsley – sprinkled on at end of cooking |

- ❖ Marinate meat in wine overnight.
- ❖ Remove meat from marinade and brown with bacon in olive oil.
- ❖ Add remaining ingredients including wine and pressure-cook 20 minutes, or simmer 90 minutes.

*Serve with rosemary new potatoes.*

## Sun~Dried Tomato Meat Burgundy

| | |
|---|---|
| 3 lb. | beef or lamb roast |
| 1 can | stewed tomatoes |
| 1 C | burgundy wine |
| 1/2 C | sun-dried tomatoes |
| 2 | carrots – diced |
| 2 | celery stalks – diced |
| 1 | onion – chopped |
| 1 | green pepper – chopped |
| 3 | garlic cloves – crushed |
| 2 T | tomato paste |
| 3 t | olive oil |
| 1/2 t | thyme |
| | S&P |

### Pressure-cooker Instructions

- ❖ Brown beef on all sides, add remaining
- ❖ ingredients and pressure-cook 35 minutes.

Oven Instructions

- ❖ Put all ingredients inside an oven roasting bag and place on a roasting dish, make slits in the top of the bag, and roast 3 hours at 325°F.

*Remove meat, slice and serve with cooking sauce and new potatoes.*

## Russian Beef Stroganoff

| | |
|---|---|
| 1 lb. | fillet beef – sliced into strips |
| 2 C | mushrooms – sliced |
| 3/4 C | sour cream |
| 1/4 C | white wine |
| 1 | onion – sliced |
| 2 | garlic cloves – crushed |
| 2 T | butter |
| 1 T | lemon juice |
| | nutmeg |
| | basil |
| | S&P |

- ❖ Sauté onion and mushrooms, add meat and brown.
- ❖ Add remaining ingredients and simmer until beef is cooked, about 5 minutes.

*Garnish with chopped parsley and serve on noodles or rice.*

## Thai Beef Red Curry

| | |
|---|---|
| 1 lb. | beef fillet – sliced into strips |
| 3 C | coconut milk |
| 1 batch | *Thai Red Curry* |
| 1 T | fish sauce |
| 2 | lime leaves – sliced |
| 2 t | oil |
| 1 t | brown sugar |
| 1 | chili – minced |

- ❖ Sauté onion, add curry and cook 3 minutes.
- ❖ Add beef and brown 3 minutes.
- ❖ Add 2 C coconut milk and simmer until beef is cooked.

❖ Add remaining ingredients and heat through.

*Garnish with chopped basil and serve with rice.*

## Veal and Orange Stew

| | |
|---|---|
| 2 lb. | veal – cubed |
| 1 C | chicken broth |
| 1 C | white wine |
| 8 | mushrooms – quartered |
| 5 | bacon rashers – sliced |
| 3 | carrots – sliced |
| 2 | onions – chopped |
| 1 | orange – juice and zest |
| 3 T | flour |
| 2 T | vinegar |
| 2 | garlic cloves |
| | S&P |

❖ Marinate veal in wine and garlic

❖ Remove and brown with bacon and onions, stir in flour.

❖ Add remaining ingredients including marinade and pressure-cook 20 minutes, or simmer 1 hour.

*Garnish with parsley and orange slices and serve with new potatoes.*

# Lamb

## Lamb and Apricot Stew

| | |
|---|---|
| 1 lb. | lamb – cubed |
| 2 | eggplants – cubed and purged |
| 1 C | dates – pitted |
| 1 C | chick peas – soaked |
| 1/2 C | dried apricots – chopped |
| 1/2 C | blanched almonds – toasted |
| 1 | onion – chopped |
| 1 t | cinnamon |
| 1 t | sesame seeds – toasted |
| 1/2 t | allspice |
| | S&P |

❖ Sauté onions, add lamb and cook until brown.

❖ Add chickpeas, cover with water and bring to a boil.

- ❖ Add spices and pressure-cook 10 minutes, or simmer 30 min.
- ❖ Add eggplant, dates and apricots, pressure-cook 5 minutes, or simmer 20 minutes.

*Garnish with almonds and sesame seeds, serve with rice or couscous.*

## Lamb and Vegetable Stew

| | |
|---|---|
| 1 lb. | lamb fillet – cubed |
| 1 can | tomato puree |
| 1 can | tomato paste |
| 1/2 C | water |
| 1/2 C | raisins |
| 2 | carrots – diced |
| 1 | onion – chopped |
| 2 | celery stalks – diced |
| 2 | garlic cloves – crushed |
| 2 T | oil |
| | chili powder to taste |
| | S&P |

- ❖ Sauté onion chili and lamb until brown,
- ❖ Add carrots and celery, and cook 5 minutes.
- ❖ Pour in tomato puree and paste, add water and raisins and S&P.
- ❖ Pressure-cook 10 minutes, or simmer 25 minutes.

*Serve on couscous or rice or perhaps with potatoes.*

## Greek Lamb Souvlaki

| | |
|---|---|
| 1 lb. | lamb – cubed |
| 1/4 C | lemon juice |
| 3 | garlic cloves – crushed |
| 1 T | olive oil |
| 2 t | oregano |

- ❖ Kebab meat and marinate in remaining ingredients for 4 hours, barbecue.

*Serve with Greek salad.*

## Greek Moussaka

| | |
|---|---|
| 3 C | ground lamb |
| 2 | eggplants – sliced and purged |
| 1 C | yogurt |
| 1/3 C | wine |
| 1/3 C | parsley – chopped |
| 1/4 C | olive oil |
| 1/4 C | Parmesan cheese grated |
| 1 can | tomato paste |
| 4 | tomatoes – chopped |
| 2 | onions – chopped |
| 2 | garlic cloves – crushed |
| 2 | egg yolks |
| 1 T | flour |
| | S&P |

- ❖ Sauté onion, garlic and lamb.
- ❖ Stir in tomatoes, tomato paste, parsley and wine, simmer 15 minutes.
- ❖ Sauté eggplant until soft and light brown.
- ❖ Place 1/3 of eggplant in baking dish, spread with half lamb mixture.
- ❖ Repeat layers and top with eggplant.
- ❖ Combine egg yolks, flour and yogurt, pour over eggplant and top with Parmesan cheese.
- ❖ Bake 40 minutes at 350°F until golden.

*Serve with salad.*

## Moroccan Lamb

| | |
|---|---|
| 1 lb. | lamb fillet – cubed |
| 1 C | raisins, prunes or dates |
| 1 | apple – chopped or dried apricots |
| 1 | onion – chopped |
| 3 | garlic cloves – crushed |
| 2 T | ground pepper |
| 2 T | honey |

| | |
|---|---|
| 2 T | oil |
| 3 t | ginger – grated |
| 2 t | cinnamon |
| 1 t | allspice |
| | parsley |
| | salt |

- Combine lamb, salt, pepper, ginger, garlic, onion, apple, parsley and oil, add water to cover.
- Pressure-cook 20 minutes, or simmer 1 hour.
- Add prunes and cinnamon, simmer 10 minutes.
- Add honey and simmer 5 minutes more.

*Garnish with toasted almonds and sesame seeds and serve over couscous.*

# Pork

## Orange Marmalade Pork

| | |
|---|---|
| 1 lb. | pork – thinly sliced |
| 3 | potatoes – cooked and cubed |
| 1 C | green beans |
| 1 C | cherry tomatoes - halved |
| 1/4 C | orange marmalade |
| 3 T | Dijon mustard |
| 2 T | basil – chopped |
| 1 T | olive oil |

- Sauté pork until cooked.
- Add potatoes, tomatoes and green beans, sauté 3 minutes.
- Mix in marmalade and mustard, serve when marmalade is melted.

## Mexican Orange Pork

Carol~Yacht Elyxir

This recipe is traditionally made with bitter oranges (*naranjas agrias*). If bitter oranges are unattainable it is possible to achieve the same citrus tartness with a blend of orange and lime juice.

| | |
|---|---|
| 1 lb. | pork – cubed |
| 1/2 C | water |
| 1/4 C | orange and lime juice or bitter orange juice |
| 1/4 C | milk |

| | |
|---|---|
| 1 | onion – chopped |
| 3 | garlic cloves – crushed |
| 1 T | oil |
| 1 T | lime juice |
| 1 t | oregano |

- ❖ Combine garlic, pork and wate, simmer until the water has evaporated, about 1 1/2 hours, or pressure-cook 20 minutes.
- ❖ Add milk and orange juice, simmer uncovered until meat is brown and the liquid has evaporated.
- ❖ Drain fat from meat and season to taste.

*Serve hot with fresh tortillas and salsa.*

## Mexican Chili Pork

Carol~Yacht Elyxir

| | |
|---|---|
| 1 lb. | pork – cubed |
| 3/4 C | water |
| 1 | onion – chopped |
| 2 | garlic cloves – minced |
| 2 | minced chilies |
| 1 t each | anise seed, oregano and cumin |
| 1 | stick cinnamon |
| 1 | bay leaf – crumbled |

- ❖ Combine pork, onion and 1/2 C water, simmer 45 minutes, or pressure-cook 20 minutes.
- ❖ Simmer remaining ingredients in a small pan for 10 minutes, remove cinnamon stick.
- ❖ Add chili sauce to pork and simmer until thick.

*Serve warm with fresh tortillas or tacos and salsa.*

# Elephant

Fran from the yacht *Aka* is a friend I never met. She contributed many wonderful, practical recipes to this book, and I decided to include her accompanying note as it captures the spirit of food and cruising.

Thanks for inviting us to be a part of your adventure. Cooking is an adventure – just ask my husband. I've only poisoned him once; he simply got a little sick. We've been cruising since 1979 so we are on a pretty tight budget. Part of cruising for me is going to the markets and checking out what the locals eat. As it's all locally grown, it's the cheapest place in town, saving me more money that I can then spend on fabric. I love getting deals and love to eat, I'll experiment with something forever. I know I've a winner when my husband says, "You guys have gotta come over to our boat; Francene makes a mean Mexican."

*I will look forward to your book. I'm a cookbook addict, and my husband says that's why our waterline is down. He lies; it's his windsurfer.*

Elephant Stew is my favorite recipe from Fran's collection, and although I've never had the opportunity to prepare it myself, it lends itself to a whimsical side of cooking. There have been times in my cruising life when I find myself over my head with food, and I feel like Alice in Wonderland trying to decide what cake to eat. I hope this following recipe will give you food for thought, and when times in the galley get overwhelming, take deep breath and make elephant stew.

## Elephant Stew

| | |
|---|---|
| I large | elephant |
| | brown gravy |
| 2 | rabbits |
| | S&P |

Cut elephant into bite size pieces – this should take about 2 months.

Add brown gravy to cover and season to taste.

Cook over a kerosene fire for about 4 weeks at 450°F.

*Makes 3,800 servings.*

*If more guests are expected add 2 rabbits. However do so only if necessary as most people do not like hare in their stew.*

Chapter 15

# Bread, Cakes and Cookies

# Breads

## Speedy Wraps

Fran~Yacht Aka

Fran claims that these wraps can be made anywhere in the world

"Cheap and easy they are perfect when you run out of bread and crackers or just feel like a change. They don't require an oven, as they are made on a frying pan so it's a good recipe to share with your local friends. You can wrap anything inside especially left-overs. We eat these faster than I can make them. I know you've seen recipes like this, but the hot water and baking powder makes all the difference. These will melt in your mouth. The biggest secret is a heavy rolling pin and rolling them out as thin as possible."

| | |
|---|---|
| 4 C | flour |
| 1 1/4 C | hot water |
| 1/2 C | oil |
| 2 t | baking powder |
| 2 t | salt |

- ❖ Sift flour, add remaining dry ingredients and mix well.
- ❖ Add oil and water, knead together to make a dough.
- ❖ Let mixture rest 15 minutes, this gives the baking powder time to get to get to know the hot water.
- ❖ Make dough into small balls, about walnut-shell size, roll them out as thin as possible on a floured area using a heavy rolling pin, sprinkle flour as you roll.
- ❖ Lay wraps on wax paper or foil, overlapping them a little.
- ❖ Fry each wrap in a lightly oiled pan, medium heat, when brown specks appear, flip and cook the other side.

## Lesley's Crêpes

Lesley~Yacht Taitoa

| | |
|---|---|
| 1 C | flour |
| 1 C | milk |
| 1 | egg |
| | water |

- ❖ Combine flour, milk and egg, add enough water or milk to make a runny mixture.

- Heat and lightly grease a medium frying pan, pour 1/4 C batter in the pan and roll the mixture around the pan to coat the bottom.
- Free edges with a spatula and turn when bubbles appear, cook other side.
- Repeat the process, greasing the pan with butter after each crêpe.

*Serve hot off the pan.*

## Tips on Bread Making

- **Water temperature** should be lukewarm, 80°F, if the water is too warm, it will kill the yeast and the bread won't rise.
- If **bread collapses** after rising, there may be too much water or the weather is warm and humid.
- **Let bread rise** while covered with a dishtowel in a draft-free place.
- If **bread does not rise**, maybe you forgot the yeast, the water was too hot or the bread was in a draft.
- To test if **bread is cooked**, knock on the top, a hollow sounds tells that it is done.

## Beer Bread

Robin~Yacht Chinook

| | |
|---|---|
| 2 3/4 C | self-rising flour |
| 1 can | beer |
| 1 T | sugar |
| 5 t | baking powder |
| pinch | of salt |
| 1/2 t | dried herbs |

- Mix dry ingredients together and stir in beer.
- Bake 40 minutes at 355°F until done.

## Italian Flat Bread

| | |
|---|---|
| 1 1/2 C | flour |

- 3/4 C warm water
- 12 black olives – sliced
- 8 sun-dried tomatoes – sliced
- 5 T olive oil
- 1 T yeast
- 2 sprigs rosemary
- 2 t coarse salt

❖ Combine flour, yeast, salt, tomatoes and half the olives.

❖ Add water and 3 T olive oil, mix to a soft dough and knead until smooth and elastic.

❖ Press dough into a 10" round, place on an oiled baking tray and prick with a fork.

❖ Cover with plastic wrap and let rise until double in size.

❖ Press in remaining olives and rosemary, drizzle with olive oil.

❖ Bake 20 minutes until golden.

## Oatmeal Bread

Carol~Yacht Elyxir

- 1 C boiling water
- 1 C warm water
- 1 C oats
- 1 C white flour
- 1 C whole wheat flour
- 2 T oil
- 2 T honey
- 2 T yeast
- 2 T sesame seeds
- 1 T salt

❖ Combine oats, boiling water, oil, honey and seeds, let cool.

❖ Add warm water, flours and yeast.

❖ Mix well and knead, let rise until double in size, and punch down and knead again.

❖ Shape into loaf, place in bread pan and let rise another 30 minutes.

❖ Bake 45 minutes until done.

## Pressure Cooker Bread

Kristin~Yacht Maiden

Our replacement cook on the first leg of the Whitbread race was Kristen, as Jo had broken her arm while we were doing the Fastnet Race. Kristen was a professional cook and amazed us all with the great meals she served using freeze-dried foods, but her biggest accomplishment of all was her fresh bread. Halfway across the Atlantic Ocean, Kris produced her first two loaves.

Wow! Jeni's comment was, "This is the best cheese sandwich I've had all month, in fact it's the only cheese sandwich I've had all month." When it comes to hot bread on a boat, there is a basic rule – it can only be eaten once, so best get on with it.

| | |
|---|---|
| 4 C | flour |
| 1 C | warm water |
| 1 T | yeast |
| 1 t | sugar |
| 1 t | salt |

- ❖ Dissolve sugar and yeast in warm water until it foams.
- ❖ Add 1 t salt to flour, then yeast, knead dough for 5 minutes.
- ❖ Let rise 30 minutes.
- ❖ Punch down and knead 7 minutes.
- ❖ Place dough in a greased floured tin that fits inside your pressure cooker, let rise again 15 minutes.
- ❖ Place lid on pressure cooker with no weight and heat 5 minutes, open lid.
- ❖ Place bread inside warm pressure cooker with a small spacer tin, such as an empty tuna can, on the bottom.
- ❖ Bake 8 minutes on high heat, 20 minutes on half heat, and 15 minutes on low.

## Salt Water Bread

| | |
|---|---|
| 4 C | flour |
| 1 1/2 C | warm salt water |
| 1 T | yeast |
| 1 T | sugar |

- Dissolve yeast and sugar in water.
- Miz in flour and knead into a soft dough.
- Let rise until double in size, punch down, and knead again.
- Shape into loaf, place in bread pan, and let rise another 30 minutes.
- Bake 45 minutes until done.

## Scallion Flat Bread

| | |
|---|---|
| 2 C | flour |
| 2/3 C | water |
| 1/4 C | oil |
| 6 | scallions – sliced |
| 1 t | sesame oil |
| 1 t | sugar |
| 1/2 t | salt |

- Mix flour, sugar, salt, oil and water into a soft dough.
- Divide dough into six balls and roll out into pancakes.
- Brush cakes with oil and scallions, roll up tightly and then roll flat again.
- Brush with oil and cook both sides in frying pan.

## Wholemeal Bread

| | |
|---|---|
| 2 1/4 C | warm water |
| 1 1/2 C | white flour |
| 1 1/3 C | whole wheat flour |
| 3/4 C | wheat germ |
| 4 T | honey |
| 3 T | oil or butter |
| 3 T | yeast |
| 2 t | salt |

- ❖ Mix flour, yeast, salt, wheat germ and flour together.
- ❖ Add water, oil and honey, knead well, let rise till double in size.
- ❖ Punch down and place in a pan, bake until done.

## Cornbread

| | |
|---|---|
| 2 C | cornmeal |
| 1 1/2 C | milk |
| 1 | egg |
| 3 T | oil |
| 4 t | baking powder |
| 1 t | salt |
| | *sugar |

- ❖ Place baking dish in oven and preheat oven to 450°F.
- ❖ When oven has reached tempeture, remove dish and swirl oil around the inside, return to oven.
- ❖ Combine cornmeal, baking powder and salt.
- ❖ Beat egg and milk together, pour into cornmeal mixture.
- ❖ Mix quickly and pour battter into heated dish.
- ❖ Bake until golden, about 20 minutes.

## Rasta Cornbread

Containing the Rastafarian colors red, gold and green, this cornbread is a colorful accompaniment to any dish.

| | |
|---|---|
| 1 C | cornmeal |
| 1/2 C | milk |
| 1/4 C | flour |
| 1 | egg – lightly beaten |
| 2 T | scallions – sliced |
| 2 T | red pepper – chopped |
| 2 T | green pepper – chopped |
| 4 t | butter – melted |
| 1 t | baking powder |
| 1 t | honey |
| | pinch of salt |

- ❖ Mix dry ingredients together.

- Stir in beaten egg, butter and milk, add scallions and peppers.
- Bake 20 minutes in a greased dish at 425°F.

## Bread Rolls

Jenn~Yacht Ocean Light II

| | |
|---|---|
| 2 C | whole wheat flour |
| 2 C | white flour |
| 1 1/2 C | milk |
| 2 T | baking powder |
| 2 T | oil |
| 1 | egg |

- Combine flour and baking powder.
- Stir in milk, egg and oil to make a sticky dough.
- Form into rolls and bake on a tray 15 minutes.

## Herb Rolls

| | |
|---|---|
| 1 batch | *Bread Rolls* dough |
| 1 t | dried herbs |

- Make *Bread Rolls* dough with added herbs.

*Serve with spaghetti.*

## Cheese and Onion Rolls

| | |
|---|---|
| 1 batch | *Bread Rolls* dough |
| 1/2 C | grated cheese |
| 1/2 C | onion – chopped and sautéed |

- Make *Bread Rolls* dough with added cheese and onion.

*Serve with soup.*

## Seedy Rolls

| | |
|---|---|
| 1 batch | *Bread Rolls* dough |
| 1/2 C | sunflower seeds |
| 1/4 C | poppy seeds |

1/4 C sesame seeds

- ❖ Save 1/4 C seeds to roll buns in before baking
- ❖ Make *Bread Rolls* dough with seeds

*Serve with soup or lentils stews.*

## Reading Between the Lines

Empanadas are Patagonia's equivalent to the American burger or the Kiwi meat pie. Similar to a Cornish pastie or Indian samosa, empandas are a trianglar pieces of short pastry stuffed with a meat and vegetable mix, then deep-fried. They are sold on most street corners, small cafés, or in bars, and are best washed down with a mate tea, coffee or beer.

We had arrived in Puerto Williams, 50 miles from Cape Horn, and were gleaning some knowledge from the local expedition yachts about rounding Cape Horn. Jean-Paul from *Ksar* advised us to obtain weatherfax information from the Argentine service along with the Chilean and New Zealand maps we had been receiving. We duly tuned in our frequency and eagerly awaited our map. The first map arrived; we were thankful that the information was helpful as we set off for Cape Horn. Conditions deteriorated, and we were forced to wait for calmer weather 10 miles north of the Horn in Caleta Martial. We were not alone as *Ksar* also joined us. When the next Argentine map arrived, and we were surprised to discover a large blob on the chart right at Cape Horn. Thinking we had missed something of vital importance on the weather forecast, we radioed *Ksar* to ask for his advice.

"Humm," replied Jean-Paul in his very French accent. "Dooes zee blob appear in zee shape of a triangle?"

With a worried look, John replied, "Yes."

"And iz zere a semi-circle to zee right?" Jean-Paul questioned.

"Seems so" remarked John.

A loud laugh came over the radio. "Zat is nothing to worry about. Zee large blob iz just where zee weatherman haz placed his morning empanda and zee circle iz hiz cup of coffee, it appens quite often."

# Pizzas

## Pizza Crust

Vicky Witch

| | |
|---|---|
| 3 C | flour |
| 1 C | water – very warm |
| 1/4 C | oil |
| 1 T | sugar |
| 1 T | yeast |
| 1 t | salt |

- Mix all ingredients, except flour, until yeast is dissolved.
- Add 1/2 the flour and mix well.
- Add remaining flour and mix to a sticky dough, don't kneed too much, just enough so it sticks to your fingers.
- Cover mixture and let it rise for an hour, punch down and spread onto a greased tray.
- Layer base with favourite topping.
- Bake 20 minutes at 400ºF.

## Quick Pizza Crust

Pat~Yacht Danzante

| | |
|---|---|
| 2 C | flour |
| 2/3 C | milk |
| 1/4 C | salad oil |
| 2 T | salad oil |
| 2 t | baking powder |
| 1 t | salt |

- Heat oven to 425°F
- Mix flour, baking powder and salt together.
- Add milk and 1/4 C salad oil, stir vigorously until mixture leaves side of bowl.
- Knead until smooth and roll into a 13" circle on lightly floured board.
- Place dough on a greased tray and turn up edge 1/2" and pinch in place.
- Brush top with 2 T salad oil and layer on pizza topping.
- Bake 25 minutes at 400ºF.

## Easy Pizza Crust

Barbara~Yacht Heidi

| | |
|---|---|
| 2 1/2 C | flour |
| 1 C | warm water |
| 2 T | oil |
| 1 T | yeast |
| 1 t | sugar |
| 1 t | salt |

- Stir yeast in water until dissolved, mix in sugar, let rest until it bubbles.
- Mix in flour and salt, let rise 20 minutes until it is spongy to touch, divide in half for two pizzas.
- Oil hand and press 1/2 the mixture onto greased tray, top with favorite topping.
- Bake 20 minutes at 425°F.

## Pizza Tomato Sauce

| | |
|---|---|
| 1 can | tomato sauce |
| 1 can | tomato paste |
| 1 | onion – chopped |
| 3 | garlic cloves – crushed |
| 1 t | chilli pepper flakes |
| | Italian herbs |
| | basil - chopped |

- Combine ingredients and spread over pizza base before adding favorite toppings and cheese.

## Pizza Toppings

Pizza toppings are as varied as the base recipes and are totally up to your taste buds. Although most pizzas start with a tomato sauce topped with vegetables, meats or seafood and cheese, others can just be a simple pesto sauce. Here are some ideas for you to try.

- **Cheese –** grated, avoid processed cheese as it won't melt.
- **Vegetables** – olives, mushrooms, green pepper, onion, avocado, pineapple and artichoke hearts.

- **Seafood –** smoked oysters, mussels or salmon, anchovies, prawns, baby clams and baby octopus
- **Meats –** salami, ham, ground beef, Canadian bacon and pepperoni.

# Scones and Muffins

## Drop Biscuits

Jenn~Yacht Ocean Light II

| | |
|---|---|
| 4 C | flour |
| 1 C | milk |
| 1/3 C | butter |
| 2 | eggs |
| 3 T | brown sugar |
| 8 t | baking powder |

- Combine all dry ingredients, cut in butter and stir in milk and eggs.
- Drop dollops of mixture onto a cookie tray.
- Bake 12 minutes at 450°F until done.

## English Scones or Quick Pizza Base

| | |
|---|---|
| 3 C | flour |
| 1 C | milk |
| 6 T | butter |
| 5 t | baking powder |
| 1/8 t | salt |
| 2 T | *sugar if serving the scones with jelly |
| | *1/3 C currants – dried |

- Sift flour, salt and baking powder together, cut in butter and add milk to form a stiff mix.
- Form a block 1" high, cut into 3" squares and place on a floured tray with a gap between each scone.
- Bake 18 minutes at 350ºF.

## Apple Nut Muffins

| | |
|---|---|
| 1 batch | *Lesley's Muffins* |
| 1 | apple |
| 1/2 C | nuts |
| 1 T | orange zest |
| | cinnamon, ginger and nutmeg |

- ❖ Make a batch of Lesley's Muffin mix.
- ❖ Add remaining ingredients.
- ❖ Bake 20 minutes at 350°F.

## Banana Oat Muffins

| | |
|---|---|
| 1 batch | *Lesley's Muffins* |
| 1 C | mashed bananas |
| 1/2 C | oats |
| 1/2 C | bran |
| 1/2 C | walnuts |
| 1 T | lemon juice |
| 1 1/2 t | baking soda |
| 1/2 t | nutmeg |

- ❖ Make a batch of Lesley's Muffin mix minus1/2 C flour.
- ❖ Add remaining ingredients.
- ❖ Bake 20 minutes at 350°F.

## Cereal Muffins

Carol~Yacht Elyxir

| | |
|---|---|
| 2 C | breakfast cereal – wheat germ, bran, oatmeal, or a combination |
| 1 1/4 C | milk |
| 1 1/4 C | flour |
| 1/2 C | oil |
| 1/2 C | sugar |
| 1 | egg |
| 1 T | baking powder |
| 1/4 t | salt |

- ❖ Combine milk, egg and oil, mix in cereal and soak 2 minutes.
- ❖ Add remaining ingredients.

❖ Bake 20 minutes at 350ºF.

*Makes 12 muffins.*

## Chocolate Muffins

| | |
|---|---|
| 1 batch | *Lesley's Muffins* |
| 1/2 C | orange juice |
| 1/2 C | chocolate chips |
| 1/4 C | cocoa |
| 1 t | cider vinegar |

❖ Make a batch of Lesley's Muffin mix.

❖ Add remaining ingredients.

❖ Bake 20 minutes at 350ºF.

## Date Nut Muffins

Cara~M/V St. Elias

| | |
|---|---|
| 1 1/2 C | dates, prunes or dried apricots – chopped |
| 3/4 C | white |
| 3/4 C | bran |
| 3/4 C | boiling water |
| 1/2 C | whole wheat flour |
| 1/2 C | walnuts or pecans – chopped |
| 1/2 C | sugar |
| 1/4 C | oil |
| 1/2 t | baking soda |
| 1/2 t | vanilla or almond extract |

❖ Combine prunes or other fruit and boiling water, oil and extract.

❖ Mix together flour, bran, sugar and baking soda, add prune mixture and walnuts.

❖ Bake 12 minutes at 350ºF.

## Lesley's Muffins

Lesley~Yacht Taitoa

| | |
|---|---|
| 2 C | flour |
| 1 C | milk |

| | |
|---|---|
| 1/4 C | oil or butter |
| 1/4 C | sugar |
| 2 | eggs |
| 2 t | baking powder |

- ❖ Mix oil/butter, sugar and eggs together.
- ❖ Add remaining ingredients.
- ❖ Bake 20 minutes at 350°F.
- ❖ Makes 12 muffins.

## Zucchini Bran Muffins

| | |
|---|---|
| 1 batch | *Lesley's Muffins* |
| 1/2 C | bran |
| 1/2 C | zucchini – grated and squeezed |
| 1/3 C | walnuts – chopped |
| 1/2 t | ginger |

- ❖ Make a batch of Lesley's Muffin mix and add remaining ingredients.
- ❖ Bake 20 minutes at 350°F.

# Cakes and Loafs

## Tips on Baking Cakes and Loafs

- ❖ The following cake and loaf recipes require the oven to be **preheated** before adding the item for cooking.
- ❖ The cakes are all baked in a 8 x11 **glass dish.**
- ❖ All pans are prepared by **greasing the inside** with butter.
- ❖ A **cake is baked** when it springs back when slightly touched.

## Apple and Oat Loaf

| | |
|---|---|
| 1 1/2 C | flour |
| 2 | apples – grated |
| 1 C | oats |

| | |
|---|---|
| 1 C | brown sugar |
| 1 C | raisins |
| 1 C | water |
| 1/2 C | butter |
| 2 | eggs – beaten |
| 3 t | baking powder |
| 1 t | baking soda |
| 1 t | all spice |
| 1/2 t | cinnamon |

- ❖ Bring butter, soda, spice, cinnamon, sugar, apples, raisins and water to a boil, allow to cool.
- ❖ Beat in eggs and oats, sift in flour and baking powder, combine well.
- ❖ Bake 45 minutes at 350ºF.

## Apple Cake

| | |
|---|---|
| 2 C | apples – peeled and diced |
| 1 C | sugar |
| 1 C | flour |
| 1/2 C | pecans – chopped |
| 1/4 C | vegetable oil |
| 1 | egg |
| 2 t | cinnamon |
| 1 t | baking soda |
| 1/2 t | salt |
| 1/4 t | nutmeg |

- ❖ Beat egg, stir in apples, oil, sugar, cinnamon, nutmeg and walnuts.
- ❖ Sift in flour and baking soda, stir in remaining ingredients.
- ❖ Bake 40 minutes at 350ºF.

## Banana Loaf

| | |
|---|---|
| 1 1/4 C | flour |
| 1 C | bananas – mashed |
| 1/2 C | oats |
| 1/2 C | sugar |
| 1/3 C | butter |

| | |
|---|---|
| 2 | eggs |
| 2 t | baking powder |
| 1 t | vanilla |
| 1/4 t | baking soda |
| | lemon zest |
| | pinch of salt |
| | *grated coconut |
| | *sultanas or raisins |
| | *nutmeg and cinnamon |
| | *nuts or seeds |

- ❖ Cream butter and sugar together until fluffy, add eggs, and beat well.
- ❖ Sift in flour, baking powder and baking soda, while adding bananas.
- ❖ Stir in vanilla and salt.
- ❖ Bake 1 hour at 350°F.

## Banana Cake

| | |
|---|---|
| 1 3/4 C | flour |
| 1 C | bananas – mashed |
| 3/4 C | sugar |
| 1/2 C | milk |
| 1/4 C | butter |
| 1 | egg |
| 1 t | baking soda |
| 1 t | baking powder |
| 1 t | vanilla |

- ❖ Cream butter and sugar together until flufy, add beaten egg and vanilla.
- ❖ Sift in flour, baking powder and baking soda, add milk and stir in bananas.
- ❖ Bake 45 minutes at 350ºF.

## Caribbean Ginger Loaf

| | |
|---|---|
| 1 1/2 C | flour |
| 2/3 C | fruit juice, coconut milk or milk |
| 1/2 C | raisins or dried tropical fruit |

1/2 C honey
1/2 C maple syrup
1/2 C oil
1 egg
2 t ginger
1 t baking soda
1 t cinnamon
1/4 t salt

- Blend oil, honey, syrup, egg and fruit juice together until smooth.
- Sift dry ingredients, add liquid and dried fruit, mix well.
- Bake 70 minutes at 350ºF.

## Chocolate Cake

2 C flour
1 C sugar
1/2 C water
1/2 C butter
3 eggs
3 T cocoa
1 t baking powder

- Cream butter and sugar together until fluffy, add eggs.
- Dissolve cocoa in boiling water and add to eggs alternately with sifted flour and baking powder.
- Bake 45 min at 350ºF.

*Ice with Chocolate Icing.*

## Date Loaf

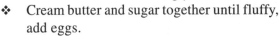

2 C flour
1 C walnuts – chopped
1 C dates – chopped
1 C water – boiling
1 C brown sugar
1 egg beaten
1 T butter
1 t baking soda

| | |
|---|---|
| 1 t | baking powder |
| 1/4 t | vanilla |
| | *replace dates with died apricots |

- Mix dates, water, soda and butter, stir until butter melts then let rest 30 minutes.
- Beat sugar, egg, walnuts and vanilla into date mixture.
- Sift in flour and baking powder, mix well.
- Bake 45 minutes at 350°F.

## English Muffin Loaf

Barbara~Yacht Heidi

| | |
|---|---|
| 6 C | flour |
| 2 C | milk |
| 1/2 C | water |
| 2 T | yeast |
| 1 T | sugar |
| 2 t | salt |
| 1/4 t | baking soda |

- Combine 1/2 flour with yeast, sugar, salt and baking soda.
- Heat liquids until warm, add to dry ingredients and beat well.
- Add remaining flour to make a stiff batter
- Oil and dust 2 bread pans with cornmeal, and spoon in mixture.
- Sprinkle tops with cornmeal and let rise 45 minutes.
- Bake for 30 minutes.

*Makes super toast.*

## Ginger Cake

| | |
|---|---|
| 2 C | flour |
| 1/2 C | butter |
| 1/2 C | sugar |
| 1/2 C | milk |
| 1/4 C | crystallized ginger – chopped |
| 1/4 C | walnuts – chopped |
| 1/4 C | raisins |
| 2 | eggs – beaten |
| 3 T | maple syrup |

| | |
|---|---|
| 1 t | baking powder |
| 1 t | ginger |
| 1 t | all spice |
| 1 t | baking soda |

- ❖ Cream butter, sugar and syrup together until fluffy.
- ❖ Sift in four, baking powder and spice, mix in eggs.
- ❖ Stir in ginger, walnuts and raisins.
- ❖ Dissolve baking soda in milk and add to mixture.
- ❖ Bake 45 minutes at 350ºF.

## Hawaiian Carrot Cake

| | |
|---|---|
| 1 1/2 C | flour |
| 1 1/2 C | carrot – grated |
| 1 C | sugar |
| 1 C | coconut – grated and toasted |
| 1 C | macadamia nuts – chopped |
| 1/2 C | oil |
| 1/2 C | canned crushed pineapple – drained |
| 2 | eggs |
| 1/2 t | salt |
| 1/2 t | baking powder |
| 1/2 t | cinnamon |
| 1 t | vanilla |
| | *may replace macadamia nuts with walnuts |

- ❖ Sift together flour, sugar, salt, baking soda, baking powder and cinnamon.
- ❖ Combine oil, vanilla and eggs, stir into flour.
- ❖ Add carrots, pineapple, coconut and walnuts.
- ❖ Bake 1 hour at 350ºF.

*Ice with* Cream Cheese Icing, *with a little added coconut.*

## Orange Poppy Seed Loaf

Dyan~Yacht Ascension

| | |
|---|---|
| 2 C | flour |
| 1/2 C | sugar |

| | |
|---|---|
| 1 C | oil |
| 1/2 C | milk |
| 1/2 C | orange juice |
| 3 | eggs |
| 3 T | poppy seeds |
| 1 t | vanilla |
| 1 t | baking powder |
| 1/2 t | salt |

- ❖ Beat eggs, sugar, milk, oil and vanilla together.
- ❖ Add remaining ingredients and mix well.
- ❖ Bake 50 minutes at 350°F.

*Ice with lemon icing.*

## Papaya Cake

| | |
|---|---|
| 3 C | flour |
| 2 C | papaya – mashed |
| 1 C | raisins |
| 3/4 C | sugar |
| 1/2 C | butter |
| 2 | eggs |
| 2 T | yogurt or milk |
| 1 T | lemon juice |
| 1 T | orange marmalade or orange zest |
| 2 t | baking soda |
| 1/4 t | each – cinnamon, nutmeg and ginger |
| | pinch of cloves |

- ❖ Cream butter and sugar, add eggs one at a time, beating well after each addition.
- ❖ Mix in papaya and marmalade.
- ❖ Sift in flour and spices, add yogurt and lemon juice, fold in raisins.
- ❖ Bake 45 minutes at 350°F.

## Pumpkin Loaf

| | |
|---|---|
| 2 C | flour |
| 1 C | pumpkin – cooked and puréed |
| 1/4 C | hazelnuts – chopped and toasted |

| | |
|---|---|
| 1/4 C | brown sugar |
| 1/4 C | sugar |
| 1/4 C | raisins |
| 2 | eggs |
| 1 | orange – juice and zest |
| 1 T | butter |
| 1 t | baking powder |
| 1/4 t | baking soda |
| 1/4 t | each – cinnamon, nutmeg, ginger and allspice |
| | pinch salt |

- Cream butter and sugar together until fluffy
- Stir in eggs, zest, juice and pumpkin.
- Sift in dry ingredients, add raisins and nuts, mix well.
- Bake in greased bread pan for 45 minutes at 350°F.

## Sultana Cake

Karen~Yacht Kamaraderie

Sultana and fruitcakes have a strong tie to my sailing adventures. Summer holidays Down Under revolve around Christmas, and a sailing trip away wouldn't be complete without leftover Christmas cake stashed away in a locker, to be sliced up and served with a cup of tea after a day of sailing.

On preparing for the Sydney-Hobart yacht race one year, I was up the mast doing a rig check when a call came from dockside that someone was looking for me. I called out asking what they wanted, and the gentleman replied that he was a workmate of mum and dad's visiting Australia from New Zealand. As a favor, mum had asked if he could deliver me a home-baked sultana cake for the race, and it was the best Christmas present mum could have sent.

During the Whitbread race, when we were getting ready to depart Freemantle, Australia for New Zealand, the whole town felt sorry that we would be spending Christmas at sea. Christmas cakes came flooding down to the boat. So generous were the bakers of these cakes that we had to make a public news announcement that we could not possibly accept any more cakes. We were conscious of all the weight onboard and cakes were too heavy versus freeze-dried food.

I remember one cake in particular that was an incredible work of art. The cake sides were covered with marzipan icing that was woven into a straw basket. The top of the cake was a sculptured entirely from marzipan – a miniature fruit basket loaded with fruits and berries, each beautifully colored and shaped resembling the real thing. It was far too beautiful to eat.

I owe great thanks to my Nanna, Ann Searle and Christine Webb, who have all baked memorable cakes for my sailing races, and I have fond memories of sharing cake slices with fellow crew members on Whitbread, Sydney-Hobart, and Kiwi Coastal Classic races.

When Mike, our first Kiwi expedition member, joined *Mahina Tiare* for the passage from Hawaii to Seattle he came toting a sultana cake his wife Karen had made for the passage, what a sport! I guess sultana cake is as symbolic to Kiwis as brownies are to Americans.

| | |
|---|---|
| 2 1/2 C | flour |
| 2 1/4 C | sultanas/raisins |
| 1 1/2 C | sugar |
| 1 C | butter – softened |
| 3 | eggs |
| 2 t | almond extract |
| 1 t | baking powder |

- ❖ Boil sultanas, then simmer 7 minutes, strain, add almond extract and butter, and cool.
- ❖ Beat eggs and sugar together.
- ❖ Sift flour and baking powder into sultanas, mix well, add to eggs.
- ❖ Bake 75 minutes at 300°F.

*Keeps for 1 month wrapped wax paper then newspaper.*

# Icings

## Cream Cheese Icing

| | |
|---|---|
| 1 C | confectioners sugar |
| 1/4 C | cream cheese |
| 2 T | butter |
| 1 t | vanilla |
| 1/2 t | lemon zest |

- ❖ Beat butter and cream cheese, add confectioners sugar, vanilla and zest, combine well.

## Chocolate Icing

| | |
|---|---|
| 2 C | confectioners sugar |
| 2 T | water |
| 1 T | cocoa |
| 1/4 t | butter |
| 1/4 t | vanilla |

❖ Sift sugar and cocoa, add butter and enough water to mix to a spreadable consistency, flavor with vanilla.

## Lemon Icing

| | |
|---|---|
| 2 C | confectioners sugar |
| 2 T | lemon juice |
| 1 t | lemon zest |
| 1/4 t | butter |

❖ Sift sugar, add butter and enough lemon juice to mix to a spreadable consistency, flavor with zest.

# Cookies and Bars

## Brownies

Dyan~Yacht Ascension

| | |
|---|---|
| 2 C | sugar |
| 1 1/3 C | flour |
| 3/4 C | cocoa |
| 1/2 C | boiling water |
| 1/3 C | vegetable oil |
| 2 | eggs |
| 1 t | vanilla |
| 1/2 t | baking soda |
| 1/4 t | salt |

❖ Combine cocoa and baking soda, stir in oil.

❖ Stir in water, add remaining ingredients and mix well.

❖ Bake in cake pan for 20 minutes at 350°F.

## Date Bars

Cowpuccino's Coffee House~Prince Rupert

2 C oats
2 C pitted dates – 1 x 500g pkg
1 1/2 C flour
1 1/2 C brown sugar
1 1/4 C butter
1 1/2 t baking soda
1 t vanilla
1/2 t salt

- Simmer dates in 2/3 C water until mushy, add vanilla.
- Mix dry ingredients together, cut in butter.
- Press 1/2 dry ingredients into a greased 8 x 12 pan, spread with dates and crumb remaining mixture on top.
- Bake 30 minutes at 350°F.

## Louise Squares

1 1/4 C flour
1/2 C desiccated coconut
1/2 C sugar
1/3 C butter
1/4 C raspberry jam
2 eggs – separated
2 T sugar
1 t baking powder

- Cream butter and 2 T sugar together until fluffy, beat in egg yolks.
- Sift flour and baking powder together and stir into creamed mixture.
- Press mixture into a greased 8 x 12 pan and spread with raspberry jam.
- Beat egg whites until stiff but not dry, mix in 1/2 C sugar and coconut, spread meringue over jam.
- Bake 30 minutes at 350°F or until meringue is dry and lightly colored.

*Cut into squares while warm.*

## Macadamia Butter Cookies

Ralph~Yacht Morning Cloud

| | |
|---|---|
| 2 1/2 C | flour |
| 1 1/3 C | salted macadamia nuts – chopped |
| 1 1/4 C | sugar |
| 1 C | butter |
| 1 | egg |
| 1 t | baking soda |
| 1 t | vanilla |
| | *chocolate chips |

- ❖ Cream butter and sugar together until fluffy, beat in egg and vanilla.
- ❖ Mix in flour, baking soda and nuts.
- ❖ Drop 1 T balls on tray and press flat with a fork dipped in remaining sugar.
- ❖ Press a chunk of nut into the center of each cookie.
- ❖ Bake 15 minutes at 375°F.

## Oatmeal Chocolate Chip Cookies

Jenn~Yacht Ocean Light II

| | |
|---|---|
| 2 1/2 C | oats |
| 2 C | flour |
| 1 1/2 C | sugar – white and brown mix |
| 1 C | butter |
| 1 C | chocolate chips |
| 1/2 C | pecans – chopped |
| 2 | eggs |
| 1 t | vanilla |
| 1 t | baking soda |
| 1 t | baking powder |
| | pinch of salt |

- ❖ Cream butter and sugar together until fluffy, mix in eggs and vanilla.
- ❖ Add combined flour, baking soda and salt, stir in oats, nuts and chocolate.
- ❖ Drop 1 T balls on tray and bake 15 minutes at 375°F.

*Makes 3 dozen.*

## Oatmeal Raisin Cookies

Pat~Yacht Danzante

| | |
|---|---|
| 3 1/2 C | oats |
| 1 1/2 C | flour |
| 1 C | raisins |
| 1 C | butter |
| 3/4 C | brown sugar |
| 2 | eggs |
| 1 t | vanilla |
| 1 t | cinnamon |
| 1/4 t | salt |
| | *substitute dried cranberries, yogurt covered sutanas or pecans for a more exotic cookie |

- ❖ Cream butter and sugar, together until fluffy, beat in eggs and vanilla
- ❖ Stir in oats and raisins.
- ❖ Drop 1 T balls on tray and bake 15 minutes.

## Secret Granola Bars

Cowpuccino's Coffee House~Prince Rupert

| | |
|---|---|
| 1 1/2 C | oats |
| 1/2 C | chocolate chips |
| 1/2 C | raisins |
| 1/2 C | sunflower seeds |
| 1/2 C | Rice Krispies |
| 1/2 C | sweetened condensed milk |
| 1/3 C | butter – melted |

- ❖ Mix all ingredients together.
- ❖ Press into a greased 8 x 12 pan.
- ❖ Bake 25 minutes for 325°F until golden.

Chapter 16

# Desserts

## Desert Crêpes ~ Lesley's

Yacht Taitoa

- Make Lesley Crêpes.

*Serve hot off the pan sprinkled with sugar and lemon juice, Pineapple Flambé or Warm Mango Sauce.*

# Fruit Deserts

## Apple Cobbler

| | |
|---|---|
| 3 | apples – sliced |
| 1 C | oats |
| 1/2 C | flour |
| 1/2 C | walnuts – chopped |
| 1/4 C | sugar |
| 1/4 C | brown sugar |
| 1/4 C | butter |
| 1 | lemon – juice and zest |
| 1/2 t | cinnamon |
| 1/8 t | nutmeg |
| | pinch of salt |

### Oven Option

- Combine sugars, oatmeal, flour, spices and lemon zest, rub in butter and add nuts.
- Mix apples and juice together in a buttered dish, top with oatmeal mixture.
- Bake 45 minutes at 325°F.

### Pressure Cooker Option

- Place apples in a buttered 6 C soufflé dish and top with oatmeal mixture.
- Cover with buttered foil and place place in drainer basket.
- Pour 1 1/2 C water in to pressure cooker and place basket inside.
- Pressure-cook 25 minutes.

*Serve with ice cream, whipped cream or custard.*

## Banana or Pineapple Flambé

A quick favorite one-dish desert of my mum's results in a sure way to use up ripe bananas. It looks impressive when set alight and the rum makes it an instant hit with company. You may also mix the bananas and pineapple.

| | |
|---|---|
| | bananas – 1 per person, or fresh pineapple – sliced into rings |
| 1/4 C | rum |
| 1/4 C | brown sugar |
| 1/4 C | butter |

❖ Melt butter in skillet, add sugar and heat.

❖ Add fruit and stir until butter and sugar caramelizes.

❖ Pour in rum into the pan and set alight.

*Serve immediately.*

## Baked Papaya

| | |
|---|---|
| 2 | ripe papaya - peeled and sliced |
| 2 T | brown sugar |
| 2 T | lemon juice |
| 2 T | brandy |

❖ Place in papya in a buttered baking dish.

❖ Sprinkle with sugar, lemon juice and brandy.

❖ Bake 30 minutes at 350°F.

*Serve with ice cream, whipped cream or custard.*

## Canned Fruit Cobbler

Dee~M/V Penguin

| | |
|---|---|
| 1 can | peaches, apples, berries or apricots |
| 1 C | flour |
| 1/2 C | brown sugar |
| 1/2 C | white sugar |
| 1/4 C | butter |
| 1 | egg |
| 2 T | lime juice |
| | corn starch or tapioca |
| 1 t | cinnamon |

- ❖ Place drained fruit in a baking dish and add lime juice.
- ❖ Heat half the canned fruit juice in a pan, add cornstarch or tapioca to thicken, pour over the fruit.
- ❖ Mix flour, sugars, butter and egg together, place on top of fruit.
- ❖ Bake 20 minutes at 375°F.

## Fruit Freeze

Dee~M/V Penguin

| | |
|---|---|
| 1 can | evaporated milk |
| 1 can | fruit – drained or equivalent volume of fresh berries |
| 1 C | sugar |
| 1 t | vanilla |

- ❖ Blend all ingredients together and pour into a bowl.
- ❖ Cover fruit mix with foil or plastic wrap and freeze.

*Serve with chocolate chips and whipped cream.*

## Peaches Drowned in Red Wine

| | |
|---|---|
| 6 | peaches – sliced into wedges |
| 7 T | sugar |
| 2 | whole cloves |
| 1 | cinnamon stick |
| | red wine – preferably Chianti |

- ❖ Place peaches in container and sprinkle with sugar.
- ❖ Add spices and cover with red wine.

*Refrigerate overnight and serve cold.*

## Strawberry Dip

I first had this dessert 20 years ago at the St. Francis Yacht Club. We had sailed from New Zealand into San Francisco, and Henry, the gentleman on the yacht beside us in Sausalito invited us out for dinner. I was in awe, never before had I seen such elegance: a huge table with a carved ice statue of King Neptune and dancing dolphins took center stage in the dining room. This dessert appeared simple, but was so exquisite in its presentation that I still have vivid memories of its arrival and the joy it was to leisurely dip and devour each strawberry.

- 6 strawberries per person – rinsed, but not hulled
- 1 C brown sugar
- 1 C sour cream
- *quartered apricots can substitute for strawberries

The St. Francis Yacht Club served two small pots – one of sour cream and the other of brown sugar – for each person, along with the strawberries in a dish, though this presentation is a little impractical on a yacht.

A bowl for each ingredient is placed in the center of the table and each person dips a strawberry first in the sour cream and then brown sugar.

## Tropical Fruit Cobbler

### Filling

- 3 bananas
- 3 mangos
- 3 pineapple slices
- 1/3 C brown sugar
- 1/3 C orange juice
- 1 lemon – juiced

### Topping

- 1 1/2 C flour
- 3/4 C rolled oats
- 3/4 C brown sugar

| | |
|---|---|
| 1/2 C | coconut grated |
| 1/3 C | butter |
| 1/2 t | cinnamon |

- ❖ Mix filling ingredients together in a buttered baking dish.
- ❖ Rub topping ingredients together using fingers, spread over fruit.
- ❖ Bake 20 minutes at 375°F.

*Serve with ice cream, whipped cream or custard.*

# Puddings

## Fruit Sponge

| | |
|---|---|
| 1 C | flour |
| 1 can | fruit |
| 1/2 C | butter |
| 1/2 C | brown sugar |
| 2 T | milk |
| 2 | eggs |
| 2 t | baking powder |
| 1 t | vanilla |

- ❖ Cream butter, vanilla and sugar together, beat in eggs.
- ❖ Sift in flour and baking powder, add milk and mix well.
- ❖ Place fruit in bottom of baking dish, spoon in mixture.
- ❖ Bake 40 minutes at 350°F until sponge springs back when touched lightly.

## Bread Pudding ~ Jamaican

| | |
|---|---|
| 3 C | milk |
| 8 | bread slices – buttered and sliced into strips |
| 1/2 C | honey and/or brown sugar |
| 1/2 C | dried mixed tropical fruit – pineapple, pa paya, citrus peel, dates and coconut |
| 1/4 C | raisins |
| 1/4 C | rum |
| 3 | bananas |
| 2 | eggs |

1 T lemon juice
1 t vanilla
1/4 t each – nutmeg, cinnamon and ground ginger

- Slice bananas and mix with lemon juice.
- Layer bread in buttered baking dish, followed with layer of bananas and fruit.
- Continue layering bread and fruit, ending with bread.
- Beat milk, honey, rum, eggs, vanilla and spices together, pour over bread.
- Bake 45 minutes at 325°F until egg has set.

*Serve hot or cold.*

## Lemon Meringue Pie

Lorena~Cape Horn

### Base

2 C flour
1/3 C butter
1/4 C sugar
3 eggs – yolks
1 t baking powder

- Rub flour and butter together, mix in sugar and baking powder, add egg yolks.
- Press mixture into buttered pan and poke with a fork.
- Bake 15 minutes until golden.

### Filling

1 can condensed milk
1/2 C lemon juice
2 t lemon zest
1/4 t vanilla

- Whip condensed milk with lemon juice to taste and pour into base.
- Bake until set, about 5 minutes.

### Meringue Topping

1/4 C powered sugar
3 egg whites
1/4 t vanilla

- Beat egg whites until stiff, beat in sugar 1T at a time until thick and glossy, stir in vanilla.
- Top pie with meringue and bake 10 minutes until golden.

## Mango Cream Pie

Base

| | |
|---|---|
| 2 C | plain cookies – crushed |
| 1 C | coconut – grated |
| 1/2 C | brown sugar |
| 1/3 C | melted butter |
| 1 t | cinnamon |

- Combine cookie crumbs, coconut, sugar and cinnamon, mix in melted butter.
- Press mixture into a baking dish.

Filling

| | |
|---|---|
| 1 1/2 C | mango – mashed |
| 3 | eggs – separated |
| 1 can | condensed milk |
| 1/2 C | lime juice |
| | lemon zest |
| | *can replace mango with papaya, pine apple, or guava |

- Combine egg yolks, condensed milk, fruit juice and zest.
- Beat egg whtes until stiff and fold into fruit, pour into dish.
- Bake 1 hour at 300°F.

*Serve hot or cold.*

## Microwave Mexican Flan

Dee~M/V Penguin

| | |
|---|---|
| 1 can | evaporated milk |
| 1 can | sweetened condensed milk |
| 2/3 C | sugar |

| | |
|---|---|
| 4 | eggs |
| 1 t | vanilla |

- ❖ Beat eggs, milk, condensed milk and vanilla together until fluffy.
- ❖ Prepare a shallow dish of warm water in which a large bowl can easily sit.
- ❖ Melt sugar in frying pan until it caramelizes, don't burn.
- ❖ Pour caramel into bowl and swirl around to evenly coat the base and sides.
- ❖ Pour beaten mixture inside caramel coated bowl, cover with plastic wrap.
- ❖ Microwave on high for 12 minutes.

*Chill and flip out onto a plate before serving.*

## Marshmallow Mousse

Dee~MV Penguin

| | |
|---|---|
| 18 large | marshmallows |
| 1 1/2 C | cream |
| 2 shots | liquor – kahlua, crème de menthe or melted chocolate |

- ❖ Melt marshmallows with 1/3 of the cream.
- ❖ Whip remaining cream and add to marshmallow mixture.
- ❖ Fold in liquor and pour mixture into small dishes or medium bowl.
- ❖ Cover with plastic wrap and chill.

*Serve cold.*

## Rice Pudding

| | |
|---|---|
| 3 1/2 C | milk |
| 1 C | rice |
| 1/4 C | brown sugar |
| 1/4 C | raisins – soaked in rum |
| 1/4 C | nuts - chopped |
| 2 T | lemon zest |
| 2 T | butter |

| | |
|---|---|
| 2 t | vanilla |
| | cinnamon and nutmeg |

- Sauté rice in butter until rice is coated, stir in remaining ingredients.
- Pressure-cook 10 minutes, or simmer 25 minutes until rice is tender.

*Serve garnished with chopped nuts.*

## Indonesian Rice Pudding

- Make rice pudding as above then make the following spiced coconut milk.

| | |
|---|---|
| 1 C | coconut milk |
| 2 T | lemon zest |
| 1/4 t | cardamom |
| | *crushed pineapple |

- Heat milk and ingredients until just about to boil.
- Leave for 5 minutes then pour onto rice pudding.

*Serve warm or cold.*

# Dessert Sauces

## Caramel Sauce ~ Quick

| | |
|---|---|
| 3/4 C | evaporated milk or 2/3 milk and 1/3 cream |
| 1/3 C | brown sugar |
| 2 T | butter |
| 3 drops | vanilla extract |
| | *melted chocolate for chocolate sauce |

- Place all ingredients in a pan and cook gently while stirring for 7 minutes.
- Remove from heat and beat till glossy.

*Serve hot or cold.*

## Mango Sauce

| | |
|---|---|
| 2 | mangos – peeled and chopped |
| 1/3 C | sugar |
| 1/4 C | water |
| 1 T | lemon juice |

- ❖ Combine half of the mangos with sugar, water and lemon juice.
- ❖ Bring to a boil and simmer 3 minutes.
- ❖ Purée the mixture until smooth and return to pan, add remaining mango and heat through.

*Serve hot with* Lesley Crepes, *ice cream, or cold with* Mango Cream Pie.

## Maple Syrup ~ Mock

Fran~Yacht Aka

A very good substitute when you run out of the real thing.

| | |
|---|---|
| 1 C | brown sugar |
| 1/2 C | water |
| 1 t | vanilla |

- ❖ Boil water and sugar until sugar dissolves.

*Cool and add vanilla.*

Chapter 17

# Chutneys, Relishes and Jams

# Chutneys

## Fresh Green Papaya Chutney

| | |
|---|---|
| 1 | green papaya – grated |
| 1/4 C | lemon juice or vinegar |
| 1 t | salt |
| 1 t | ginger |
| | ground pepper to taste |
| | *cucumber or tomatoes with a clove of crushed garlic may be substituted for the papaya. |

❖ Combine all ingredients and test for flavor.

*Serve with curry and fish dishes.*

## Banana Chutney

| | |
|---|---|
| 4 C | bananas – mashed |
| 2 1/2 C | malt vinegar |
| 2 C | raisins |
| 1 1/2 C | brown sugar |
| 2 | garlic cloves – crushed |
| 2 T | ginger – grated |
| 1 T | chili sauce |
| 1 t | Gram Marsala |
| 1/2 t | cinnamon |
| 1/4 t | cloves |

❖ Purée raisins with 1 C vinegar, ginger, garlic and chili.

❖ Combine all ingredients and simmer stirring occasionally for an hour, or until thick.

❖ Pack into sterile jars.

## Cranberry Chutney

| | |
|---|---|
| 2 C | cranberries |
| 1/2 C | onion – sliced |
| 1/2 C | water |
| 1/4 C | currants |
| 1/4 C | sugar |

| | |
|---|---|
| 1 | apple – peeled and diced |
| 1 | orange – juice and zest |
| 6 T | cider vinegar |
| 5 T | brown sugar |
| 1/2 t | ginger – grated |
| 1/4 t | salt |
| 1/4 t | nutmeg |
| 1/4 t | curry |

- ❖ Simmer onion, sugar and water for 20 minutes.
- ❖ Add vinegar, apple, spices and zest, simmer 30 minutes.
- ❖ Stir in cranberries, currants and juice, simmer until cranberries pop.
- ❖ Let cool, cover and refrigerate.

## Mango Chutney

| | |
|---|---|
| 5 C | ripe mangos – diced |
| 2 1/2 C | cider vinegar |
| 2 C | brown sugar |
| 2 C | raisins |
| 3/4 C | onion – chopped |
| 1/4 C | ginger – chopped |
| 1/2 T | chili peppers |
| 1 t | salt |

- ❖ Combine all ingredients and bring to a boil.
- ❖ Simmer 30 minutes, or until mixture is thick.
- ❖ Cool 15 minutes, stir well and bottle.

*Makes 12 cups.*

## Tomato Chutney

| | |
|---|---|
| 1/2 C | cider vinegar |
| 1/2 C | brown sugar |
| 1/4 C | raisins |
| 1/4 C | nuts |
| 5 | tomatoes – diced |
| 2 | onions – chopped |
| 2 | apples – chopped |
| 2 | celery stalks – diced |

| | |
|---|---|
| 1 | green pepper – diced |
| 1 | red pepper – diced |
| | citrus peel |
| | ginger – grated |
| | S&P |

- ❖ Combine all ingredients and bring to a boil.
- ❖ Simmer 30 minutes, or until the mixture is thick.
- ❖ Cool 15 minutes, stir well and bottle.

*Makes 12 cups.*

# Relishes

## Asian Relish

| | |
|---|---|
| 1/4 C | sesame seeds |
| 3 | scallions – chopped |
| 1 | garlic clove – chopped |
| 2 T | soy sauce |
| 2 t | ginger – chopped |
| 1 t | rice vinegar |
| 1 t | sesame oil |
| 1/4 t | sugar |
| | salt |

- ❖ Blend all ingredients together.

*Serve with* Asian Marinated Fish *marinades and sauces.*

## Tomato and Cucumber Relish

This refreshing relish goes well with fish, chili dishes and curries.

| | |
|---|---|
| 1/2 C | tomato – cubed |
| 1/2 C | cucumber – cubed |
| 1/3 C | yogurt |
| | fresh mint |
| | S&P |

- ❖ Combine ingredients, chill and serve.

## Nanna's Tomato Relish

This tangy relish has been a long time staple item on nanna's condiment shelf. I have fond memories of summer sandwiches liberally spread with relish containing slabs of Sunday's cold cut roast beef and tasty cheddar cheese.

| | |
|---|---|
| 6 C | tomatoes – diced |
| 2 1/2 C | vinegar |
| 2 C | brown sugar |
| 4 | onions – diced |
| 1 | apple – chopped |
| 3 | chilies – chopped |
| 1 T | mustard |
| 2 t | salt |
| 2 t | salt |
| 1 t | curry |

❖ Simmer tomatoes, apple, onions, chilies and 2 1/4 C vinegar for 1 1/2 hours.

❖ Mix remaining ingredients into a smooth paste and stir into relish.

❖ Boil 5 minutes to thicken, pack into sterile jars.

*Makes 6 cups.*

## Pink Onion Relish

| | |
|---|---|
| 2 C | water |
| 1 | red onion – sliced thin |
| 1 T | salad oil |
| 3 t | vinegar |
| 1 1/2 t | vinegar |
| 1/2 t | mustard seed |
| 1/4 t | cumin seed |
| | salt |

❖ Bring water and half vinegar, to a boil.

❖ Add red onion and simmer 3 minutes, drain and cool.

❖ Add remaining ingredients and season to taste.

*Serve with bean chili.*

# Jams and Jellies

## Tips on Jam Making

- Select fruit that is in **good condition** and not overripe.
- A stainless steel **pressure cooker** is ideal for jam making.
- Watch and test jam frequently **towards the end of the cooking** time as it can easily burn.

### Three Methods for Testing if Jam Will Set

- Dip wooden spoon into jam allowing mixture to drip; when two drops merge on the end of the spoon, the jam will set.
- Place a little jam on a cold plate from the fridge, let cool, press the mixture with a finger, and a wrinkle should form.
- Place a little jam on a plate, draw a channel through the jam with a knife; the gap should remain open and not cave in.

### Sterilizing Jars

Sterilize jars and lids by cleaning them thoroughly in hot soapy water; then follow one of these procedures.

- Place jars in a oven for 30 minutes at 250°F.
- Cover jars with water and boil for 15 minutes.

## Pineapple Jam

| | |
|---|---|
| 6 C | pineapple – chopped |
| 4 C | sugar |
| 2 1/2 C | water |
| 4 | lemons – juice and zest |

- Combine all ingredients and refrigerate overnight.
- Simmer 1 hour uncovered, stirring only at the end of cooking. .
- Bottle in hot sterilized jars and cover when cool.

## Mango Jam

| | |
|---|---|
| 4 C | ripe mangos – chopped |
| 3 C | sugar |
| 1/2 C | water |
| 1/4 C | lemon juice |

- ❖ Combine mangos, water and lemon juice, bring to boil and simmer covered 15 minutes until mango is tender.
- ❖ Add sugar, stirring until dissolved, then boil uncovered without stirring until jam sets.
- ❖ Bottle in hot sterilized jars and cover when cool.

## Orange Marmalade

| | |
|---|---|
| 2 lbs. | oranges |
| 8 C | water |
| 6 C | sugar |
| 2 | lemons – juiced |

- ❖ Cut oranges in half and squeeze out juice, scrape out pulp and discard seeds.
- ❖ Thinly slice orange skins and simmer with water until peel is tender, about 20 minutes.
- ❖ Add remaining ingredients and gently heat, stirring until sugar dissolves.
- ❖ Boil uncovered, without stirring, until marmalade sets, about 25 minutes.
- ❖ Bottle in hot sterilized jars and cover when cool.

Chapter 18

# WATER MANAGEMENT

## Water Capacity

- Carry a minimum of **1.5 gallons of water** per person, per day, for offshore passages.
- Always carry **extra water** in rigid plastic jugs for emergency.
- Have at least four 5-gallon **collapsible jugs** onboard for transporting water by dinghy.
- Rig a **water-catchment** system utilizing your sun awning or a separate foredeck awning. While sailing, rainwater can be caught in a bucket or canvas catcher hanging at the gooseneck.
- A **simple option** to obtain water in a downpour is to place a towel across the deck to dam and direct water into the deck fill after the rain has thoroughly washed the decks.

## Hints on Galley Water Consumption

- Using a **foot-pump** instead of pressure water.
- Installing a **saltwater** foot-pump in the galley may reduce water consumption by 50%. Rinse briefly with fresh water.
- Dishwashing

  Provide each crewmember with their own **drinking mug** so that it doesn't have to be rinsed after each drink.
  Use **small dinner plates** rather than large as there is less surface area to wash.
  A **paper towel** might be better than a sponge for wiping up messy jobs, as it doesn't require rinsing.
  **Avoid stacking dirty plates** after a meal so you don't have to scrub the bottom of the plate.
  **Heated water** is more efficient for washing dishes than cold.
  Use salt water for washing dishes and rinse them fresh water. Rinse briefly with fresh water.
  Choose **biodegradable** soap that lathers well in salt water for seawater dishwashing.

- Cooking with **salt water**

  beans, soak in 100% salt water
  eggs, hard boiled: 100% salt water,
  whole potatoes and carrots: 50% salt water
  rice: 50% salt water
  oats: 25% salt water

## Warnings About Contaminated Water

- **In the tropics**, drinking water may be scarce and expensive. Supplies may come from rain catchment, slightly brackish wells, expensive desalination plants, or may be transported to small islands by barges. The water on high islands comes from springs, natural rain catchment reservoirs and rivers. Any of these may be contaminated, although generally water coming from deep wells and springs is potable.
- When **obtaining water from shore**, ask around about the quality, especially from other yachties, as the locals build up resistance to bad water. Check sanitation: Does the water flow from a river with a village upstream? Is it clear rather than turbid?
- **Avoid contaminated water** by catching your own rainwater or using a watermaker.

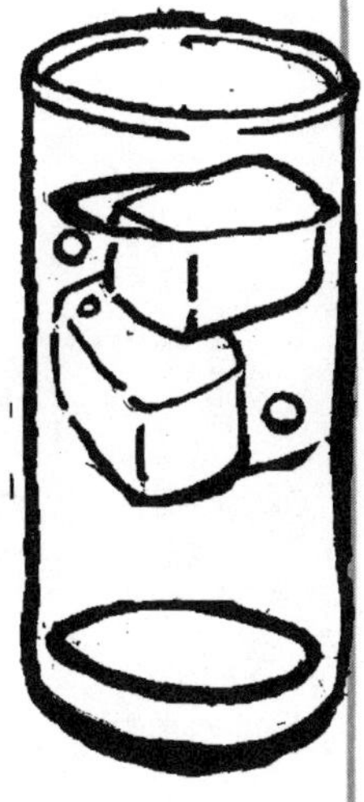

- **Babies and children** are more susceptible to serious diarrhea from contaminated water than are adults. For cruising babies and young children, always boil water for at least three minutes or filter using high-quality water filter systems.
- **Ice and containers** in contact with contaminated water should also be considered unsafe. It is safer to drink directly from a can or bottle, but water on the outside may be contaminated and should be wiped off.
- **Carbonated beverages** are safe as a result of the acidity caused by the carbonation. Some noncarbonated "bottled" water may simply represent recycled packaging with contaminated water.
- **Hot drinks or coconut milk** straight from the nut are not contaminated but do not drink from coconuts that have been opened for more than 1/2 hour, as these may cause food poisoning.
- **Ice cream** made with contaminated water or milk is a risk.

## Water Treatment

- The most effective way to treat drinking water is to **bring it to a vigorous boil** for several minutes and then allow it to cool. Boiling destroys all the diarrhea producing organisms, but some single-celled parasites such as *Entamaeba histolytica*, which causes amoebic dysentery, may take longer to destroy.

- The best way to treat tank water is with iodine. Purifying tablets are available from pharmacies, REI, or sporting goods stores. Two-percent tincture of iodine from the first aid chest can also be used. In addition you can get iodine crystals, add water periodically, and thus have a continuous supply of iodine solution. Five drops per liter or quart are needed for clear water, and ten drops for cloudy water. If the water is extremely cold, it needs to be heated for the chemical reaction to take place. After adding iodine, allow the water to stand at least 30 minutes. Iodine may be purchased inexpensively from chemical supply stores. Adding a squeeze of citrus juice will mask any after taste caused by purification.

- **Chlorine** may also be used for treating water, though it is not quite as effective as iodine.

| Chlorine Strengths | Clear Water | Cold or Cloudy Water |
|---|---|---|
| 1% | 40 drops per gallon | 80 drops per drops gallon |
| 4-6% (household bleach e.g. Clorox) | 8 drops per gallon | 16 drops per gallon or 1 teaspoon per 10 gallons |
| 7-10% | 4 drops per gallon | 8 drops per gallon |

## Water Filtration

- **Pre-filter shore water** before putting it in you tank by running it through an in-line filter that rids the water of chlorine, sediment and minerals. Systems IV F7-BGH, $30 (West Marine sku #193755).
- Install, at a minimum, a **water filter**: Amtec CBC-10 filters giardia and cryptosporidium; $25 for unit and $12 for filter (special order from West Marine).
- For a **pressured system** consider installing a Seagull IV Water

Purifier $250 for unit and $50 for replacement filters. General Ecology Inc, 151 Sheree Blvd, Exton, PA 19341 800-441-8166, e-mail gecology@ ix.netcom.com, www.general-ecology.com

- Another more expensive option is a **UV water sterilizer** like the Water Fixer, $350.
- If you plan on extensive hiking ashore in less developed areas, consider carrying a **hand-operated water purifier**. PUR Traveler: $69.95, 2229 Edgewood Ave. S, Minneapolis, MN, 800-845-7873.

## Treating Water Tanks

- **Bacteria** grows inside water tanks in the tropics, resulting in a foul taste in your water. You may think the water and tanks are wonderfully clean and clear until you start sailing to windward, when the sediment and bacteria get shaken up.
- **Sanitize your water tank** and hoses once or twice a year by mixing 1/4 cup of liquid dishwashing detergent and 1/8 cup of household bleach. After the solution is dissolved, pour it into your boats empty tank. Add 10 gallons of warm water, and rock the boat to ensure the solution is well mixed in the tank. Then open each tap on board, including showers, until the sanitizing solution appears at the faucets. Let the solution remain in the tank and lines for at least an hour to enable complete disinfecting. Next, open all taps and allow all the solution to run out. Follow this with at least two full rinses of the tank to ensure that all the sanitizing solution is flushed out.
- To **treat water in your water tanks** (as long as they aren't aluminum), use 1 teaspoon of household bleach per 10 gallons of water. Increase the amount of bleach if the water is cloudy.
- Treat **water stored in jugs** with chlorine or iodine.

## Care of Aluminum Water Tanks

- Chlorine, contained in many large city water supplies, and bleach should be avoided in aluminum water tanks, because it reacts with the aluminum, causing aluminum chloride, a white pasty oxidation in your tanks that clogs filters.

- You need to rinse your tanks and then treat them with **Aquabon** (chlorine dioxide) which oxidizes the inside of the tank, forming a protective coating.
- **Once the tanks are treated** with Aquabon, you must pre-filter chlorine-treated water when filling your tanks. Don't use bleach as a water treatment, as chlorine will penetrate the Aqua Bond coating causing oxidation. Granulated activated charcoal pre-filters that screw into your dock water hose are available from West Marine for approximately $30. These pre-filters, which will remove sediment as well as chlorine, are an excellent idea whenever filling from a pressure water source on shore.

## Watermakers

- Carry a small **hand-operated watermaker** for emergencies. The PUR Survivor 06 watermaker costs only $526 and is small enough to fit into any abandon-ship bag.
- Most watermakers in the past have required 110-volt power, so can only efficiently be used while you're running a generator. The **PUR 12-volt watermakers** are an excellent solution to avoiding filling your tanks with contaminated water from shore and avoiding the complexities and cost of higher output watermakers. The product number is the gallons per day rating, and the prices are: 40E ($1,998), 80E Modular ($2,929), 160E ($3,398). The Power Survivor 80E uses 8 amps of 12-volt power to make 3.5 gallons of fresh water per hour. Ours worked flawlessly for six years of heavy use in conditions ranging from high-salinity calcium rich waters of tropical atolls to 33 degree waters of Antarctica. After 800 hours of operation the unit needed to be re-built ($400 kit). We are now using the 160E, which actually makes 180 gallons per day, far more than we need!
- It is important to follow the directions explicitly on **installation and biociding** the membrane when not in use.

Chapter 19

# Foreign Provisioning

# World Provisioning Guide

Provisioning worldwide is becoming far less difficult as foreign trade and manufacturing expand.

**Mainland** provisioning ports may have large supermarkets that are clean and temperature-controlled, with a high turnover providing excellent selection with moderate prices. The variety of goods will never rival that of a North American store, but you will not want for much. Plan large provisioning shops in accordance with the areas you plan to cruise, or before crossing large expanses of ocean. Most often these are areas in which you will be spending hurricane season, such as Australia, New Zealand, Venezuela, and South Africa.

**Small Island Nations** have less selection than mainland countries, and the governing body for the islands determines the overall selection. The main port for entry and customs clearance generally contains the largest stores and often a thriving local produce market.

French Polynesia, for example, is extremely French, and even the potatoes are shipped from France buried in crates of French soil. In 1988, Continent superstore opened in the main port Papeete, totally cleaning up all local competition. You can't even buy locally grown bananas there, and all local fruit costs double what you would pay at the village market. A quarter of the store is stocked with frozen produce, and California cherries and strawberries are available for those willing to pay the price.

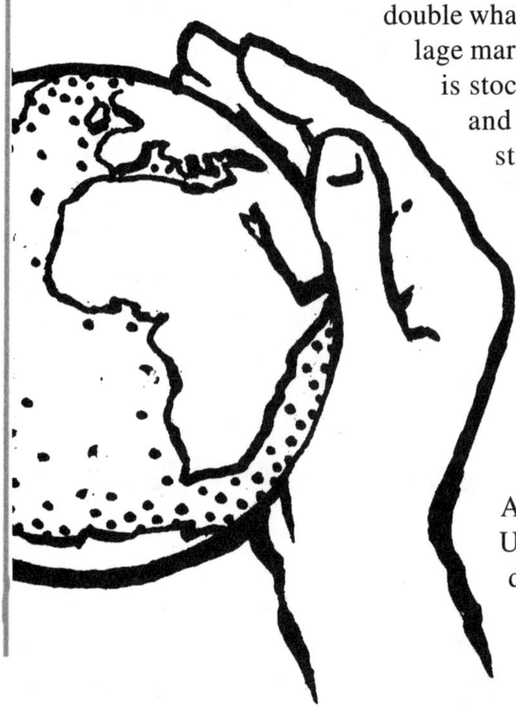

Most other package goods are imported from Europe, including cheeses. New Zealand supplies fresh produce, frozen meat and butter; Fiji, cookies and crackers; Australia, fresh produce; U.S., cereal and fresh produce; and Chile, cookies and wine. It's amazing how one superstore can afford to import so much and keep its prices reasonable.

Cruising through the other South Pacific islands will be a matter of hit-and-miss as to what's available. Rarotonga and Fiji have a New Zealand influence, while American Samoa relies on supplies form the U.S. Super bulk-buy stores are now opening in the South Pacific providing for the local market of hotels, restaurants and large families.

Outside the main ports, small village stores contain basic supplies of long-lasting goods. Fresh produce is often harder to find, and if excess is not sold on roadside stands, you may have to ask around. Meat is often out of the question, as most stores don't contain refrigeration.

**Remote Cruising** lends itself to being resourceful and relying on the provisions you have. For a couple cruising, this is not too difficult, as you are basically forced to make-do with what you have, so it is rather like being at sea. Hopefully, you provisioned wisely in your last major port of call. You may often be able to supplement your diet with items you trade, discover or are able to purchase in the areas you visit.

I met one cruising boat that had taken a local lad aboard as they cruised through the Society Islands, offering to pay his ferry ride home from their last port of call. He proved to be most helpful in his skills of diving and fishing, scaling coconut trees, and preparing local recipes. In return, he really enjoyed the sailing and the opportunity to share his knowledge.

## Arrival and Food Quarantine

- Many countries have strict **quarantine laws** applicable to agricultural products. These products may contain diseases that are a risk to the country's environment and generally require inspection if not confiscation.
- For current information on provisioning and the latest on agricultural restrictions for foreign ports become a member of the **Seven Seas Cruising Association** and receive their monthly bulletin written by cruisers. SSCA, 1525 S. Andrews Avenue, Suite 217, Fort Lauderdale, FL 33316. E-mail: office@ssca.org.

- As master of a vessel you are responsible for ensuring that your crew is aware of quarantine restrictions applicable to the country you are entering.
- An example of strict quarantine is **New Zealand's agricultural clearance requirements**. You may check out their web site at: www.quarantine.govt.nz. Though few countries are as stringent as New Zealand, many countries confiscate fresh produce.

  All **meat** onboard must be declared. This includes beef, sheep, pig, poultry and venison, but not fish. It also includes canned, fresh, frozen, dehydrated, vacuum packed and freeze-dried products.

  **Fresh provisions** such as vegetables and fruits may not be landed and will be confiscated and destroyed.

  **Anything that can sprout** – such as popcorn, sprouts and seeds and beans – will also be taken away.

  **Honey** is not allowed, as it may be contaminated with a virus that kills the honeybees.

  **Eggs and egg cartons** will be confiscated.

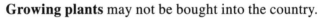

  **Stored products** will be inspected, assessed and, depending on the disease risk, released or destroyed.

  **Growing plants** may not be bought into the country.

  **Garbage** from overseas stores – e.g., meat, eggs, fruit and vegetables – must be disposed of in special bins as directed by the Quarantine Officer.
- **Before arriving** into port, I do a clean-out of all fresh food storage areas, taking an inventory of which items I have left. Knowing beforehand what the country's agriculture restrictions are helps in using up supplies that are likely to be confiscated. Anything that looks unhealthy I toss overboard a day before making landfall. Quite often its heartbreaking, especially if I have over-provisioned and have good produce left. On the other hand, it's great to be able to see the bottom of the fridge, and to anticipate reprovisioning in a new port.

## Where to Provision in Foreign Ports

- If available, do your bulk purchasing in a **large air-conditioned supermarket** with a guaranteed high turnover of products, ensuring that your purchases are as fresh as possible and free from weevils.
- Some supermarkets **discount** for large orders and some offer **free transportation** back to the boat.
- Get a local person to help you shop. **Hiring a taxi** driver for bulk items and busy trips to the market and town makes the trip less daunting.
- **Local markets** vary in quality worldwide, but most often they are colorful, cheap, and contain the best selection of fresh local produce.

## Guides for Foreign Shopping

- Have a good knowledge of the **metric system**.
- At the least, learn **hello and thank you** in the local language of the country you are visiting. These two words and a pleasant smile go a long way in communication.
- If you are unfamiliar with the language carry a **translation dictionary** with you.
- Take your own **canvas tote bags** for carrying home your purchases.
- **Arrive early** at public markets for the freshest foods and best selection.
- In the local markets the **produce changes daily**. If you see an item that you need, it's best to buy it that day rather than wait for a day when it may be all sold out.
- **Educate yourself** about local food, recipes, diseases, and endangered species.
- I carry **a snapshot** of our boat when out shopping. When I meet a storekeeper or market stall owner who has good produce, I introduce myself and give them a photo. This makes future provisioning easier and often I can request green tomatoes, bananas, and fruit and vegetables to my liking.
- Many supermarkets **do not have people to help pack your**

**groceries**, so you need to take someone with you to give you a hand; otherwise, you hold up the customers behind you as it's nearly impossible to unload your cart, reduce the packaging, and sort your groceries into their designated bag.

- In many countries, the locals shop every day and goods are packaged in small quantities. I often ask at the deli for cheeses and meats to be put into **larger packets and doubled-wrapped**.
- **Budget** for a meal or two out at a local restaurant. This way, you get a feel of what's available as you scan the menus.
- Take a cue from the locals and **dress accordingly**. Don't wear fancy jewelry or revealing clothes.
- **Be considerate**. Don't draw attention to yourself by being loud and demanding.
- If **security** is an issue, always go shopping with someone else.
- Ask before **picking or gathering** fruits and coconuts that you see lying about, as they may be someone's property.

## Food Items Readily Available Worldwide

Bread - white
Butter
Cheese: processed or long life
Cookies: very plain and rather uninteresting
Cooking oil
Cake mixes
Corned beef - canned
Flour – white
Fruit - canned
Milk powder
Pasta – basic white spaghetti noodles
Pulses – beans, lentils
Rice - white
Sugar - white
Soft drinks - Coke or Pepsi
Tuna - canned
Vegetables – canned
2 minute noodles

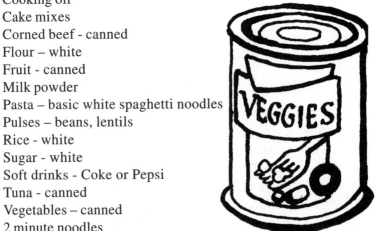

## Items Hard to Find or Expensive in Remote Cruising Grounds

- Antibacterial Soap.
- Baking Mixes: pancake, muffin, bread, waffle, bread, brownie, and cookie. Most often available in American ports and large bulk buy super stores that import goods.
- Beans and seeds for sprouting
- Breakfast Cereal: variety may be hard to find outside North America but basic brands such as corn flakes and rice crispies are frequently available and not too expensive.
- Biodegradable Soap.
- Cans: whole chickens, chilies, pie filling, boneless chicken, ham, turkey, roast beef, and ready to go meals.
- Chicken Breasts either frozen or fresh are often expensive or unavailable. Boneless, skinless, and iced glazed breasts are available throughout the world at Costco Warehouse stores. Although they take up more space than freezing fresh breasts they are often a good buy.
- Chocolate chips may be difficult to find or in the tropics may come melted together. An option is to cut up dark chocolate bars.
- Condiments, including mayonnaise, peanut butter, bacon bits, maple syrup, American brand ketchup, hot sauces.
- Dish soaps vary in quality. Some local brands may not suds up well and may not be biodegradable.
- Ethnic ingredients such as bamboo shoots, baby corn, water chestnuts and curries.
- Fruit Juice concentrated without large amounts of sugar may be unavailable.
- Health bars and other nutritious individually wrapped snacks.
- Ham slices for sandwiches may be of poor quality and expensive.
- Ice cube bags the disposable plastic pocketed bags that are easy to use for making ice cubes for drinks.
- Hot drinks including herbal teas, hot chocolate ground coffee and assorted black teas.

- Nuts and seeds are often only available in small packets.
- Pastas of any specialty: lasagna, spinach, whole-wheat.
- Paper towel rolls vary in size throughout the world, so install a holder with a center bar that goes through the roll. The quality of paper even varies with some falling apart as soon as they get wet an others acting like grease proof paper.
- Raisins and other dried fruit.

## Cruising the Aisles

We cleared into Chile in the city of Puerto Montt and spent a week at Marina Del Sur, provisioning before sailing south. After cruising to Cape Horn, Argentina, and Antarctica, we arrived back in Puerto Montt 18 months later and chose this city as our departure for an eight-week passage to the Marqueses via Easter Island and Pitcairn, knowing that our next major provisioning port would be Hawaii several months later.

I'd learned many shopping hints during our stay in Chile, and provisioning the second time around was far less daunting and overwhelming than when we first arrived. The biggest improvement was being able to speak and understand more of the language. I only had a basic knowledge of Spanish when we first arrived and was rather shy about using it. The Chileans are most friendly, and though most don't speak English, they go out of their way to encourage communication, always with a big smile. At first, when I was out and about, I always carried a small pocket Spanish dictionary, but as my confidence and vocabulary grew I found that I didn't need it.

My first visit into town is taken rather casually; I'm like a submarine with it's periscope up, just surveying the scene and doing a mental inventory of what is available and their prices. Before heading into town, I've already asked fellow cruisers and the marina office what is the best supermarket to shop at. Puerto Montt is easy to navigate. The bus from the marina takes you along the port waterfront to downtown, where both the largest supermarkets are situated next to each other and a colorful thriving local produce market fills the surrounding streets and plaza.

*Supermarcado* is the largest store, and I cruise it's aisle with a slightly glazed look, absorbing and plotting, ready for my next passage in a few days time through the islands of shelves. My shopping mission is small: a canvas carry bag of items that we'll consume over the next few days. I wander through the local market, where wheelbarrows overflow with bananas, cherries and grapes. Parcels of cilantro and piles of tomatoes form colorful displays among heads of cabbage and lettuce. In between the stands of fruit and vegetables are other stalls with mounds of smoked shellfish looking interesting and inviting, but we have been warned to avoid them at all cost as they may be affected by red tide.

Under a gaily-colored umbrella a man calls out from behind a bench with a large chopping board. He reaches beneath the table and produces a gigantic salmon from an iced tub, and then skillfully fillets the fish according to the instructions of the customer. A glass cabinet nearby displays smoked trout and salmon fillets wrapped in plastic ready for purchase. They share shelves with curling-stone-sized local cheeses sealed in bright waxes and large jars of cloudy local honey.

A slight pause in front

of the cabinet produces an excited response from the vendor, who eagerly asks if I would care to try a small sample. With a flourish, he cuts off a slice of cheese and passes it to me on the blade; next is the salmon, followed by a wooden stick dipped in the honey. I purchase a piece of salmon knowing this is one stand I'll return to.

Two days later, I again catch the bus into town. I'm now carrying five canvas carry bags and two large duffel bags. I exit the bus and tour the market stands. I introduce myself to a stall keeper whose produce looks the healthiest, mentioning that I'm off a sailboat and will be leaving for Easter Island in a few days. In our conversation, I explain that I will be returning on Saturday, and tell him the items I will be requiring from his stand, the state of ripeness, and the quantities. I hand over a picture our yacht sailing in Tahiti. With a toothless smile, he shakes my hand and introduces himself as Luis.

I enter the supermarket and exchange my jacket and bags at the baggage counter for a numbered disk in return. Collecting a shopping cart, I steer down the rows of shelves, loading the cart with non-perishable items. Canned goods are easy to choose as their labels contain bright-colored pictures of the contents. Condiments are my next selection: mayonnaise, mustard, ketchup and imported salad dressings, followed by olive oil and vinegar.

Toilet rolls are cheap, but paper towels are more expensive than in North America. In the health food section, I select local herbal teas, small expensive packets of raisins, dried fruit and nuts. Nestle has a high market-share, producing popular two-minute noodles, small packets of cookies and hot chocolate that is inexpensive. Cereals, rice and pasta are easily found and added to the cart, which is then topped up with flour, sugar and cleaning supplies.

As I approach the checkout, I produce my credit card and wait patiently as a separate counter is opened up to accept it. Two young boys appear, and they are very efficient at carefully packing items for long-distance travel, as the supermarket supplies many isolated estancias (ranches) and salmon farms. Boxes and balls of twine are at the ready, waiting to truss up my purchases, complete with handles.

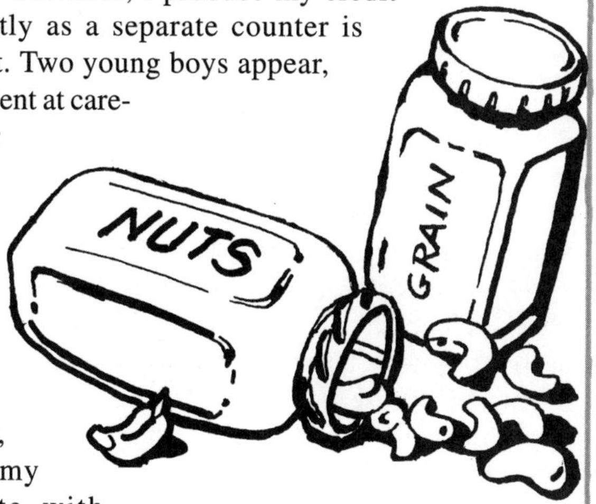

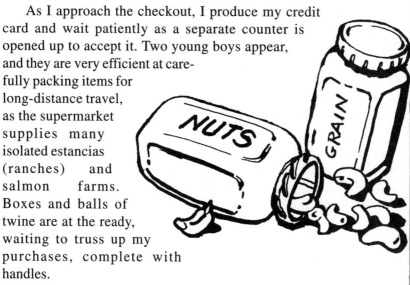

I politely refuse the boxes, handing over my baggage-claim number and explaining that I'd like the items packed into my own bags. To eliminate any unnecessary packaging onboard, I request that they take the foil cereal packs from their boxes. The boys grin and tear them apart with relish. It's sure a relief to have some help, as in some countries – such as Argentina and French Polynesia – I've discovered that I'm on my own in the checkout department.

Ten minutes later, my stuffed bags and I are loaded into a waiting taxi, and for $2US, I am whisked away through town back to the boat. On board it's a hectic couple of hours as the boat is pulled apart for access to stowage spaces under the floorboards and bunks, and behind the main saloon settee. I'm also busy transferring bulk items into smaller daily-use containers that are kept in the galley and handy squeeze-bottles. Remaining supplies are stored in large plastic sealed containers or into Ziploc bags for protection.

Saturday I meet a welcoming Luis at his stand and select the fruits and vegetables that are unavailable in the supermarket and of better quality. He adds up the amount and gives a 10 percent discount for such a large order. I stow the produce into canvas bags and leave them beneath his counter for collection on my way home. I call by the salmon stand and choose a smoked salmon fillet and bright red waxed cheese from the northern Lake District.

It's now time for the final showdown at the supermarket, and I enter ready for action. I'm purchasing perishable goods and their selection takes longer. In the deli department I ask the assistant to slice and wrap ham and cheese into 2 kg. double-plastic-wrapped packages. This took me a while to figure out; when I provisioned for Cape Horn, I bought packs of six slices each on a plastic-wrapped polystyrene tray, resulting in a lot of unwanted plastic rubbish.

Quickly, I grab an empenada for lunch; I'll eat it on the taxi ride home. I collect four roasted chickens that smell divine, and proceed to the in-house bakery section, which emits delicious aromas and where I smartly sweep up loaves of hot sliced wheat bread. Nearby, I carefully deposit into the cart a fresh carton of brown eggs that I've checked for breakages. I gather up items I still need from the produce section – yogurt, butter and bacon from the open fridge. In the frozen section, I choose pastry for quiches, frozen vegetables, imported shrimp, flash-frozen Chilean fish fillets, and chicken. We don't eat much red meat, but it is readily available and best purchased fresh in the meat department.

I blaze through the checkout, pile into a taxi, swing by the market to collect my bags and say farewell to Luis, and then head back to the marina. Loading the fridge and freezer takes planning, and two hours later the fridge containers are loaded, labeled, stacked and the freezer is full of small Ziploc bags, each one containing an easy-to-thaw meal of fish, meat or vegetables. I slump down on the settee, three roasted chickens sitting before me, and proceed to pull off their flesh, stuffing it Ziploc bags for freezing. Next, three dozen eggs each get a light coating of Vaseline, and are returned to their box and stowed away in a sliding locker.

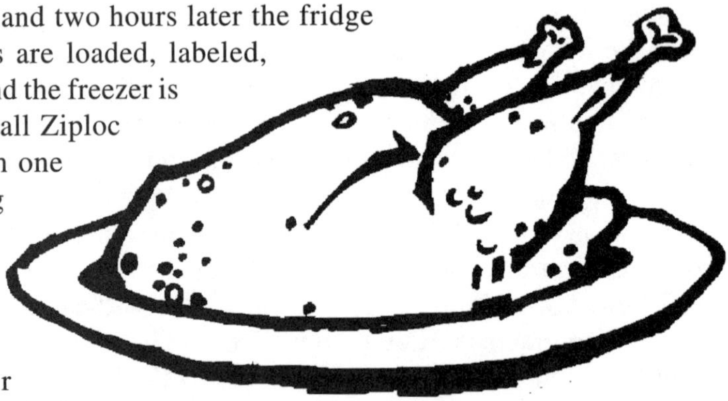

I'm done and totally "fooded" out. I've saved one chicken for tonight's dinner, but hardly have enough energy to prepare a meal. Thank goodness we are leaving on Monday and I'll have Sunday to recover.

# Food and Waterborne Illnesses

## Amoebic Dysentery

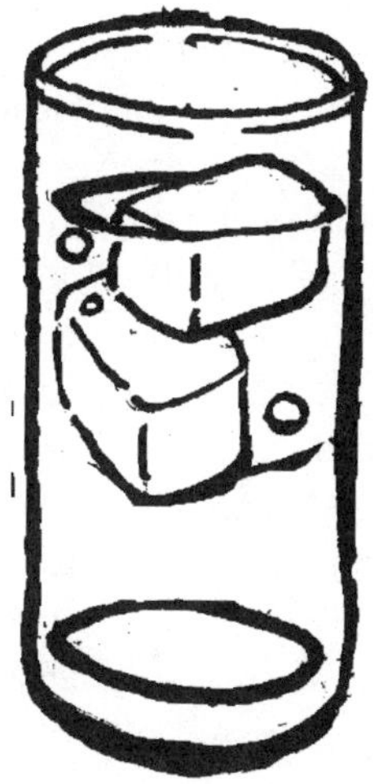

If cruising in areas where amoebic dysentery from contaminated water and vegetables is known to occur, laboratory stool exams should be carried out annually or at least upon return. Also have your stools checked if you have any chronic diarrhea or cramping, particularly with fever. If amoebiasis goes untreated, it can cause dangerous liver problems. Giardia from contaminated water, another less severe form of amoebic infection, should be treated too. It does not cause blood in the stool or fever, but it can cause cramping, nausea, gas, and loose stools.

## Botulism-Canned Food Poisoning

Botulism is a highly dangerous food poisoning from improperly canned foods. It can be acquired not only from ingestion of toxic food but from touch and inhalation of toxic fumes! Even if there is no odor, gas, or signs of food spoilage, botulism can still be present in food. The toxins affect the nervous system and progress to paralysis and respiratory failure. Prevention is essential. These measures include: meticulous sterilizing technique for canning goods, careful can storage to prevent rust and punctures of cans, and prudent inspection of cans before opening for signs of spoilage, i.e., bulging ends. Hissing or exploding contents on opening is definitive of spoilage. Any suspect cans should not be opened and should be discarded, and thrown overboard if at sea. Cooking contents for 30 minutes will destroy botulism toxins. Honey from any source or country should not be given to infants younger than one year due to a risk of developing an infantile variety of botulism.

## Cholera

Cholera is acquired from contaminated food and water and is a severe infectious diarrhea that occurs in epidemics, particularly in Asia and Africa. However, the infection may also be mild and self-limiting for two to seven days. Alternatively, it may be a massive diarrhea that can be fatal.

In areas where cholera is common, special preventive measures should be taken. Some endemic regions require cholera vaccinations; refer to *Health Information for the International Traveler* for a list because it is not highly effective and only provides partial protection. Otherwise, the vaccination is not recommended protection for four to six months. Recent studies using an oral vaccination have been promising, however. The cholera organism is easily destroyed by chlorination and heating of water. Avoid eating uncooked vegetables and drinking contaminated water.

Symptoms: diarrheal stools from cholera have the appearance of "rice water," and may also be associated with some vomiting, fever, and abdominal cramps. If fluids and electrolyte levels in the body cannot be maintained, severe dehydration progressing to shock and death may occur quite rapidly, otherwise recovery is easily achieved. Treatment includes replacing body fluids and electrolytes at the same rate of loss using oral rehydration solution. In severe situations, intravenous fluid replacement is necessary, and medical assistance required. Do not use Lomotil or Imodium in cases of severe watery diarrhea.

## Hepatitis A

Hepatitis A is a viral infection of the liver acquired from contaminated food, water, and shellfish in areas of poor sanitation. Cruisers in tropical regions and in developing countries who don't travel the usual tourist routes may be at greater risk for infectious hepatitis. People visiting areas with high incidences of hepatitis A and B should consider protection with a new preventive vaccine named Havrix. Prevention for infectious hepatitis requires avoiding contaminated foods, shellfish taken from contaminated water, and suspect water. Water should be considered contaminated and possibly harboring hepatitis in areas with poor sanitation, for example if there is a village or animals upstream.

Symptoms of the illness begin with mild flu-like symptoms: anorexia, malaise, fever, nausea, vomiting, and headache. It is during the initial 14 days of hepatitis that it is most contagious. The infection can be transmitted by direct contact, using the same dishes, poor hygiene and sanitation, lack of hand washing, and from kissing. Jaundice does not always occur with hepatitis. If jaundice occurs, the yellow eyes and skin appear 3-10 days after the flu-like symptoms, and may be associated with dark urine, light colored stools, and itchy skin. Affected persons are no longer infectious once the jaundice is obvious. The jaundice peaks in 1-2 weeks, and the patient will start to feel better despite the worsening color.

Positive diagnosis of hepatitis involves blood tests. Antibiotics will not help hepatitis. Debilitating convalescence with listlessness, depression, and poor appetite may last from several weeks to four months. Care should be taken to ensure adequate rest during this time to promote healing and prevent lasting liver damage. In severe cases, with significant fluid loss from diarrhea and with reduced fluid intake, one could become seriously ill. Encourage the patient to drink small amounts at frequent intervals especially in hot weather. If significant dehydration should occur, medical help should be sought for intravenous fluid and electrolyte replacement. This can usually be accomplished even in poorly equipped medical facilities.

Hepatitis A virus is excreted in the urine, stool, and saliva for the first two to three weeks. Appropriate isolation measures should be taken to prevent others from contacting infected material.

The compromised liver function associated with hepatitis can be minimized by abstinence from drugs that are metabolized in the liver and from alcohol, for up to one year. A low fat diet is recommended with hepatitis because the liver is involved with digestion. Aspirin preparations should be avoided with hepatitis because of the possibilities of increased bleeding tendencies.

## Salmonella

Salmonella bacteria occur in infected meat, poultry, raw milk, eggs, and egg products. Salmonella infection causes gastrointestinal upset 12 to 48 hours after ingesting infected food.

Symptoms are nausea, abdominal cramp, diarrhea, fever, and sometimes vomiting. The upset lasts 1 to 4 days and is usually mild. Treatment involves plenty of fluids and a bland diet. Salmonella occurs on the shell of freshly-laid eggs. When using unwashed eggs do not use cracked eggs and ensure that the shell does not come into contact with the contents. Never let foods containing uncooked eggs remain at warm temperatures for more than an hour. Salmonella reproduces in food held at temperatures 40° to 140° and is killed when food temperatures reach 140°. To avoid salmonella contamination in raw chicken, clean all equipment, surfaces, and containers used in preparation with hot soapy water.

## Staphylococcal

Staphylococcal food poisoning occurs from eating food contaminated with staphylococci bacteria and results in diarrhea and vomiting. Food becomes contaminated when people with staphylococcal skin infections, such as boils, handle food that is then left at room temperature, allowing the bacteria to grow. Foods likely to become contaminated are custard, cream-filled pastry, milk, processed meats and fish. Symptoms of nausea, vomiting, abdominal cramp, diarrhea, headache, and fever last less than twelve hours.

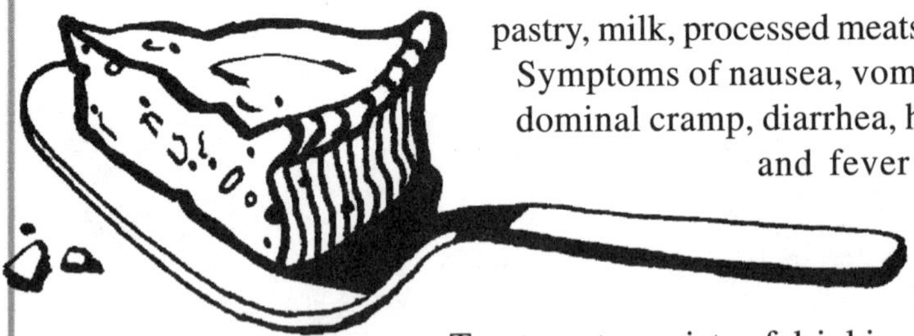

Treatment consists of drinking adequate fluids with electrolyte replacement and complete recovery is usually ensured.

## Worms

Intestinal worms are common in some less-developed communities and are easily acquired from eating inadequately cooked pork, beef, fish, and from water. They are relatively harmless, and treatment can usually wait until the next port.

Symptoms may be vague and go unnoticed. Drug therapy for pinworm, which causes rectal itching among children, and roundworm, which can be seen in the stool as large, earthworm size creatures, is Pyrantel-Pamoate (Antiminth) or Vermox (Mebendazole), usually available world-wide in pharmacies.

# Poisonous Animals

## Ciguatera - Fish Poisoning

Ciguatera affects reef fish sporadically and unpredictable between latitudes 35 North and South. The type and location of poisonous fish varies even in one lagoon and may change at different times. The only way to tell if a fish has ciguatera is to check it with a Cigu-test kit. (Available from Oceanit Test Systems of Hawaii. (808) 539-2345; www.cigua.com) Cooking will not destroy the toxins. Some island cultures test fish for ciguatera by feeding it to a cat first. The toxin is cumulative so that larger reef fish like barracuda and red snapper that are higher on the food chain are more poisonous. Pelagic (ocean going) fish such as tuna and mahi mahi, are least likely to be affected.

Eating a small portion of the affected fish may not produce symptoms, but eating more at a second meal could increase the toxin levels enough to produce poisoning.

Ciguatera poisoning affects the nerves and gastrointestinal system. It is fatal in three percent of cases in the Pacific but rarely in the Caribbean.

Symptoms can start immediately or up to 30 hours later. Severe cases may occur earlier, and milder cases may be precipitated by alcohol ingestion.

### Clinical Features Include:

General weakness; tingling and numbness, especially of face, hands and feet, respiratory failure in severe cases.

Reversal of temperature perception - hot feels cold and cold feels hot.

Red itchy rash and sometimes hives.

Varying degrees of gastrointestinal symptoms: nausea, vomiting, diarrhea, and/or abdominal cramps.

Uncomplicated episodes usually subside in 24 hours, but residual weaknesses, numbness, and temperature perception reversal may last for many months. Flare-ups may occur with ingestion of alcohol or more ciguatera toxic fish.

Prevention:

Check with knowledgeable locals on types and location of safe reef fish.

Eat only smaller reef fish, testing with a small portion first.

Avoid ingesting fish organs as these have higher levels of toxin than flesh.

Never eat tropical moray eels because they have a high incidence of ciguatera.

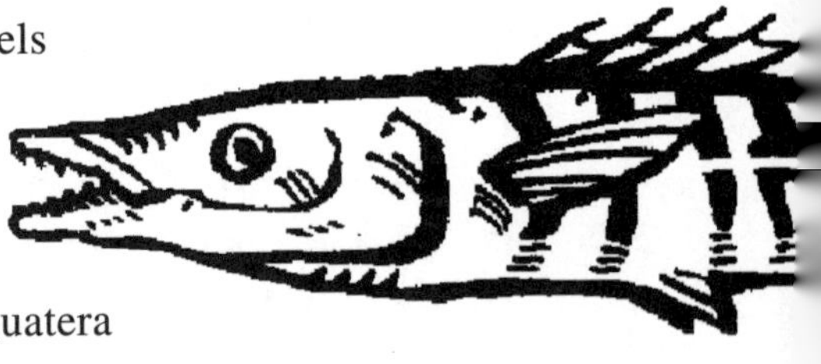

Test the fish on an animal or adult, as children are more susceptible to ciguatera poisoning.

Treatment:

Induce vomiting and use laxatives to remove any remaining unabsorbed toxins.

Bed rest and reassurance.

Resuscitation in extremely severe cases.

Medical assistance and hospitalization for observation of all but mild episode. Book References: **The Ship's Medicine Chest** (Chapter: Poisoning, and Dangerous Marine Animals).

## Paralytic Shellfish Poisoning

Paralytic shellfish poisoning (PSP) or red tide is caused by a consuming a toxin produced in blooming red algae that accumulates in crabs, clams, lobsters, mussels, oysters, scallops, and whelks. PSP occurs even after food has been cooked and attacks the nerves. The algae blooms occur in both the Pacific and Atlantic oceans above 30°N and below 30°S

Symptoms: tingling and numbness around the lips and mouth that spreads to the face and neck beginning 5 to 30 minutes after eating. Nausea, vomiting, and cramps follow. 25 percent of people develop muscle weakness which may progress to paralysis of the arms and legs and those needed for breathing resulting in death.

## Puffer Fish Poisoning

Puffer fish are highly toxic if eaten. Fortunately, they are easy to identify by their ability to inflate themselves with water or air. All varieties throughout the world contain tetraodon poisoning, including porcupine and ocean sunfishes. Although the Japanese consider these a delicacy, preparation by anyone but an expert is not advised.

Symptoms of poisoning are similar to ciguatera.

## Endangered Food to Avoid

- **Triton Shells** are the only natural predator of the crown-of-thorns starfish, which can destroy coral reefs rapidly if the natural balance is thrown off.
- **Lobster** take several years to reproduce and have been over-fished in many areas by locals and cruisers.
- **Turtle** are protected in French and U.S. territories, as they are in Fiji during certain months of the year. Refuse offers of turtle meat, shells, or anything (jewelry, combs, etc.) made from them and diplomatically explain to the local people that sea turtles are no longer found on many beaches and islands because of over fishing and illegal harvesting.
- **Whale meat**. Politely refuse any offers off whale meat. Whales are an endangered mammal and even if the country you are visiting has permission to hunt whales you don't want to encourage the locals to do so.

Chapter 20

# Pelagic Fishing

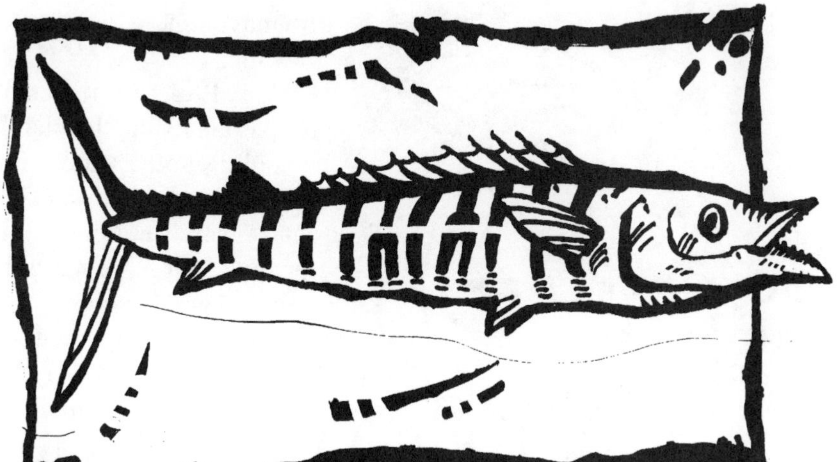

# "Fishing with Big Poppa Gus"

If it's canning that conjures memories of my nanna (grandmother) then its fishing that brings my grandfather to life. My poppa Gus was a colorful character, always enjoying the simple pleasures of life like working in the garden, a local Saturday rugby match, and fishing. A favorite photo shows him casually leaning on the swing clothesline, a slow smile on his lips, sparkling eyes. While one hand is hanging on a wire the other holds a 25-lb. red snapper, a result of a quiet morning spent out on the bay in his boat, away from nanna's yakking.

Nanna and poppa would join us in autumn as we cruised around the Northland coast. We'd go hiking with nanna, listening to her chatter the whole day as we marched up bush clad peaks and swam in cold stony rivers, dad always hoping that the fast pace he set would tire her out so maybe she'd be quiet for awhile.

Pop would stay aboard, a fishing line lazily dangling in the water. Locals would swing by and call out, "There's nothing left in the bay mate, we've been cleaned out this summer." He would listen, smile, and ask if they had heard a cricket match score, changing the subject as he nonchalantly reeled in his line with another beauty of a snapper on the hook.

We'd sail through a flock of birds working, a sign that kawai fish were also around. Pop and I would stand by the two lures, each with a line in hand. As the fish bit and we hauled them in hand-over-hand. Pop would quietly say he'd give me 50 cents for every fish I caught over his. Time and time again my line would be pulled in, a struggling fish taken off the hook then the line quickly tossed out as dad cut donuts through the birds. My heart would pound with excitement trying to beat my pop and I'd be totally mindless of the blood splattering about as the caught fish flapped around my ankles.

Now when I haul in my line, a large pelagic fish fighting for his life, I say a prayer for pop. Each fish has his name on it, a silent tribute to a wonderful man. It's not the 50 cents that come to mind but a passion I learned from him for something that is so intriguing as hauling in a mighty fish for so little effort.

# Fish You Can Catch

## Tuna ~Yellow Fin, Big-Eye, Bonito, Skipjack and Albacore

Tuna are the most common fish to catch on a tropical ocean passage. When caught on a meat line they are not so large as to be out of control once landed. Tuna can survive in depths up to 1000 ft. They are red-blooded and once landed they need to be bled to rid the meat of blood. They are tubby little guys, shaped like a rugby ball, ranging from one to three feet in length. They hit hard on the lure and tend to dive deep. Tunas carry a lot of meat and a single fish can provide several meals. The best meat comes from around the tummy and you need to fillet around the dark red meat that runs the length of the side bones as well as the meat that contains the strings of white tough muscle. Yellow fin tuna, easily identified by its yellow crescent tail and fins, is the most delicious of the tunas with firm rose-colored meat. Black skipjack and big eye tuna's meat tends to be quite red and bloody, containing many strips of white sinuous tissue, it would probably taste good only if you're stranded in a liferaft!

## Mackerel ~ Spanish, Pacific, Wahoo

Wahoo is my favorite fish. I rarely catch wahoo in the middle of the ocean but as we get closer to land I am more likely to hook one.

It is a long blue, black, and white-striped fish resembling a barracuda with a smiling face. It's easily handled once caught and requires little bleeding. Wahoo's white flesh is firm and it cooks, barbecues, marinates, and freezes well. It is particularly good in ceviche and poisson-cru.

## Mahi mahi ~ Dolphin Tuna, Dorado

Considered the prince and princess of the tropics, mahi mahi have two dazzling color costumes. While swimming, their display is cobalt spots on an indigo back with pearl sides. When excited, their back becomes an iridescent emerald, their sides turn golden with fluorescent blue spots, and the their fins turn azzure. Mahi are surface dwellers, they like to linger around floating debris and can sometimes be viewed swimming alongside the boat. Tahitian fisherman chase down mahi in a speedboat with a joy stick control in the bow. When they draw alongside a tired fish, they then spear it to bring it aboard. This requires great skill as mahi have exceptional eyesight and attain speeds of 40 m.p.h.. Reaching full length at six months they are a long, lean, compressed fish. The male is easily distinguished from the female by it's higher rounded forehead. They mate for life and I once caught a male mahi and watched as the female swam alongside her partner as I reeled him. It is sad to watch them die for they rapidly flash through their wardrobe of colors, paling to a spotty milky white. They don't require bleeding and their flesh is lean, soft and juicy, rather like chicken.

## Billfish ~ Black, Blue, and Striped Marlin, Swordfish, and Sailfish

I have never caught a game fish and quietly, on the side, I'm quite happy that I haven't. I could not imagine fighting to get one of these creatures aboard not matter how small it is, let along one over 1,000 pounds. I'm sure that they are good sport but I'm more than happy with a nice quiet fish that's easy to pull in. I learned of one cruising boat that caught a swordfish as they arrived in Rangiroa. As the guy was reeling the fish alongside it hunted him down, jumped out of the water, and stabbed him right through his calf with its bill. Ouch!

# Lures, Lines and Equipment

As I've mentioned I'm not into game fishing and this equipment information is what we have for basic trolling (otherwise called meat fishing). I think "meat fishing" sounds like I'm out to catch a great white shark so I prefer to call it trolling. You can very easily make up your own lures and I've heard many fish tales from people catching fish dragging almost anything covering a hook. I'm not going to offer any instructions on how to make your own lure from scratch but I will mention what has worked for me. The best advice I can give is ask around. Talk to fellow cruisers, local fishermen, visit shops that carry lures and check out what's in stock.

Carry a small selection of lures and if you haven't caught a fish in a few days or so try another. Fishing is not an instant happening, you can only have patience, give it a try, and just visualize Mr. Fishy sitting on your plate.

## Line

Use a 150 ft. length of 200 lb. monofilament line terminated with a sturdy stainless swivel and closed hooked catch to attach lure leaders.

## Reel

We have just a simple round plastic reel that the line gets wound around by hand. This is rather a new addition to our fishing wardrobe. Previously I used a 8" x 12" piece of plywood with a V cut out at each end to hold a wrapped line.

A more user-friendly option is having a winding reel mounted on the rail.

## Leader

The leader is an 8' length of 200 lb. stainless steel wire that passes through your lure and is attached to your hook. The leader allows you to easily change your lures from your main line and is long enough so you don't disturb the water too much causing the fish to notice something amiss.

Made of wire so that the fish don't bite through it, the leader is crimped with an eye one end to hook into your line. The other end is crimped onto the hook with a sleeve after passing through the lure.

## Crimper and Sleeves

If you are serious about catching a fish I suggest you invest in a hand-crimping tool and matching bags of sleeve sizes. John bought me one as a present last year. He had repeatedly witnessed my distress when my pliers squish job failed and I would loose both fish and lure. Now making lures is fun and it easy to replace hooks when they get broken or straightened out by a big fish.

## Wirecutters

This tool gives you a nice cut through your trace line, making it easier to thread the sleeves.

## Lures

There are two main types of lures suitable for ocean trolling and both try to mimic the food fish eat.

- A **flying fish** lure is most commonly a 6" Rapala painted metallic blue and silver to resemble a small fish. Rapalas come fitted with two small triple hooks that soon rust, one situated on the belly and the other at the tail. They have a spoon protruding above the fish lure's mouth to make it ride better. I had reasonable luck catching wahoo with a Rapala close to land and around reefs but not out in the ocean. I find trying to retrieve the lure from inside the wahoo's mouth quite a chore as they tend to swallow it good and hard.
- If you are keen enough, you can rig your own fish lure. "Louie the Fish," a keen fisherman and bone carver from American Samoa told me that the best lure is to use the real thing. Collect a flying fish that lands on deck. Insert a wire trace inside the fish's mouth and exit out the underside of the belly; attach a single hook and insert it into the belly so that just the curved hook is showing. Connect it to your line and troll it behind. Boy, those flying fish are so stinky, I don't really relish the thought of poking them about!
- **Squid** are also eaten by big fish, yet I've still not cut open a fish stomach and found one inside. Squid have a tendency to turn many colors thus attracting fish. Squid lures are my favorite and give you a creative license to make you own, choosing your

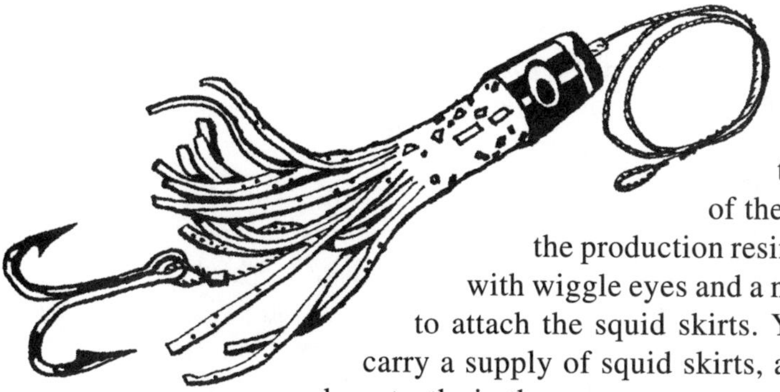

materials and colors.

At the top end of the market are the production resin cast heads with wiggle eyes and a neck for you to attach the squid skirts. You need to carry a supply of squid skirts, as the fish's sharp teeth rip them up.

Zuker is my favorite brand with the overall head size being about 2 ¼" and the color a deep blue. As for skirts, an 8" pink and yellow mix has been my most successful the past four years for catching mahi, wahoo and tuna.

I troll a second lure, a cheaper smaller pink squid of one brand or another often with a single hook, though most often it's the Zuker that gets the strike.

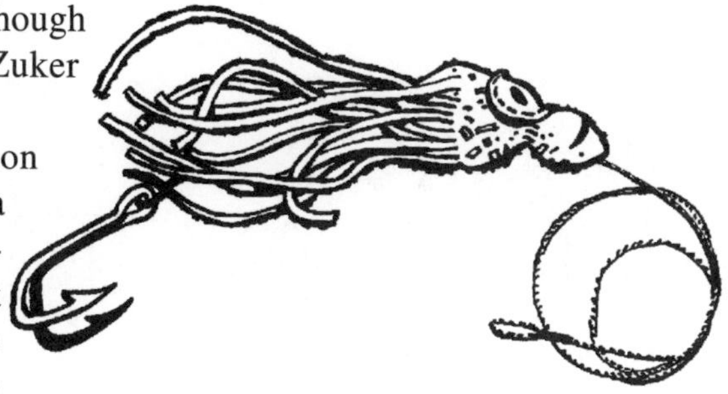

A cheaper version of the Zuker is a simple rugby ball-shaped lead weight with a hole down the length. The lead gets inserted inside an 8" plastic squid then threaded with a wire trace and hook. I've only been using it this year and have already caught a couple of fish though, I tend to find this lure a little heavy so it trolls rather deep.

## Lure Colors

Your choice of lure colors is totally up to you, and you need to experiment. Keep in mind the fish you are targeting and note what the common food source is for that fish in the area. I sometimes open up the stomach of fish to see what they have been feeding on. Shades of metallic pink and gold have worked best for me as these resemble the color of squid when they flash. Green, blue and silver mimic the colors of small bait fish, and if you are in an area of pelagic algae or seaweed try matching their green to amber colors.

Fish scrutinize the surface for food so choose a color opposite from the weather conditions to create a distinction. If it is bright and sunny use dark purples, deep blues and maroons. On cloudy days, try lighter shades of color.

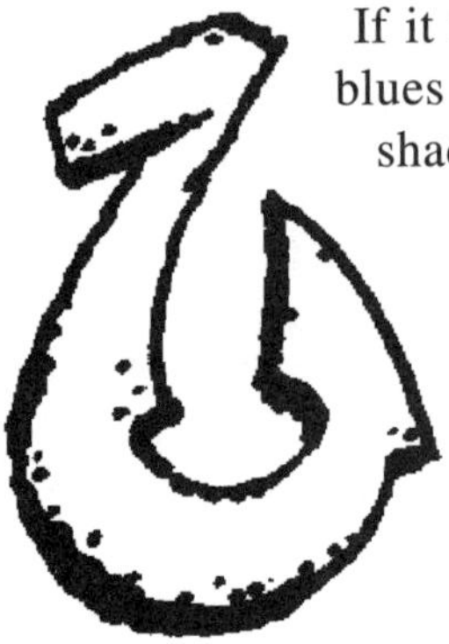

### Fishing Hooks

I use a double 2 ½" barbed stainless steel hook with my lures. They are more expensive than steel but are stronger, last longer, don't rust or stain everything, and it's easier to keep a sharp point on the hook with a small file. Rig the hook so that it trails inside the hem of the skirt. Small plastic beads threaded on the wire help space the distance from the hook to the lure.

## Setting the Line

### Trolling Distance

There are many different theories as to how much line to let out. I'm pretty much a set-and-forget person and pay out 100' run it over the middle rail of the stanchion and cleat the line off on the aft deck cleat. Others say adjust the line throughout the day, especially if you are not having any luck, the shortest distance being a boat length.

### Speed

Boat speed is not too critical, though the general consensus is the faster the better. Our average speed is 6 to 8 knots and this works well. I've talked with many boats that average faster speeds than us and they too catch fish.

### Clip and Rubber

To set the hook in the fish's mouth so not rip it right out, you need to set up a shock absorber in the line.

- The simplest method is to clip up a loop of line with a **clothespin**. When the fish takes the line it trips the peg and has a few feet of line to run with allowing it to swallow the hook.

- Another option is to install a **rubber link** in the line. The rubber is tied into the line taking the shock of the fish hitting the line.

### Alarm

You can get elaborate and rig a bell on the line that rings when you have a fish in tow but a clothespin works just as well.

### Remember

Remember all the time that the line is there.

- **Announce to the crew** that the fishing lines are out and mention that they can no longer turn the boat in a hurry in case they run over the lines and foul the propeller or rudder.
- **Never leave the lines in the water** if you are in little wind or making no way through the water as the lines may foul your propeller or rudder.
- Remember to **look aft and see** if you have caught a fish. On a recent passage the crew set the lines after we had not been fishing for a few days due to bad weather. At the end of the day Jimbo pulled in a line and discovered a battered fish head on the hook. Oops, we'd dragged the poor fish for half the day not even remembering to check and see if we had caught anything.
- I generally don't rig an alarm to encourage crew to look aft frequently to see if we have a fish. Quite often we incidentally gather seaweed or **flotsam on the hook** that then needs to be removed.

## When Do I Catch My Fish?

### Time

The best time for catching fish is at sunset. Often this is rather an inconvenient time as I'm in the middle of preparing the evening meal having already defrosted something to eat. However, fresh fish is always welcome! Sunset is not a guaranteed time catch time and I've caught fish in all hours of the day, bright sunshine to gray skies.

## Flotsam and Jetsam

Fish hang around floating debris, so swing off course to trail your lures beside floating matter.

## Currents

Fish follow the warmer ocean currents so keep an eye on the seawater temperature.

## Landfall

Within a day or so of making landfall is a good time to be fishing. Even if you don't need the fish, someone ashore will be very thankful. It's fun arriving into port and being able to offer fresh fish to the officials and friends.

## Birds

A flock of feeding, diving birds indicates that bigger fish are driving smaller fish to the surface in a feeding frenzy. This only happens coastwise as these feeding birds roost ashore each night. It's great sport to go cruising through the middle of the flock hoping to catch a fish. It's often a good idea to start the engine to continue doing runs through the working birds. You have to be quick as the whole ensemble moves about quite erratically.

## Nighttime

You don't want to leave your lures out at night. It does not make for good seamanship and I heard a tale from Crystal on the Irish yacht Turn-nah-nog that they caught a wicked creature one night. With bulging eyes, spiky fins, and razor teeth there was no way they wanted it aboard even to save their lure, so they cut him away.

## Have I Caught a Fish?

Once you set the lure you need to study how much tension is on the line and the direction it leads due to swell and wind. When a fish strikes, the line will go taut, the alarm will sound, and the fish will either break to the surface or swim. A fish can easily swim the same speed as the boat, fooling you into thinking it got away. Slowly pull in the line until the fish breaks the surface and starts to tire. Sometimes you might miss the alarm and not notice the fish until it is being dragged behind which is very obvious due to the disturbed water.

## Landing the Catch

Once the fish is on the hook, it's best to start reeling it in as soon as possible so that it doesn't get away. Towing the fish tires it out and brings it to the surface where it's easier to pull in. Fresh air also starts to kill the fish. You need to be quick if you are in an area of sharks, as your fishy may soon become chomped.

While one person is reeling in the fish, John and I set about assembling all the necessary processing equipment: gaff hook, rum, sail tie, cutting board, knife, bucket, dish soap, scrub brush, and container. As a fish catching event is rather messy, I have an old swimsuit that I quickly change into, unfortunately its not very glamorous for the finale trophy photo.

1. When the fish is along side you need to **gaff** it through the gills. Our gaff hook is extendable and can reach the water while standing on the deck.
2. Now we are up to three people to land one fish; one on the line, John on the gaff hook, and someone pouring **rum** down the gullet of the fish as it is pulled out of the water. Rum, you may well ask, but it works wonders to sedate the fish and saves a lot of the bloodshed and violence other methods produce. Any cheap alcohol will do; gin, whiskey, or rum. I use an old squeeze honey bottle and water the rum down. We generally have an overzealous crew in the rum pouring department and it requires a whole bottle to calm a fish as a lot goes astray while the fish goes through it's thrashing and jittery phases. I then refill the bottle after each catch.

   Another step in to place the fish in a garbage bag. Once its eyes are covered and it is quiet you then can fillet the fish inside the bag thus reducing the amount of clean up.
3. Now the fish is quiet, but don't let that fool you. We next slip an old webbing **sail tie** with a loop over its tail so two people can lift the fish aboard, then tie it down with the sail tie.
4. If you have caught a **red-blooded fish** such as a tuna and are not planning on filleting it straight away you will need to bleed it so that the meat is not rich in blood. I generally make and

incision behind the head and hang the fish by the tail over the side for about 5 minutes.

5. I position the fish over our large **plastic cutting board** and proceed to fillet it with a sharp knife.
6. John is the cleanup crew and stands by with **bucket, scrub brush, and dish soap**. It pays to keep your filleting area wet with salt water so the fish blood does not dry and stain.
7. Once the fish is filleted, place the fillets in a **container** and send below to the chef.
8. **Clean up** begins with a scrub down and rinse of myself after which I go below to change. The scrub bucket brigade follows, cleaning all equipment and decks.

### Cookie Cutter Shark

If you ever land a fish that has a two-inch disc of meat removed from the flesh, don't panic and throw it back thinking it has a skin ulcer. This hole is caused by the cookie cutter shark, an amazing little fellow who flashes his body bright colors to attack fish, who think it's a squid. Once the fish is close by the cookie cutter shark flips back his head, opens its jaws wide, bites the fish, and does a tail spin, thus removing a perfect circle of flesh form the fish. As yet they have never been known to bite humans.

## Filleting a Fish

Filleting a large fish is rather daunting the first time so it helps to have the right equipment. My knife is an 8" stainless steel fillet knife with a protective sheath made by Dexter Russell and available from West Marine or any commercial fishing supplier in the U.S. It always gets sharpened after each catch.

### Filleting a Small Fish
### Mackerel and Mahimahi

1. Place the fish on its side on the cutting board with the belly towards you.

2. Cut through the skin behind the head and slice halfway through the fish as if you were cutting off the top quarter of its head. Work your way alone the spine and across the belly avoiding the stomach as shown in the diagram.

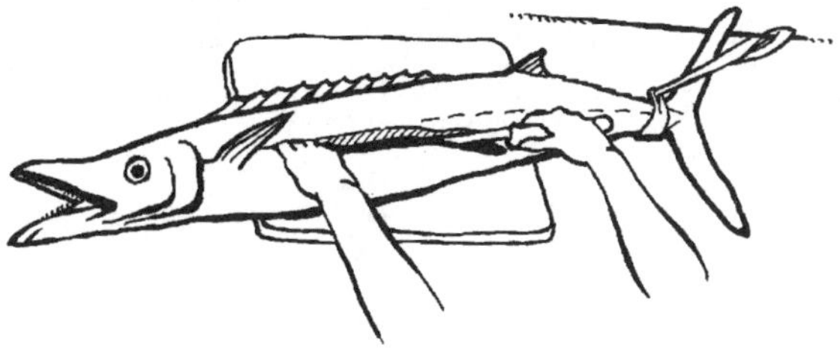

3. Turn the fish around.
4. Insert the knife, held horizontal at the tail, and work your way up the length of the fish's back along the dorsal fin. Keep the knife blade horizontal along the dorsal fin and the tip of the blade just hitting the spine Stop when you reach the cut you made to the head.

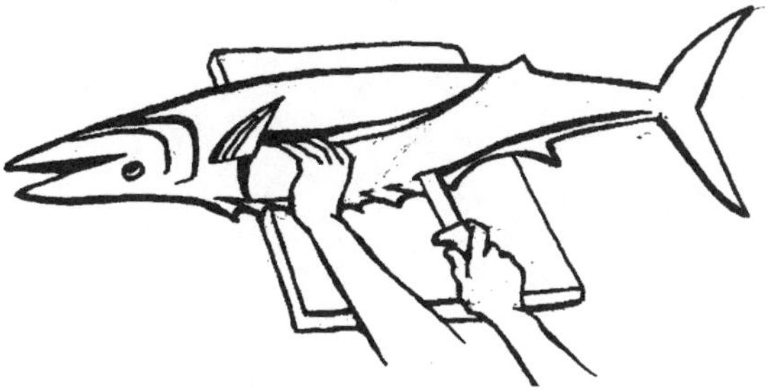

5. Turn the fish around and, starting at the tail, again cut through the other side as you did in step 4, until you reach the stomach.

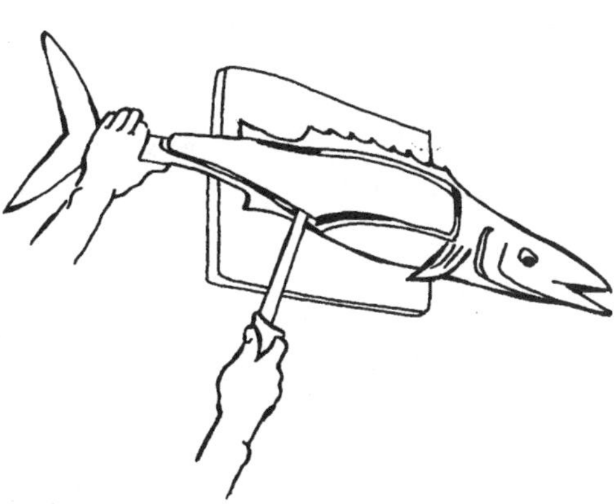

6. Starting at the tail lift up the fillet and with the knife held horizontal cut your way up the spine to release the fillet. Skirt around the stomach area.

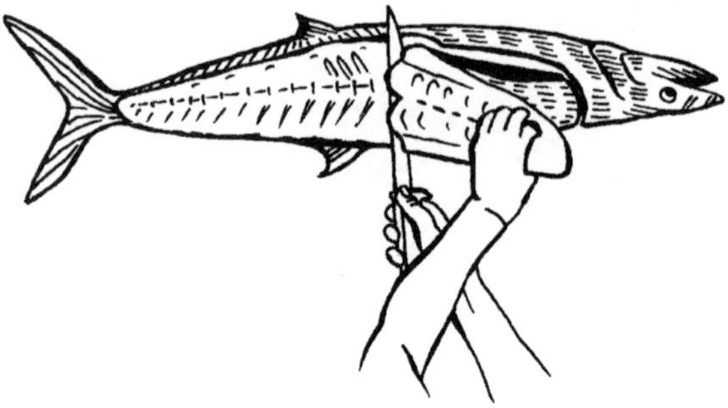

7. Turn the fish over and repeat on the other side.

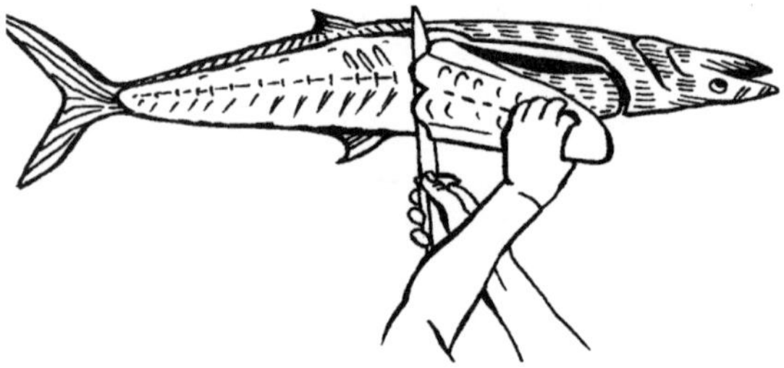

8. Throw away the carcass.

9. By now your knife has lost its sharp edge which is good as you don't want a knife that is too sharp to remove the skin.

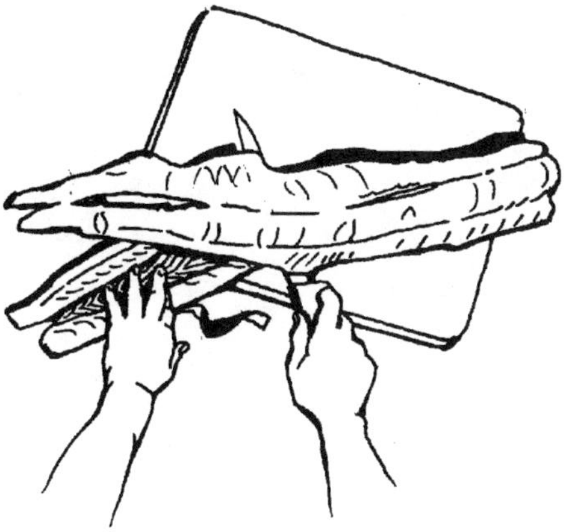

10. Place a fillet on cutting board with the skin side down. Insert the knife at the tail end and while keeping the knife pressed flat to the board hold the tail skin and cut along the length of fillet removing the skin.
11. Cut away the rib cage from the fillet remove any bones. Slice away any dark meat and veins.
12. Repeat for other fillet.
13. Rinse fillets and place in a container.

## Filleting a Large Fish

### Tuna

Filleting a large tuna is a little harder, as the fish is tubby and the rib cage a lot stronger than mahi and wahoo. Fillet the fish as you would any other but as it is larger, you need to do it in sections.

1. Place the fish on its side on the cutting board with the belly towards you.
2. Cut through the skin behind the head and slice halfway through the fish as if you were cutting off the top quarter of its head. Work your way along the spine and across the belly, avoiding the stomach as shown in the diagram for mahi and wahoo.

3. Insert the knife, held horizontal at the tail, and work your way up the length of the fish's back along the dorsal fin. Keep the knife blade horizontal along the dorsal fin and the tip of the blade just hitting the spine. Stop when you reach the cut you made to the head.
4. Lift the fillet up and cut it away from the rib cage.

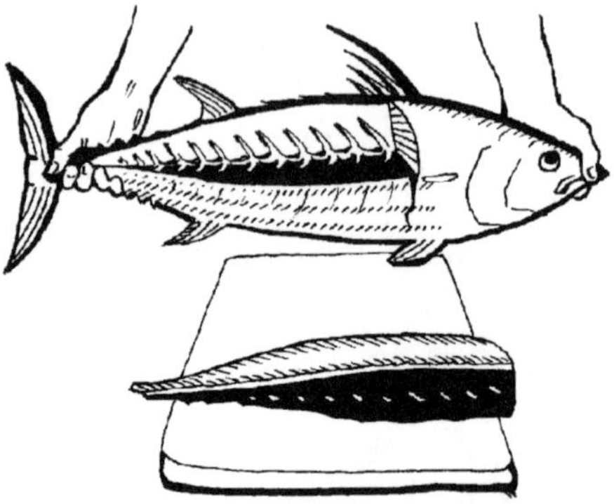

5. Turn the fish around and starting at the tail, again cut through the other side as you did in step 3, until you reach the stomach. Once again lift up the fillet and remove it from the rib cage.
6. Turn the fish over and repeat on the other side. Throw away the carcass.
7. Place a fillet on cutting board with the skin side down. Insert the knife at the tail end and, while keeping the knife pressed flat to the board, hold the tail skin and cut along the length of the fillet removing the skin.
8. Remove any bones, dark meat, and sinuous veins.
9. Repeat for the other four fillets.
10. Rinse fillets and place in container.

# Preserving Fish

Once the fresh fillets are in the galley I then clean them up some more.

## Fresh Fish

I cut up the choicest fillets to use for dinner, either that night or the following day, and place them in a Rubbermaid container in the fridge. I usually cook up extra fillets then mix them with mayonnaise for lunchtime salad or sandwiches. If the fish is a white flesh I also leave an extra fillet out for poisson-cru or if it's a nice tuna I set a small fillet aside for sushi or sashimi.

## Freezing Fish

Depending on the condition and size of the meat I then prepare it for freezing. The bigger the fillets of fish, the longer they keep in the freezer. I place large fillets into gallon Ziploc bags and remove the air. They then get placed in another Ziploc for double protection. Small pieces of meat get cut into bite size cubes and packed into small Ziploc bags ready for *Fish Tacos* or *Fish in Herbed Tomatoes*.

## Pickling Fish

Fish pickled in sterile jars will keep for several weeks.

| | |
|---|---|
| 4 | fish fillets |
| 1 C | olive oil |
| 3 C | vinegar |
| 3 | garlic cloves - chopped |
| 10 | peppercorns |
| 2 t | red pepper flakes |

- **Sauté fish fillets** with garlic and red pepper 3 minutes each side, let cool.
- **Pack fish into sterile jars** with a few pepper corns and fill with 3/4 vinegar and 1/4 oil.
- **Cover jars** tightly.
- Fish is then drained and mixed into a salad, rice dishes or pasta sauces.

## Canning Fish

See Chapter 2.

## Smoking Fish

See Chapter 2.

## Other Resources

- The Cruiser's Handbook of Fishing, By Scott and Wendy Bannerot. International Marine ISBN 0-07-134560-4

This new book is a fantastic reference covering all you need to know on how to fish, shrimp, crab, spearfish and cast nets while out cruising.

Chapter 21

# Seasickness

# Turning Green

I occasionally am asked if I have ever poisoned anyone, and I can truthfully say that I don't think I have. Most people aren't satis fied with that answer and ask if I have ever served a meal that was a disaster. The reply to this question is, yes! It was not so much the meal as the circumstances.

At 19 I had volunteered as cook on a 10 day coastal voyage aboard the New Zealand youth sail-training 105' square-rigged ship, *The Spirit of Adventure.* The passage I chose was a rugged one from the small town of New Plymouth on the West Coast of the North Island to the Manakau Harbour farther north along the coast. Two years earlier, I had been a trainee aboard *The Spirit* and ever since been looking at options to sail aboard again. At 18 it was possible for me to return as a watch leader, but the organization stated that a mate had to be 21 or over. I was disappointed at not being able to sail again for another three years, so I questioned if the cook's position had an age limit.

"No," was the reply.

"Great, sign me up!"

It was not until I was in the galley stowing supplies to feed six crew and 25 trainees – who were 17-year-old boys – that I started to have self-doubts. Walking into the freezer, I was overwhelmed by the quantity of food I was responsible for. Would there be enough of everything? Could I cope? Then there was the sudden panic when I realized I had been in a vegetarian phase for over a year, and I wondered if I still remembered how to cook meat. I doubted that many of my fellow shipmates would be sympathetic to vegetarian meals.

On meeting with the Captain, I was advised that we were to spend first night in port and leave first thing in the morning. I had not chosen the provisions; they were a standard fare that got loaded onboard for each voyage. Reading through my stores list, I decided on corned beef for the first night meal. It had always been one of my least favorite meals, and I thought it best to get it over with, hoping that things could only get better.

It's a basic meal – a simple matter of boiling three-pound chunks of meat in water for over an hour until tender, and accompanied with mashed potatoes and peas, it couldn't be easier. I was on schedule with the beef simmering away when the Captain came into the galley and stated that weather conditions were deteriorating and a cold front was coming our way. As New Plymouth was not very sheltered, and we were tied up in the berth for the tender of the Maui natural gas platform rig, it was decided that we would put to sea and head up the coast.

We departed and dinner was served while we pounded our way north in large swells. The trainees sat around the dining tables, a jovial group eagerly sounding out each other and rather smug with the idea that their adventure was under way. Apple pie and ice cream followed, and I breathed a sigh of relief that my first meal was over.

The seas began to build rapidly the farther north we headed, and soon trainees were turning green and coming to the realization that they were becoming seasick.

With darkness and mounting seas, it was decided, for safety reasons, to keep the trainees inside the saloon rather than on deck. Soon came the cry, "Get me a bucket, I'm going to be sick." Others quickly joined in, and it wasn't long before all five small buckets were occupied with seasick heads. The crew were dropping like flies; those tough guys who had sat around the dinner table making jokes were now quiet and gray. I dashed down to the galley and returned with five 10-gallon buckets used for swabbing the decks and vegetable peelings and spread them about.

The sight was rather bizarre – 25 guys slouched around the saloon floor with a wayward hand clutching a bucket, and every few minutes a head would duck into a bucket, generally followed by a few others. In any other situation, you would think they were bobbing for apples. This continued throughout the night with none of the trainees daring to go forward to their bunks; they felt safer in numbers.

By morning conditions had improved, and after a hearty breakfast of plain porridge, dolphins appeared surfing on the bow wave, spirits were raised and smiles appeared. Never again on future expeditions did I serve boiled corned beef. My secret disguise for it was to chop it up and bake it with barbecue sauce. I never wanted a repeat of 25 green trainees.

## Dehydration

- **Your body is about 70% water** and you've got to top it up to keep yourself bright-eyed and bushy-tailed! In the tropics you need to drink more water than usual, a minimum of 2-3 liters a day.

- **Breathing depletes one liter per day**, and sweating depletes up to one liter per hour. When a breeze cools your skin, you will be unaware of losing fluid, as your clothes aren't becoming damp and sweaty. The hotter it is, the more you exercise and perspire, and the more you will need to drink.
- **Water shortages**, contaminated shore water, and unappealing tank taste pose problems when the cruiser needs to drink more water.
- You need to have a way of **measuring your water intake**. It is your responsibility to avoid dehydration.
- **Once dehydrated**, you become a liability on board, not an asset. You cannot rely on thirst to tell you when you need water, as you can become seriously dehydrated to the point of going into shock without becoming thirsty.
- **Diuretics** (fluids that cause your body to lose an equal amount of water) include coffee, black tea, cola and beer.

## Symptoms of Dehydration

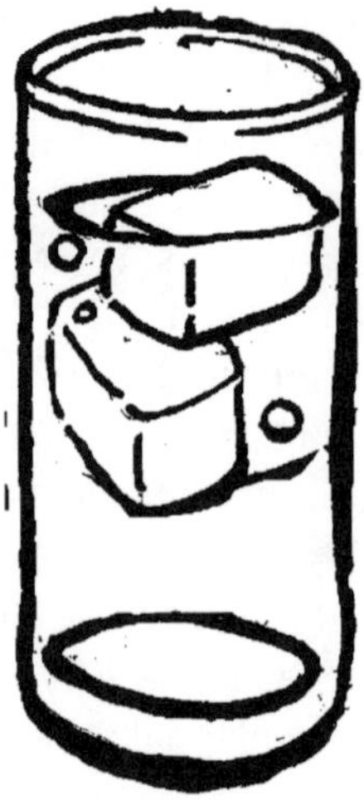

- **Symptoms of dehydration** are similar to food poisoning or flu, but it is the body slowly going into shock due to the lack of moisture in the cells, including the brain.
- **Lack of hydration** can cause or affect the following: anxiety, constipation, cystitis, depression diarrhea, drowsiness, excessive sleeping, headaches, heat stroke, irritability, liver damage, lack of concentration, loss of motivation, kidney stones, seasickness, and yawning.
- Dehydration is the **most common and serious medical problem** we see during our sailing expeditions, and headaches possibly due to dehydration were the most common medical complaint on the past three Whitbread Around The World Races.

## Symptoms of Seasickness

- **Rare is the sailor who never gets seasick**! Fortunately, motion sickness is usually only a problem for the first day or two of the passage until the ship sails beyond the refractory sea swells from land, or if the seas are rough and before the sailor adapts to the motion of the boat.

- Motion sickness is a **physical disorder caused by sensory conflict** between the inner-ear balance center and visual perception. Staying on deck and looking at a stationary point on the horizon reduces the sensory conflict. Taking the self-steering vane or autopilot off and hand-steering often works well.
- Those **most prone to motion sickness** are the very old, very young, and women. Female hormones make women more susceptible to seasickness just before and during menstruation and during pregnancy. It is primarily a hereditary condition, with 20% of the population resistant, 20% extremely susceptible, and the rest somewhere in between.
- **Motion sickness begins with** skin pallor, cold sweating, drowsiness, yawning, and increased salivation. It may progress to symptoms of dizziness, headache, drowsiness, malaise, severe depression, and even reduced survival instincts. Gut symptoms of queasiness, nausea, vomiting and dry heaves follow. If you have a history of seasickness, take medications before casting off.
- **Once seasickness nausea has begun,** it is too late to take oral preparations. Keep a variety of preparations on board, including rectal suppositories. The result of taking seasickness medication varies for each person; therefore, it may be necessary to try more than one remedy at different times.

## Cautions and Care of the Seasick Sailor

Motion sickness can be seriously debilitating, causing physical safety problems on board as well as serious dehydration.

- Look after your seasick shipmates; they **may be weak, dizzy,** and unable to concentrate, making them incapable of looking after themselves.
- Don't allow them on deck without a **safety harness** on.
- Suggest that they stay in the cockpit and **use a bucket** instead of leaning over the side to vomit. A sick person may be so severely depressed they wouldn't care if they did fall overboard, or if a ship ran down the yacht.
- **Never assume they are capable** of maintaining a safe watch.

- **Be attentive** to their needs. A seasick individual needs to be protected from the cold and the sun. Their body temperature and blood pressure will be low and they may be at risk of hypothermia, even in the tropics. They may lack the motivation and energy to put on more clothing, so help them with warmer garments. Conversely, they may be frying in the sun, unable to move and protect themselves.
- After vomiting, the seasick person's loss of body fluids and electrolytes (salts), low blood pressure, and increased blood viscosity can lead to serious problems. Encourage the person to **take small amounts of fluids with electrolytes** every 15 minutes. Glucose and electrolyte fluids (such as oral rehydration salts, Gatorade, or Pedialyte) should be given, and the victim may also tolerate eating dry crackers. A mixture of one quart of water, 1 teaspoon salt and 1/2 teaspoon baking soda with lemon flavoring will also replace lost electrolytes.
- If the patient is **unable to take oral fluids** and is in progressive dehydration, fluids may be administered rectally, or parentally by needle under the skin.
- **Rehydration** is critical to overcoming seasickness.

# Prevention of Seasickness

## Tips to Avoid And Reduce Seasickness

- Refrain from **eating fatty and spicy foods** the day before starting a passage.
- **Eliminate coffee and alcohol** at least 48 hours before starting, and during ocean passages.
- **Increase your water** intake to 2 to 3 liters (roughly 2 to 5 quarts) per day.
- Continue the intake of fluids **or if shaky drink Gatorade**, **ORS** (oral rehydration salts) or some other electrolyte replacement.
- **Eat some food** in small amounts – such as dry crackers, cookies, crystallized ginger, tinned fruit (this really works), and hard candies

- If not steering, position yourself where there is **least motion** – from amidships to the stern. Preferably out in the fresh air, tethered in the cockpit.
- **Keep away from odors**; stay in a cool shady place. A cool wet cloth placed on the back of the neck and forehead may help.
- **Lie on your back**, with head supported and still.
- **Look at a fixed place on the horizon**. If you can't keep your eyes on a fixed object, keep them closed to reduce sensory conflict between the inner ear balance center and visual perception.
- **Diversional activities**, especially steering the boat (but not reading), may reduce symptoms.
- **If sailing close-hauled,** it may be better to drop off a few degrees to a close reach and take an extra day or change your destination to another landfall for a more comfortable trip.

## Alternative Remedies for Seasickness

These have the advantage of no noxious side effects, and help many but not all seasickness sufferers.

- **Ginger Powder Capsules**: Two taken every 4-6 hours may alleviate nausea symptoms. Ginger snap cookies and crystallized ginger are an old fishermen's prevention. A few slices of ginger root in hot water is also refreshing and worth trying, as is ginger ale.
- **Acupressure Wristbands**: These are straps with pressure nodules worn strategically around the wrist to exert pressure on

specific acupressure points that prevent nausea. Conflicting reports exist about their effectiveness, but if it works for you, it has the strong advantage of no drug side effects.

- **Homeopathic Remedies**: including Alpha MS from Boericke and Tafel, 1011 Arch St., Philadelphia, PA 19107 USA. We have had excellent success with this product with no noticeable side effects.

## Medication for Seasickness

- **Nonprescription antihistamines:** include: Dramamine (chemical name Dimenhydrinate; brand names outside the U.S.., Nauseatol, Andrumin), Marezine, Antivert, Bonine (Cyclizine, Meclizine, Meclozine, Ancoloxin, Bonamine, Ancolan). Dramamine causes the most drowsiness, Bonine is the longest acting, and Marezine causes the least drowsiness.
- **Outside the U.S.**, others such as Sturgeron may be available.
- These antihistamines are for **mild seasickness** sensitivity and need to be taken prior to departure, before any nausea symptoms begin. They take at least 4 hours to be fully effective, and should be taken every 6 hours. Take at least 2 doses before departing, (e.g., 8 hours and 2 hours before departure).
- Some people may find it necessary to start taking **antihistamines** one or two days before departure to avoid seasickness. Taking anti-nausea drugs well in advance of departure also allows adaptation to the drug and its side effects.
- Most antihistamines do have a noticeable **side effect** of drowsiness, which may be hazardous if the person is also responsible for navigation, or they are on deck alone and therefore vulnerable to falling overboard.

## Prescription Drugs For Seasickness

- **Compazine and Phenergan Suppositories**: These are a good choice for the sailor once nausea and vomiting have begun. They last at least 8 hours and may have some associated drowsiness, but generally much less than with antihistamines. In rare cases, Compazine may cause an involuntary muscular rigidity (extrapyramidal syndrome), which is quickly overcome by taking an antihistamine such as Benadryl.
- **Transderm-Scopolamine**: These small drug-impregnated skin patches are placed behind the ear. The drug is absorbed through

the skin into the blood stream. These are used mainly for prophylaxis, and should be applied the night before departure. Each patch lasts for 72 hours. Caution should be taken not to get any of the drug in the eyes, otherwise blurring or loss of short-range vision due to pupillary dilation may occur, making it impossible to read the compass or chart. Wash hands well after applying. These patches have a few unpleasant side effects, and may cause some drowsiness and blurring of vision, psychosis, and hallucination in some cases, increased sweating, bladder retention, and possibly decreased heart rate.

- **Oral dextroamphetamine:** (5-10 mg. every 4-6 hours) combined with scopolamine has been used by the U.S. Navy. Consult your own physician for this one, as most MDs will not prescribe this drug to strangers.
- **Intramuscular, Injectable** prescription drugs are also used for severe motion sickness, but these shouldn't be administered without medical training. These include Phenergan, Compazine, Hydroxyzine, and Scopolamine.

Chapter 22

# Waste Management

# Waste Responsibility

It is our responsibility as cruisers to be aware of the impact we have as we travel through foreign countries. By following a few simple guidelines we can lesson our impact on the environment and discover ways to make a positive contribution to the communities and places we visit.

**MARPOL V International Treaty** was designed to reduce the amount of ship-generated garbage dumped into the ocean and applies to U.S. flag vessels anywhere in the world and to foreign flag vessels within the 200-mile Exclusive Economic Zone of the U.S. All vessels 26' and over are required to prominently display a durable placard of at least 4" x 9" in size notifying passengers and crew of MARPOL V discharge restrictions and penalties. In addition, vessels 40' and over are required to have a written waste-management plan describing the procedures used for collecting, processing, storing and discharging the vessel's garbage, and listing the person in charge of the vessel's waste management. For further information, contact: U.S.Coast Guard, Customer Information at 800-368-5647. (Monday-Friday from 8 a.m. to 4 p.m., EST.)

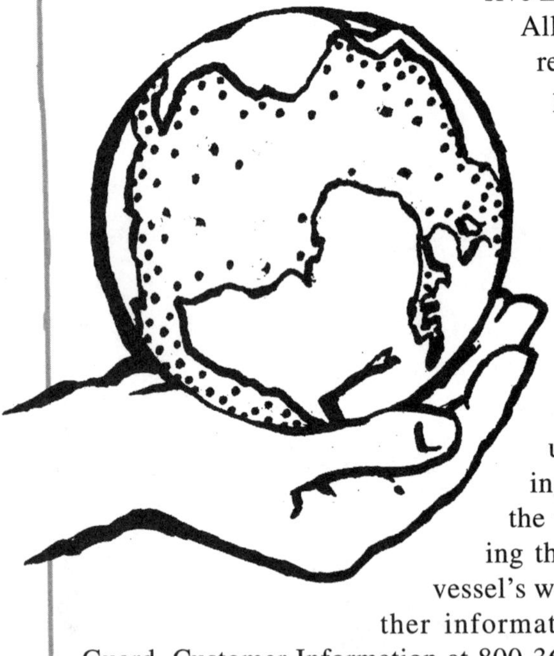

## Waste Reduction

- Instead of using "**plastic cling-wrap**" or using and disposing of Ziploc bags, use reusable snap or screw-lid containers.
- **Paper towels** are made white by bleaching with chlorine, the by-product is dioxin, a deadly toxin that pollutes waterways

near paper mills. Alternatives include using dish towels or cloth rags, when possible, that can be washed and reused (COSTCO is a good source), or buying 100% recycled dioxin-free paper towels. Another avoidable source of dioxin is white-bleached paper coffee filters. Alternatives are nylon filters, cotton, or unbleached paper filters.

- Bring as little **disposable plastic** with you as possible.
- Always snip each of the circles of **plastic six-pack holders**, with scissors, so that if they do accidentally fall overboard, they won't end up getting tangled in, or strangling, birds and marine animals.
- When you have an option, buy **supplies packaged in glass or metal**. We pull old socks over glass jars and bottles, then pack them tightly in Space Cases (similar to milk crates, they are available from West Marine), filling in extra spaces with new spare sponges.
- When cruising in **developed areas** where there is a chance of finding a glass-recycling depot, we wash glass bottles out with salt water and store them in a cockpit locker until we find a place to deposit them.
- When cruising in **less-developed countries**, we've often found that villagers are often happy to receive clean jars with lids.
- Make a point of saving **aluminum cans**, compressing them, and taking them to a recycling drop-off in the future. They don't take up much space once crushed, and are light. Recycling aluminum reduces air pollution and uses 90% less energy than making aluminum from the raw material.
- Many large motor yachts and sailing yachts have **trash compactors** in the galley. Most crews enthusiastically endorsed this product as a great way to reduce onboard waste.

## Waste Disposal on Ocean Passages

At sea, we place **two plastic shopping bags** in our galley garbage bin – one for plastic waste

and the other paper.

- ❖ **Organic waste** from the galley gets thrown overboard at sea. I buy quantities of 5" x 10" brown paper bags to use for scrap disposal at sea. The paper bag quickly disintegrates in seawater, and it's easier and sometimes safer to throw a bag overboard than stand on the side of the boat in a rolling sea scraping out a pot.
- ❖ Unwanted **glass and cans** can be filled with salt water and dropped overboard only on long ocean passages and if you lack sufficient storage to hold them until arrival in your next port. Do not drop them overboard while at anchor.
- ❖ On extended ocean passages, **waste paper** is collected in the galley bin. When it is full, it is tipped overboard. Whenever storage space permits we try and store all non-food rubbish until port.
- ❖ **Plastic, batteries** or anything we think is detrimental to the environment, are never thrown overboard and get placed in the galley plastic waste bag. When it's full or starts to smell, we try and compact it as much as possible before placing it inside a large sturdy garden-sized garbage bag. We can choose the anchor, gas, or aft fender locker to store the bag in for intelligent and responsible disposal once we reach a major port.

## Tossing It All Away

Disposal of food wastes at sea is rather bothersome, and the following incident has forced us to devise a better method for waste management.

We were on passage for Tahiti from New Zealand and it had been boisterous for a good week. The crew's stomachs were settling down and I made a big pot of spaghetti, though it was hard for most people to finish their entire serving. Plates were returned to the galley and I scrapped the leftovers onto a large dish. Ready to start the dishwashing, I handed the dish on deck, asking someone to dispose of the scrapes overboard. Soon the entire dish was sailing through the air, as the plate had been thrown like a Frisbee in an attempt to dislodge the contents, except the plate was sent along with the food. Double trouble occurred as the food contents landed all along the deck.

I now use paper bags for food scraps so that the complete package can be tossed overboard with ease.

My mum has also told me a similar story on dishwashing. When washing dishes in a bucket, be sure to check the bottom before throwing away the sudsy water. Many a galley item has been lost to Davy Jones's locker when the water is thrown out.

## Waste in Port

- When arriving in port you need to **be very cautious of where you dispose of your garbage**. Don't arrive at a small atoll and expect the locals to take responsibility for your waste. I once went ashore in a small town to do my shopping and dispose of my rubbish. Eager children gladly ran off with the garbage bag after I carefully explained I wanted it placed it in the town rubbish bin. After doing some shopping, on my walk back to the dinghy, I saw a garbage bag broken open and lying in the gutter. To my horror, I spotted my rubbish. They had explored it for anything interesting and left it in the gutter.

- Many places just push their garbage into the sea, as they have been doing for many generations. They still have a "disposable" attitude about material items. However, now the only problem is that plastic soda bottles, beer cans, plastic rice and potato chip bags and shopping bags don't biodegrade like coconut shells and woven baskets.
- I was shocked this year at the plastic garbage littering the windward shores of the remote Tuamoutu Archipelago in the eastern South Pacific, but it was not all from their small islands. I discovered a glass Coke bottle with a plastic lid from Ecuador and many products written in Asian characters and I was able to

build my own plastic figurine collection, "Toy Soldier Meets Godzilla on the Farm."

❖ If you can't wait until a major port for garbage disposal, one option is to take your burnables ashore, dig a hole below the high tide line, burn the rubbish, then bury the ashes. Burning plastics does release toxins into the atmosphere, but is better than having them eventually end up in the ocean.

When it's possible, we try to tactfully mention to the locals that throwing rubbish into the ocean may harm their marine and wildlife.

## Freon Gas

Don't vent freon into the atmosphere when recharging your refrigeration system. Newer refrigeration systems use a freon replacement gas that is not harmful for the ozone. Ozone depletion resulting in dramatic increases in skin cancer is most serious in New Zealand and Australia, but is a worldwide problem according to the National Institute of Health and the European Health Agency. Other sources of CFC (chlorofluorocarbon) pollution include halon extinguishers, aerosol spray cans, styrofoam, and foam-fitting packaging that protects electronics in shipment.

# Resources and Index

# Resources

## Recommended Galley Books

- **Cooking under Pressure** ~ Lorna Sass ~ pressure cooker tips and recipes.
- **Good Boatkeeping** ~ Zora and David Aiken ~ ideas to make your boat safer, tidier, and homey.
- **Health Information for the International Traveler** ~ U.S. Dept. of Health and Human Svcs.; Stock #017-023-00184-1 $5.00 Superintendent of Documents, U.S. Gov't. Printing Office, Washington D.C. 20402. 202.783.3238.
- **Keeping Food Fresh** ~ Janet Bailey, detailed information on storing food, uses refrigeration.
- **Offshore Cruising Encyclopedia** ~ Linda and Steve Dashew a gold mine of information.
- **Sailing the Farm** ~ by Ken Neumeyer ~ a guide to homesteading on the ocean.
- **The Cruiser's Handbook of Fishin**g ~ Scott and Wendy Bannerot ~ an excellent reference .
- **The Joy of Cooking** ~ great all-round food reference and cookbook.
- **The Top One Hundred Pasta Sauces** ~ Dianne Seed ~ superb recipes for pasta lovers.
- **The Ultimate Pressure Cooker Cookbook** ~ Tom Lacalamita Mediterranean recipes for the pressure cooker.
- **Voyager's Handboo**k ~ Beth Leonard ~ valuable information for the offshore cruising.

## Manufactures of Long Lasting Food

- Buckeye Beans and Herbs: breads, pastas, etc.
  P.O. Box 28201, Spokane, WA 99228-8201
  509.484.5000

**Bulk Freeze-Dried and Dehydrated Foods**

- Alpine Aire: 4031 Alvis Court, Rocklin, CA 95677
  Fax: 916.824.5020; www.alpineairefoods.com
- Oregon Freeze-Dry: Inc: Mountain House Division, P.O. Box 1048, Albany, OR 97321 800.547.0244
  www.ofd.com/mh; e-mail: mthouse@ofd.com

- Backpacker's Pantry: Customer Service, 6350 Gun Park Drive, Boulder, CO 80301 303.581.0518

**Canned Gourmet Cheese**

- Washington State University Creamery: Troy Hall 101, Pullman, WA 99164-4410 509.335.4014 ($10.50 per 30 oz. Tin)

**Canned Meats**

- Brinkman's Farms Inc.: 16315 U.S. Route 68, Findlay OH 45840
  419.365.5127; www.findlayoh.com/brinkmans

**Bulk Food Co-Op (catalog)**

- Mountain Peoples Northwest: P.O. Box 81106
  4005 Sixth Ave, So Seattle, WA 98108 253.333.6769
- Mountain Peoples Warehouse: 12745 Earhart Ave, Auburn, CA 95602 800.679.6733

**Organically Grown Prepackaged Foods: Soups, cereals, grains, sauces and cookware**

- Walnut Acres: Penns Creek, PA 17862 (Catalog available)
  570.837.0601

**Powered Eggs, Whites, Yolks, and Scrambled**

- REI, Inc.: 1700 45th Street E., Sumner WA 98352
  800.426.4840

## Provisioning Supplies

**Foodsaver Vacuum Packing System**

- Nationwide Marketing: 568 Howard St, San Francisco, CA 94105 1.800.777.5452 ($230)

**First Class Mail Order Spices**

- Wild West Spices: P.O. Box 471, Cody ,Wyoming 82414
  888.587.8887; e-mail: spices@wyoming.com
  Natural spice blends from the heart of cowboy country.

**Labels for Containers**

- Labeleze: P.O. Box 223, Baldwin, NY 11510
  516.379.2978; fax 516.379.2979 Kitchen and spice, clear transparent. ($4.25)

**Prolonged Life Produce Bag**

- Evert-Fresh Corp: P.O. Box 540974, Houston, TX 77254-0974
  800.822.8141 For keeping fresh produce.

**Plastic Storage Containers**

❖ Consolidated Plastics: 8181 Darrow Rd, Twinsburg, OH 44087 800.362.1000 Wide mouths and plastic caps.

**Ziploc Bags**

❖ Bradley's Plastic Bag Co.: 9130 Firestone Blvd., Downy, CA 90241 800.621.7864 Different sizes and thicknesses.

## Related Supplies and Suppliers

**Bio-DegradableSoaps, Detergents, Cleansers, Etc.**

❖ Seventh Generation Company: Colchester, VT 05446-1672 800.456.1177

**Foreign Provisioning Information**

❖ Seven Seas Cruising Association. (SSCA)
1525 S. Andrews Ave., #217, Ft. Lauderdale, FL 33301
954.463.2431 fax: 954.463.7183
www.ssca.org; e-mail: office@ssca.org

**Seagull IV Water Purification System**

General Ecology, $H_2O$ Purification: 151 Sheree Blvd., Exton, PA 19341 800.441.8166 (EST); e-mail: gecology@ix.net.com
www.general-ecology.com

## General Marine Stores

**Canned Butter, Long-Life Milk and Galley Supplies**

❖ Downwind Marine: 2804 Canon Street, San Diego, CA 92106 619.224.2733

❖ **West Marine Products**: 500 Westridge Road, Watsonville CA 95076 800.538.0775; www.westmarine.com

**West Marine** has approximately 200 stores nationwide and ships equipment to cruisers worldwide, utilizing UPS, air mail and air freight. An excellent source for galley supplies, including stoves, barbecues, cookware, non-skid dinnerware and Scoot-Guard.

Please forward any additional provisioning related resources, which will be included in our next edition. Send to: Mahina Expeditions Publishing, P.O. Box 1596, Friday Harbor WA 98250

# Index

## F

## J



## K



## L



## M

## N



## O

## P

# T

# Additional Titles From
# Mahina Expeditions Publishing

## Offshore Cruising Companion

An indispensable guide for preparing yourself and your sailboat for safe offshore voyaging. This annually updated book is the course handbook for Amanda Swan-Neal and John Neal's Offshore Cruising Symposiums.

Handbook, 220 pages, $49.95

## Sailing to Cape Horn,
## The Ultimate Adventure

Join Amanda Swan-Neal and John Neal for an unforgettable journey sailing Chile's dramatic channels. Explore uncharted canals, glorious glaciers and rustic fishing villages enroute to Cape Horn. Witness the excitement as they battle 60-75 knot winds attempting to round and land ashore on Cape Horn.

Includes practical tips on preparing for ocean cruising, storm preparation, weather tactics and landfall formalities.

Video, 60 minutes, $29.95

## Sailing to Antarctica

An Odyssey in Ice

From Cape Horn, Amanda, John and expedition crew crossed the notorious Drake Passage, sailing far south along the Antarctic Peninsula, discovering incredible wildlife and the intense beauty of this rarely-visited ice bound land.

Includes information on provisioning, anchoring, communication and navigation.

Video, 40 minutes, $29.95

## Log of the Mahina
## A Tale of the South Pacific

A tale of cruising simply, Log of the Mahina is a reminder that the beauty of sailing is not dependent on a budget. An open attitude, good seamanship and self-reliance are the most important factors. The story takes place in the islands Amanda and John have sailed to, and grown to love.

Includes appendixes; Outfitting a Small Boat for Offshore Cruising and the South Pacific Islands.
Paperback, 282 pages, 44 photos, $19.95

To order any of these items, see your local dealer or order direct from Mahina Expeditions Publishing.

# Also Available

## Weekend Offshore Cruising Symposium

The cruising symposium is an exciting 18 hour course packed with information that has taken Amanda, John and their co-presenters years to acquire. Presented logically, intelligently and professionally, the course includes demonstrations, slides and extensive documentation in the invaluable 240 page Offshore Cruising Companion. For future dates, check out: www.mahina.com or contact Mahina Expeditions.

## Mahina Tiare Sailing Expeditions

For the opportunity of increasing your confidence and safety level in a learning environment, join Amanda and John aboard *Mahina Tiare III* for an offshore passage. Expedition members are immersed for a period of two to three weeks in all aspects of operating and maintaining a modern ocean cruising boat, including provisioning, meal planning and preparation, navigation, storm sailing techniques, weather and passage planning and more.
For schedules of upcoming expeditions and satellite log updates from current expeditions, check out www.mahina.com or request the expedition brochure from Mahina Expeditions.

Mahina Expeditions, P.O. Box 1596, Friday Harbor, WA 98250, USA
Tel. 360.378.6131, Fax 360.378.6331, E-mail: sailing@mahina.com
www.mahina.com

MAHINA EXPEDITIONS
PUBLISHING
FRIDAY HARBOR

# About the Author

Amanda Swan-Neal grew up in a boat building and sailing family in New Zealand and has been traveling the world under sail, covering 125,000 miles since she was 11 years old. Her first professional cooking experience was aboard the 105' *Spirit Of Adventure*, one of New Zealand's sail-training tall ships. Later she helped design the galley, and sailed as an officer aboard the new 150' *Spirit of New Zealand.* Amanda has also worked in some of Auckland's and Sydney's finest restaurants.

Amanda was chosen as rigger aboard the British boat, *Maiden* and spent one year refitting and training before circumnavigating in the 1989-90 Whitbread Around the World Race. *Maiden* was the first all-women Whitbread entry, and won two strenuous Southern Ocean legs in their class, finishing second in their division in the race.

Following the Whitbread, Amanda was worked as a chef aboard the classic 76' Fife yacht *Tuiga* for a voyage through the Mediterranean.

In 1994 Amanda joined John Neal aboard *Mahina Tiare* and has co-conducted over 50 offshore sail training expeditions in locations from Antarctica to Alaska and the South Pacific. Amanda has lectured extensively in England, the U.S. and New Zealand and writes articles for Blue Water Sailing Magazine.

To inform and update future cruisers of provisioning stops around the world, Amanda frequently updates her own web site, ***Amanda's World:*** www.mahina.com/amanda.html.

Amanda spends an average of seven months a year at sea conducting sail-training expeditions with her husband, John Neal aboard their Hallberg-Rassy 46, *Mahina Tiare III.* When not at sea they live on San Juan Island, Washington.